BRASS BANDS
in the 20th Century

Brass Bands
in the 20th Century

Edited by

VIOLET & GEOFFREY BRAND

EPL EGON PUBLISHERS LTD.,
19 Baldock Road, Letchworth, Herts.

First published in 1979
by Egon Publishers Ltd
19 Baldock Road, Letchworth, Herts SG6 3JX

Copyright © Egon Publishers Ltd.
and Violet and Geoffrey Brand.

ISBN 0 905858 12 3

Bookjacket photography by Dick Smith.

Typesetting and design by
Art Anonymous, Biggleswade, Beds

Printed and bound in England by
Staples Printers Rochester Limited

CONTENTS

Appendices

Foreword

by Sir Adrian Boult

I always feel that many musicians who have roots in the centre or north of England should know all about the history and development of Brass Bands. I personally realise that I know far too little about it all. Such contacts as I have been lucky enough to have, have left me full of admiration both for the musicianship and competence of the conductors, and the immense skill and general artistry of the individual players.

I well remember Edward Elgar, on his introduction to a festival somewhere where they were playing the arrangement of his Second Symphony, coming away full of admiration for the many very difficult passages in that work which he has written and intended for violins, being played by cornets with equal brilliance.

This book covers the whole range of the fine history of the Brass Band movement and will be welcomed by a very large number of musicians all over the country.

Introduction

by Geoffrey Brand

Books about the brass band movement are scarce. You have to go back nearly forty years to discover anything substantial on this particular subject, though this dearth has now been broken. Two years ago when John Street, an ardent follower of the brass band movement, approached me on the possibility of writing a book on the subject, there was nothing worth laying your hands on. We decided that brass band enthusiasts should, at long last, have their own authoritative book.

During the eight years (1967-75) when I was Editor of the *British Bandsman*, I had become acutely aware of the need for such a book. My wife, Violet, had been Co-Editor (which meant that she did most of the editing, whilst I spent my time conducting and adjudicating brass bands in this country and abroad) and I knew that she would join me in any such project. We had both spent many hours answering the queries of school and college students, who were preparing anything from a primary school project to a post-graduate thesis, on the subject of brass bands. The only written material we could point them to was the *British Bandsman*, which dated back to 1887, but could only be researched in our office, or the British Museum, and a splendid book, The Brass Band Movement by Russell and Elliot, which has been out of print for many years and is thus almost unobtainable.

Equally important were the numerous bandsmen and women who contacted us over the years, asking for information about an aspect of banding which interested them. At the same time they often passed on to us their own special experience or treasured contest memories. They also wanted a book on brass bands — and we had none to direct them to.

So the idea was planted and from that time the enthusiasm and support for this book has been overwhelming. Photographs and information have come from all over the world and we trust that those who have constantly asked about its progress will now enjoy the contents.

Some of the problems have been in deciding what to leave in. Like many a good film, almost another book has been left on the wayside. Great characters and fascinating personalities have become known to us; musicians and performers, some of whom have gone on to make national, even international, reputations, have inspired us as we learned about their achievements, and their aspirations. Some were men of vision; others dreamed dreams. A great many wore the marks of dedication to their beloved banding.

Over the years countless thousands have found fulfilment through the brass band; this is no less true today than it was in the middle of the last century.

This book tries to trace the pattern of some of those people and their achievements. Our aim has been to preserve the story, and place on record, as fairly as possible, some of those events which seem to us to have been important, together with the people who were involved in them.

It remains for use to thank those who have helped to compile this book. Some, who have contributed chapters of great importance, are acknowledged — others who have sent anecdotes or photographs may not be. But to all we send thanks, coupled with the hope that you will find the book worthy of the brass band movement we all serve and enjoy.

1. How it all began

by VIOLET BRAND

Why was it that brass bands were born in the mid-nine-teenth century? Why were they principally a working-class musical activity? Why were they isolated both socially and musically for over a hundred years?

The answers to these questions lie in the social develop-ments of the period, the inventions of time and the paths which the early bandsmen allowed themselves to follow. Twentieth century bandsmen have much to thank their predecessors for — the high standard produced by contest-ing, the comradeship of the band fraternity and the estab-lishment of unifying factors. But in retrospect many thorny problems of the twentieth century were the result of decis-ions taken before 1900. What clef should brass band in-struments use? What pitch should they be in? What about a National Association? Some of these issues have still not been finally resolved and they continue to rear their heads.

It could be said that twentieth century brass bands began with the Great Industrial Exhibition of 1851, held in the Crystal Palace, on Hyde Park. Working men from the fact-ories and mines were offered special train excursions to attend the exhibition. These had two effects — the men were encouraged to use the railways and they were introduced to a whole new range of manufactured goods. Amongst the ex-hibitors was Adolphe Sax and it was at his trade stand that men from all over the country heard and saw the Sax range of brass instruments for the first time.

The *Illustrated London News* commented "The show of brass instruments in the French department is exceedingly good . . . First and foremost among the exhibitors is M. Adolphe Sax, of Paris well known in England and the Continent as the inventor and manufacturer of Sax horns, so beautifully played by Messrs. Distin." (August 23, 1851)

Adolphe Sax had perfected his valve system early in the 1840s and, shortly after, met Henry Distin in Paris. Distin was a member of a famous brass quintet and was very im-pressed with this new range of brass instruments. The group toured with them on the Continent and in England and then agreed to demonstrate them at the Great Exhibition.

Many of the men who listened were already playing with wind groups, made up of a motley assortment of instruments — bugles, cornopeans, ophicleides, French horns, baritones, trombones, clarinets, flutes — in fact any instrument which could be blown. There was an obvious need for uniformity and standardisation. The Sax family of instruments seemed to satisfy that need.

When the Mossley Band contested at Belle Vue, Man-chester, in 1853 with a complete set of Sax instruments, and

Adolphe Sax

Left: Black Dyke Mills Band 1865, ten years after converting to all brass.
Back row: W. Haigh, A Oldfield J. Greenwood, A. Fawthrop, W. Firth, S. Greenwood, J. Taylor, J. Wood.
Middle row: Joseph Rushworth, J. Smith, J. Oldroyd, T. Leach, Smith Downsborough, George Rushworth.
Front row: Bob Rutherford, J. Varley, William Rushworth (Bandmaster), J. Rothery, John Rushworth.

won, the clamour for change was on. During the 1860s and 1870s many new brass bands were formed, and many reed and brass groups transferred to the new style of instruments. Besses o' th' Barn converted to all brass in 1853 and Black Dyke Mills followed two years later. By 1895 it was estimated that there were forty thousand brass bands in the country.

In the early days, not all bands had the same number of players. The size depended on the availability of men and instruments. In fact at Belle Vue in 1853 the contesting bands varied in numbers from ten to eighteen.

The cost of instruments was an obvious problem. Besses bought a second-hand set in 1879 for £160, and whilst many admirers and friends contributed, they found the cost crippling. Not surprising, when it is also recorded that members of the band's social club paid an annual subscription of 4s.

Some bandsmen struggled to pay for their own instruments and out of an average weekly wage of 24s., this represented no small achievement. It must have been a great relief to win an instrument at a contest. Between 1871 and 1883, Meltham Mills won a baritone valued at £19 19s. and a cornet worth £14 14s., whilst Nelson Band won a euphonium worth £27, and at Belle Vue in 1887 Kingston Mills won a euphonium worth £30.

Bands were springing to life from all kinds of working class groups — missions, mills, pits and villages. Their social superiors rarely joined them in their musical activity, but often contributed money for the purchase of instruments. Mill and colliery owners took pride in financing their own band, perhaps with some relief that their workers were indulging in the innocuous activity of "banding" rather than disruptive politics.

But already social class divided those who indulged in brass band activities and those who did not. The cloth cap image hung over brass bands for well over one hundred years. Slowly, through education, changes are taking place.

Besides social divisions, musical separation was present from the start. Music festivals existed. Whether bands were invited to participate and refused, is not known but certainly separate brass band competitions were set up.

The first recorded contest that Besses o' th' Barn took part in, was not a planned event, and it was before the band changed its instrumentation. In 1821, at a procession in honour of the coronation of George IV, the marching bands were invited to perform a piece of their own choice, just to entertain the crowds. Money was collected for a prize, which

Besses won, having played 'God Save the King'. The second recorded occasion was in 1838, when celebrations were taking place to mark Queen Victoria's coronation and the trophy was shaped like a crown. Besses played 'Hail, Smiling Morn' and won.

But perhaps the contest which was to have the greatest effect on brass bands and set the future pattern, was that held at the Hall of Burton Constable near Hull, in 1845. Eighteen-year-old Enderby Jackson was present at this event and it made a lasting impact. Sir Clifford Constable had been persuaded by his sister-in-law to have an "afternoon's rivalry of brass bands" as part of his annual Magdalen Feast. They had witnessed such events in the south of France and were "most entertained". Prizes of £12 and £8 were offered, with the possibility of a further contribution from the house guests should more than two bands compete. Players in each band were limited to twelve and no drums were allowed. Richard Hall, an organist from Hull, was selected as adjudicator and music was to be "own choice". Five bands competed and the winner was Wold Brass Band, led by James Walker of York.

The young Enderby Jackson did not forget and when, at the Great Exhibition of 1851, he met two other young enthusiastic musicians, with thoughts like his own, he suggested that "as rail facilities were rapidly progressing, it would be

Besses o' th' Barn Band 1860 from an oil painting presented to the Bandmaster Mr. William Jones on May 31, 1860.

The Crystal Palace, scene of the first brass band contest in the south of England, organised by Enderby Jackson in July 1860.

wise for deputations from bands to visit railway managers, seeking their co-operation in bringing distant bands to a suitable centre" for a competition. Belle Vue, Manchester, was suggested as the "suitable centre" and work immediately began to persuade the railways and the proprietor of Belle Vue that this really was a good idea.

Eight bands took part in that first September, Belle Vue Contest in 1853, and sixteen thousand people attended. Mossley won the first prize, playing on their newly-acquired Saxhorn instruments. The Belle Vue Contest became an annual affair, and set a pattern for other national events. Three adjudicators were used in 1853, to "cut out individual preferences" and today, for most top contests, three judges are engaged.

But Enderby Jackson was not satisfied. He wanted to bring brass band contesting to London. The manager of the Crystal Palace, now re-erected at Sydenham, South East London, was a friend and he was prevailed upon to stage the first contest of brass bands ever held in the south of England, on July 10 and 11, 1860.

Seventy-two bands entered for the first day and ninety-eight for the second, although these numbers seem to have

diminished considerably when the actual day of the contest arrived.

Six platforms had been erected, out of earshot of each other and the bands were divided into six groups. Three adjudicators judged at each platform and selected two bands to go forward to the final contest at which all eighteen adjudicators sat in judgment!

The bands played "own choice" test-pieces and the final winners were: 1. Black Dyke, 2. Saltaire, 3. Cyfarthfa.

During the day, the massed bands of 1,390 players performed under the baton of Enderby Jackson. Amongst the instruments used on this occasion were ophicleides and D-flat althorns.

The support for these events seems to have been enormous, for twenty-seven thousand people attended over the two days.

The contest took place annually until 1863, by which time it had become a one-day event and attracted only twenty-one bands. Maybe it was because of the new ruling which stated: "No band will be allowed to compete unless it is tuned to the pitch of the Crystal Palace organ".

It was 1900 before London again became a centre for a brass band contest on a national scale.

However, contesting trends were being set. Working people who had never previously travelled beyond their own town or village, were going by train to regional and national events. They were going to play in a band, or to support one. From these meetings at contests, grew the contacts and friendships which are so much part of the brass band movement. In the nineteenth century it began as a national fraternity. Now in the twentieth century, it has become an international fraternity.

The other important effect of the brass band contest, which still applies today, is that bands were measuring themselves musically against each other. They spent hours prior to the event striving to achieve perfection, both by private practice and full band rehearsal. When the contest day dawned, they went to play at their very highest level. But they also went to listen. They listened to their rivals and through their listening, as well as through their practising, their level of performance improved.

This is not to say that all was well with contesting in those early days. Often the music was "own choice" and so a band would perfect one piece and stick to it. It is reported that between 1884 — 1892, Besses o' th' Barn won £1,500 from "own choice" contests. They played Alex Owen's selection of Berlioz' 'Damnation of Faust' twenty-one times

The silver cup won by Black Dyke Mills at the first Crystal Palace contest in July 1860, and still in the band's possession. Along with the cup, the band won a cash prize of £40.

and his arrangement, 'Reminiscences of Rossini's Work' twenty-seven times. A contemporary adjudicator said that there was no need to enclose him in a box, as he knew the bands by the music they played!

However, in 1854, Enderby Jackson instituted the idea of a set test-piece, arranged specially for the contest and released to all competitors on the same date. Many contest organisers incorporated the idea, but allowed an "own choice" section as well, much as the Australian and New Zealand Championships do today. By 1867, pressure for entry to the Belle Vue event had become so great, that the "own choice" section was discontinued. The set piece became the pattern.

Adjudicators in the nineteenth century were treated with far less respect than they are today, and reading reports of crowd behaviour of the period is reminiscent of newspaper articles on present-day football hooliganism.

It was reported in the *British Bandsman*, September, 1888, that following the Belle Vue contest, judges were hissed and booed, and attempts were made to subject them to "rough usage" as they left the hall.

"Mr. Godfrey found it necessary to secure the protection of a police constable".

The editor goes on to comment: "Our readers know how we have persistently denounced ruffianism, as is recorded against the Belle Vue Contest of 1888. Hitherto it has been confined to contests of less importance and has been passed over, but it is now time that every one concerned should take the matter in hand and set to work to redeem the honour and creditable name of brass bands".

Mr. Charles Godfrey announced that he would, in future, decline to adjudicate at any contest in which a Lancashire or Yorkshire band would be competing. He had been judging at Belle Vue for seventeen years.

Dr. Spark had reached the same conclusion earlier in the year after he had had a similar unfortunate experience. After giving his decision he had been rescued from the angry mob by a friend, and put on the train home, but he wrote in the *British Bandsman* (July 1888): "I found myself in the same train as the bands, when intemperate language attracted the attention of the porters and guards who protected me in a first-class railway carriage from the threatened bodily attack of the sweet-tempered men, one of whom was kind enough to say that he would tear me limb from limb."

The abuse of adjudicators went on, and in August, 1896, Sam Cope, founder and editor of *British Bandsman*, announced that he would withdraw from all adjudicating until a National Association had been formed to ensure that contests

Sam Cope, (1856–1947), founder and first editor of the 'British Bandsman'.

were conducted with "dignity and propriety".

He had been adjudicating at Hawes Contest and had decided in favour of Wyke Temperance, against Hartlepool Civic. He was turned on with "abominable language" which was "quite disgusting". He went on to say: "Unfortunately, the betting mania has reached the crowd who chiefly patronise brass band contests".

He suggested that perhaps the top bands like Wyke, Besses, Dyke and Kingston should be excluded from the smaller contests. They could be invited to demonstrate how the piece should be played, but not allowed to compete.

"Their presence at these contests as combatants, is bad for the art bad for morality and bad for inferior bands. It encourages the betting mania and creates ill-feeling among the men of these bands."

The conception of general grading had not arrived, but in 1886 Belle Vue introduced a July contest as a preliminary to the great September day. No band who had won a prize in the previous four years in September, was allowed to take part in July. Thirty bands applied for the first event, although the organisers could only accommodate twenty. The principle of grading was established.

Belle Vue introduced other contest regulations in 1889, which laid the foundations for the twentieth century.

a) Any performer on the staff of the Militia, or engaged as a regular musician in a theatre band will be regarded as a professional musician. Every performer must earn his chief income apart from playing music.

b) Slide trombones only will be allowed.

c) Conductors will be allowed to act for more than one band, but not allowed to play. Conductors may be professional.

d) Test pieces must not be played in public previous to the day of the contests.

British Bandsman July 1889

Conducting personalities were already beginning to establish themselves through the contest scene. For over twenty years Alexander Owen, John Gladney and Edwin Swift were rivals.

Alexander Owen was born in 1851 and was evidently a brilliant cornet player. He conducted Stalybridge Old Band when he was sixteen and four years later formed Stalybridge Borough. He had a very successful relationship with Black Dyke (1879-1888) and with Boarshurst. In 1884 he was invited to conduct Besses. It was said at the time that as a conductor he had taken twice as many prizes as any other gentleman. In December, 1897, he sailed to Australia, on doctor's orders. It was thought the long sea voyage would be good for him as he was suffering from insomnia.

"Those closely in touch with Mr. Owen and his work can hardly be surprised at his being attacked with insomnia. He works at tremendous pressure, travelling up and down the country, constantly giving lessons here, there and everywhere, snatching what few hours he can to pore over new scores and arrange new selections for brass bands."

Brass Band News

In May, 1898, he returned home a "new man" and lived until 1920.

John Gladney was born in Belfast in 1839 and had a good musical education. He was a clarinet player with the Hallé orchestra and at the same time the professional conductor to a number of brass bands. He made numerous arrangements for bands and had many Belle Vue successes.

The third member of this group of outstanding brass

band conductors of the nineteenth century was Edwin Swift. He was born in Linthwaite in 1842, the son of a handloom weaver. He always lived in the Huddersfield area, and was completely self-taught as a musician. He worked as a weaver in the mill, but was much more interested in music. He trained the Linthwaite Band and by the early 1870s they were rivals to Dyke and Meltham Mills. He became very much in demand as a band trainer, so gave up weaving on his thirty-second birthday.

The Belle Vue contest of September, 1894, must have been a riveting affair. Alex Owen conducted five bands, Edwin Swift five and John Gladney four. The contest was won by Besses o' th' Barn.

Many bands had no professional conductor, so that the men who led them had no more musical knowledge or training than the men who played.

However, it was possible for the average working man to increase his knowledge and improve his education through the Mechanics Institutes. Dr. George Birkbeck started the idea in Glasgow, with technical courses for the new breed of worker-mechanics. In 1823 the London Mechanics Institute was formed and, in 1824, Leeds and Manchester followed. By 1841, two hundred Mechanics Institutes existed and by 1860 there were about seven hundred and fifty, mainly in the Midlands, Lancashire and Yorkshire.

When Benjamin Heywood opened the Manchester Institute, he said: "So that the mind might take advantage of any new ideas, it has to be educated and the Mechanics Institute must make education possible, at nominal cost, in leisure time".

A class in musical instruction became part of the educational programme in many institutes. It was thought that music would act as a "humanising influence and keep people away from vicious habits". To bandsmen and their conductors it became a way of improving their standards.

It may have been because of this general lack of musical education that the controversy arose, over which clef should be used for brass band music. In November, 1887, the question was asked in the columns of the *British Bandsman* as to why publishers of brass band music sent out their solo and second euphoniums parts in bass clef.

Others joined in the discussion as to which clef was more suitable, until May, 1888, when the following opinion was offered: "On common sense principles I must vote for the use of G clef for all brass instruments. One single system of fingering should be used. That of the cornet. This would considerably facilitate not only the task of the bandmaster, but the learning of the instrument itself. One player could pass easily from one instrument to another".

By 1896 the issue had not been settled and the *British Musician* published this comment: "The use of the treble clef for all purposes has been strongly advocated in recent reports and among brass bands has been successfully carried out, but it is on a wrong basis and theoretically incorrect".

But the discussion was not over and in an article on arranging for brass bands in the *British Musician*, April, 1898, the following information was given: "The tenor trombones are generally written for in the tenor clefs, but sometimes in the bass, and in a few instances, in the treble clef. E*b* and B*b* basses are frequently written for in the bass clef, but in several English band journals, they are written for in the treble clef".

Uniformity ultimately came, but it is possible that many twentieth century teachers who want their brass players to play in orchestras and wind bands, as well as the brass band, regret that the treble clef alone (apart from the bass trombone) was selected for brass band use. Certainly it established brass band musicians as being separate from the main stream of instrumentalists.

Another controversy which concerned musical Europe during the latter years of the nineteenth century, was that of universal pitch. The problem continued to concern brass band instrumentalists and the manufacturers of instruments until the 1960s, although it was settled in other spheres much earlier.

On January 15, 1888, the editor of the *British Bandsman* commented: "It seems a thousand pities that we cannot adapt our pitch to the 'diapason normal' now becoming universal. It has been lately officially adopted in Italy and England will soon stand alone in this respect. The principle, if not the sole, hindrances are the military band instruments. Is it a question of money or method?"

But by February, 1888, further light was shed on the subject. It was pointed out that the biggest obstacle to a change of pitch was not band instruments but organs. They seemed to be at "all sorts of pitches" and it would be necessary for their owners to spend a considerable amount of money to standardise them.

"Suppose the army pitch were changed tomorrow, the first time a Guards band joined in any concert with the organ at the Crystal Palace or Albert Hall, the result would be confusion."

However, the military authorities requested the Commandant of Kneller Hall, Col. Thompson, to write a report on the subject. It had previously been assumed that brass and woodwind instruments would be ruined by a conversion to universal pitch, but he discovered that this was not so, and that both brass and woodwind could be changed with thoroughly satisfactory results. Col. Thompson calculated, in 1888, that the cost of converting all of the instruments in the British Army would be £9,000.

Since military bands did not convert to universal pitch until the 1920s it must be assumed that the cost was thought to be too great. But the discussion continued in the *British Bandsman* of June 15, 1888, when a comment from another journal was reprinted, which made the point that amateur brass bands would be affected by any decision which military bands made. Manufacturers too should be considered as they "hitherto have endeavoured to maintain the high pitch to prevent complication in their factories and to some extent shut out foreign competition". A change to low pitch would cause them to manufacture both kinds of instruments, as the amateur bands would never be able to afford to convert.

Whether it would have been easier to convert in the 1880s than the 1960s is impossible to ascertain. But certainly a further point made was true, that conversion to low pitch by military bands would mean that the difference between professional musicians and amateur bands would be emphasised and that these units would be unable to perform together. This discrepancy existed for nearly forty years, and throughout that period the instrument manufacturers had to supply both high and low pitch brass instruments to the home market. Finally it was they who forced the issue in the 1960s by refusing to manufacture high pitch instruments.

Trade played an increasingly important part as brass bands became established. Some firms already existed and others came into being because of a need. Boosey & Co., which was founded in the eighteenth century, took over the brass instrument business of Henry Distin in 1865 and the Parisian firm of instrument manufacturers Besson & Co. founded their English firm in 1858.

The manufacturers continued to experiment in order to perfect brass instruments as used in a brass band, being confident of a ready market. In the mid-1890s there were fifty-two firms manufacturing brass band instruments.

The first specialist publisher of brass band music was Richard Smith. He was a brilliant cornet player and a highly esteemed teacher of brass bands. He was one of the most prolific composers and arrangers of his time and, more importantly, made the music available for all bands. In 1857 he founded the Champion Brass Band Journal in Hull and

Left: William Rimmer, (1862–1911), outstanding cornet player with Besses and later, a professional trainer of many bands. He arranged and composed for brass bands and was music editor, at various times, to F. Richardson, R. Smith and Wright & Round.

Right: Richard Smith, founder of the first publishing company specialising in brass band music — R. Smith & Co. Ltd. Established in Hull in 1857, the company is still specialising in brass band music and flourishing in Watford, Herts.

moved the company to London in 1878. Ten years later it was possible to buy a full brass band set of an arrangement of an overture for three shillings.

In December, 1889, he was stung by an article in the *British Bandsman* which said that the only music published for brass bands was trivial and he wrote in reply: "I am quite ready to adopt as high a standard as my customers will support me in. I have determined to introduce two classical pieces during the next year and present them free to my subscribers. I will also publish them on special terms and watch the results with much interest."

In March, 1890, Richard Smith had a stroke and died. Sam Cope, founder of the *British Bandsman*, became the next editor, and in 1898 John Henry Iles became the owner of R. Smith & Co.

Similar developments were taking place in Liverpool where in 1875 a professional musician, Harry Round, joined forces with business man Thomas Wright, and founded a new publishing company — Wright & Round. Round was one of the pioneer composers of music written for, and conceived in terms of, a brass band. But at the turn of the century a man who was to become the music editor of Wright & Round was making his mark — William Rimmer. Son of a military bandmaster, he was involved in band music almost from birth. He was an outstanding cornet player with Besses and later turned to conducting. He was a great success and in the July Belle Vue contest of 1898 he conducted three bands and won the first three prizes. Many of his compositions are still being played by bands today.

Wright & Round were the first publishers of a paper which dealt solely with the interests of brass bands. *Brass Band News* appeared in Liverpool for the first time in 1881. It was edited initially by Enoch Round, who was succeeded in 1886 by William Seddon, bandmaster of the Kettering Rifles. Until his death in 1913, Seddon, through the paper, played a great part in the development of bands. He was very outspoken in some of his comments, spurring bandsmen on to higher standards of performance and deportment.

In 1898 he wrote: "All old contestants deplore the fact that the educated, well-to-do local gentry, no longer patronise band contests by their presence, as they used to do. There is no doubt that in the old days contesting bandsmen were more modest, less suspicious and envious than they are today. They were more simple minded, less conceited and consequently more easy to manage.

"Many good bands today do not contest, saying that contesting has fallen from its high estate, what with cheap judges, cheap contests, and the influx of bandsmen who look on contesting as a sport, like cock-fighting or rat-worrying."

A person of equal influence was Sam Cope, who founded the *British Bandsman* in 1887. The ambition of the new paper was to become the "pioneer of band progress". Like the *Brass Band News*, the *British Bandsman* recorded events of the time, published informative articles and opened its columns to discussion of topics of concern to bandsmen. Like all newspapers, not only did it carry the news of the day, but became an historical record as soon as it was published.

In 1894 the *British Musician* printed a report of the first meeting of the British Amateur Band Association, held in Manchester, on November 18, 1893. Twenty-two bands were represented and amongst the resolutions passed were the following:

a) Each enrolled Band should submit a list of members to the Association.

b) No man should register with more than one band.

c) No Association Band should be allowed to play under judges not approved by the Association.

d) No band should be allowed to compete with more than twenty four players.

Also recorded was the first meeting of the Lancashire Brass Band Association. It took place on the same night, just a few miles down the road, at Wigan. Twelve bands were present and many decisions reached were the same.

Local band associations have flourished throughout the years, but there has never been a democratically elected national body, empowered to speak for all.

In 1898, a man burst on to the scene with great enthusiasm, and for almost half a century it was he who provided the national unity, which bandsmen were unable to provide for themselves. He was John Henry Iles.

Whilst on a business trip to Manchester in September, 1898, he found himself with some spare time and was advised by a hotel-porter to visit the brass band contest taking place at Belle Vue.

In his own words he was "positively astounded" and he came away from that contest a "completely converted enthusiast" to the cause of bands.

When he returned to London he started to make inquiries about brass band activities in the south and soon contacted Sam Cope who naturally encouraged this enthusiasm.

Before the end of 1898, John Henry Iles had become the owner of R. Smith and the *British Bandsman.*

A few months later John Henry began to organise the *British Bandsman* War Fund in support of the *Daily Mail* Kipling Fund which was inaugurated to aid the relatives of soldiers fighting in the Boer War. To support the fund, John Henry Iles decided to organise a brass band concert in the Royal Albert Hall, bringing to participate eleven bands from all over the British Isles, including the Besses o' th' Barn, Black Dyke, Kettering Rifles and St. Albans City.

The most important work in the programme was a march by Sir Arthur Sullivan inspired by Kipling's poem 'The Absent Minded Beggar'.

. . . He's an absent-minded beggar, but he heard his country call.

And his reg'ment didn't need to send to find him!

He chucked his job and joined it — so the job before us all

Is to help the home that Tommy's left behind him! . . .

The project stirred the imagination of bands and bandsmen all over the country. Sir Arthur Sullivan was persuaded to conduct and on the night of January 20, 1900, an immense audience of ten-thousand was packed into the

PROGRAMME ·
PATRIOTIC BAND FESTIVAL
Royal Albert Hall.

January 20th, 1900.

CHAS J. FOLKARD/00

John Henry Iles in his younger days,
from a photograph taken in 1903.

Albert Hall, with half as many again turned away. Between
£2,000 - £3,000 were raised for the fund.

But for the brass band movement this event subsequently
proved to be of enormous importance.

As Sir Arthur Sullivan stood on the platform of the
Royal Albert Hall, he was obviously deeply moved by the
performance of the bands and the response of the audience.
He turned to Mr. Iles and said: "What can be done for these
fellows?"

A fortuitous remark, for Sullivan was one of the directors
of the Crystal Palace and John Henry Iles had already conceived the idea of putting on an annual brass band festival
there — but he needed support from the right quarters.

He had heard of the contest organised at Crystal Palace
by Enderby Jackson in the years 1860, 1861, 1862 and

1863, and was very impressed. It was now 1900 and once again London became the centre for a brass band contest on a national scale.

With the birth of the National Brass Band Championships, brass bands entered the twentieth century.

References
British Bandsman – 1887 – 1890 and 1898 – 1900
Orchestral Times & Bandsman – Jan. 1891 – Dec. 1892
British Musician – Jan. – Dec. 1893
British Musician & Orchestral Times – Jan. 1894 – Dec. 1898
The Brass Band Movement by J.F. Russell & J.H. Elliot – published by
                                                    J.M. Dent 1936

2. Instrumental
Developments

by BARRIE PERRINS

British Brass Band instrumentation now (1979) comprises:

1 E*b* soprano cornet
9 B*b* cornets
1 B*b* flugel horn
3 E*b* horns
2 B*b* baritones
2 B*b* tenor trombones
1 B*b*/F bass trombone
2 B*b* euphoniums
2 E*b* basses (tubas)
2 B*b* basses (tubas)

plus percussion

Nationally and internationally, contests have done much to help standardise brass band affairs, including instrumentation; likewise, improved communications and travel to other countries by individual band personnel, and bands themselves touring, have had influence on uniformity. And economic stresses during the past two or three decades have caused the number of instrument manufacturers to diminish quite rapidly which in turn has affected this trend toward uniformity.

Although brass band instrumentation is (with few exceptions) standardised in Britain, the position in other countries varies — in some cases considerably. Brass bands in the Netherlands and Switzerland, for example, sometimes comprise fifty or more players, and instrumentation and distribution of parts often differs too. In countries other than Britain, trumpets and flugel horns are frequently used in place of cornets, and baritone parts may be played on euphoniums. Even though classified as "Brass Bands", certain continental ensembles include clarinets and saxophones; and some Salvation Army bands in Britain used saxophones well into the twentieth century, the famous Chalk Farm Band, London, using them as late as 1938 (see 'Play the Music, Play!' by Brindley Boon, published Salvationist Publishing & Supplies Ltd.). Similarly, in numerous brass bands overseas, instruments such as valve trombones, helicons and sousaphones are not unusual. The 'G' bass trombone is gradually disappearing in Britain in favour of the B*b*/F bass trombone (and variations of that instrument), but "the old 'G' with its extension rod" is still quite popular elsewhere. The early part of this century saw the complete disappearance of ophicleides and helicons from British brass bands and from most brass bands overseas, being replaced by much more efficient brass basses. The growing awareness of "compensating"

29

valves, referred to in greater detail later, gradually dispensed with five-valved euphoniums and the doublophone, an instrument with two bells on which euphonium sound and trombone sound could be produced separately; the doublophone was manufactured by the Besson Company of Britain and the American Conn Company, and it was very popular in brass and military bands throughout the United States of America up to the 1930s.

The National Brass Band Championships have done much to improve instrumental development and standardise instrumentation by:

1. Rules governing what, and how many, instruments shall be played in a band, e.g. the 1902 Rules specified "No valve trombones or drums will be allowed."

2. Sponsoring music that helps players to improve, musically and technically.

3. Affording advertising facilities to, and comparison between, music publishers and instrument manufacturers, thus intensifying competition and stimulating new ideas.

4. Nurturing the Brass Band movement generally.

Admission of percussion to contests is a development of the past decade that has been welcomed, with a noteworthy increase in publication of solo items featuring percussion since then with similar response; the percussion section is no longer the "Cinderella Section" of the Brass Band!

A few exceptions to standard instrumentation in British brass bands have arisen during recent years, e.g. a representative Salvation Army band comprising musicians from the Services operated successfully with guest conductors in the mid-1950s to the early 1960s, playing French horns in place of the usual Eb (tenor) horns. And London Collegiate Brass (formerly City of London Band) comprising mainly music students in the London area, now part of Morley College activities, use French horns similarly, also trumpets in place of cornets occasionally.

The amalgamation in 1930 of the two companies, Boosey and Hawkes & Son, becoming Boosey & Hawkes Ltd. of which the Besson company later became a subsidiary, were consequential changes which led to the factory at Edgware, London, becoming the largest musical instrument manufacturing establishment in Europe. The Salvation Army factory at St. Albans, Hertfordshire, also famed for its craftsmanship for best part of a century, was taken over by Boosey & Hawkes Ltd. in 1972; and the nearby factory at Luton, Bedfordshire, of the late Mr. A.W. Philpot ceased music instrument business at about that time too. Hand-made

instruments have disappeared almost completely during the last thirty years or so, being replaced by machine produced instruments.

Among European and other foreign companies who have contributed considerably to instrument developments this century are Alexander, Courtois, Cuesnon, Hirsbrunner, Mahillon, Selmer, Willson, Conn, Getzen, Holton, Olds and Vincent Bach. Soloists and teachers have collaborated with manufacturers, pooling their knowledge for the benefit of all brass instrumentalists. And those developments have run parallel with advances in playing technique and musicianship.

Valve development in the nineteenth century revolutionised brass instrument manufacture and performance, particularly via Adolphe Sax with his sax horns which were played throughout Europe by the Distin family with astonishing effect, giving impetus to the development of the brass band. Valve design and production have played a significant part toward instrument developments during the twentieth century. Although rotary and piston valves were commonly used in brass bands throughout the world at the beginning of the twentieth century, today instruments with piston valves far outnumber those with rotary valves: and in Britain particularly, it is very rare that rotary valves are observed at all. So far as baritones, euphoniums and basses are concerned, most British brass band instruments have the "compensating" valve system, i.e. an automatic device via extra tubing controlled by a "master valve" (third valve on three-valved instruments, fourth valve on four-valve instruments) which primarily assists tuning. The British "compensating system" of D.J. Blaikley (patented in 1878) seems to be the most successful and is used universally by "bigger brass" players, in military bands and orchestras as well as brass bands, with Besson/Boosey & Hawkes instruments. With other makes of instruments, tuning improvement is sought via slides and triggers which are not automatic and are operated by players personally, adding to performance problems. In this context it may be of interest to mention the distinguished tubaist, Harry Barlow (1871 - 1932), formerly of the Hallé Orchestra and later tuba professor at London's Royal Academy of Music, who designed several 'F' tubas made by Besson; these were five-valved and not "compensated". The 'F' tuba is now almost obsolete in Britain, having been replaced by larger instruments; it was mainly orchestrally used, rarely in brass bands.

Various types of piston valve have been made, with springs in the upper part of their cases and others with springs in the lower part: and not long ago some cornets (and

Ophicleide — forerunner of the tuba (B & H Museum cat. No. 548)

trumpets) were made with "suspended" springs; today most piston valves are manufactured with springs in the lower part of their cases. Although round-cylindrical shaped now, some valves were ellipse shaped, notably by Conn of the United States of America. Length of action varies too between different makers, and different models of individual instruments. Metallurgical developments constitute the main improvements currently; valves have been made of bronze (hence "Solbron" instruments by Boosey), brass, and brass plated with silver or nickel, also valves with tin-nickel plating are available. The Hirsbrunner Company of Switzerland produces 'Trypen' valves, made from a combination of brass and plastic for its tubas. But the most efficient valves appear to be those made from monel, a copper-nickel alloy, now used extensively by most major manufacturers. In general, valve action is shorter today than it was on instruments made, for example, pre-1939, proving more efficient — and quicker to operate.

Tests with plastic tacquets, to replace those of metal, are currently proceeding in this country, and British and foreign instruments fitted with plastic tacquets are obtainable; plastic tacquets give a quieter and usually smoother action than those made of metal, but are less durable. The Yamaha Company produces tacquets which fit on to valves from the top, held in position by pre-drilled grooves — yet another manufacturing variation of recent years.

Most standard brass band valved instruments — mainly cornets, horns and baritones — have only three valves, whereas euphoniums and E♭ basses (in some cases B♭ basses too) with four valves have become increasingly popular since the mid-1920s. Today relatively few reputed brass bands have three-valved euphoniums and E♭ basses because contemporary technical and musical demands render the four-valved variety a necessity. On four-valved instruments that are "compensated", a complete chromatic sequence of notes is possible; they also make more alternative fingerings available, thus simplifying otherwise difficult music in terms of performance — and as already mentioned, better tuning is among other benefits derived from "compensated" instruments, three-valved and four-valved. Correct use of the fourth valve is now an important feature of "lower brass" instrument instruction yet, with notable exceptions, this instrumental development was not fully recognised by many players until long after its introduction; even now it is viewed with a measure of mystery in some quarters . . . Tone quality and range enlargement are two more advantages this development has given, besides enabling technical barriers to be overcome which formerly were deemed impossible other than by a few virtuosi.

The Yamaha Company of Japan introduced euphoniums and basses with all four valves positioned together, parallel with the bell, and operated by the right-hand fingers; this idea followed the American pattern, as different from the traditional British models on which the fourth valve protrudes from the "back" tubing area and is operated by the first finger of the left hand — the remaining three valves being operated by the right-hand fingers. Although Yamaha and similar four-valved instruments dispense with the need for a fourth valve clip, they are not "compensated", and the second D-flat/C-sharp (brass band parlance) below the treble stave has to be "lipped" in tune; in operation, the fourth valve seems slower when grouped with the other three valves, i.e. in comparison with the traditional "back" fourth valve position.

One personal observation on the subject of valves is perhaps worth consideration: if finger tops were made smaller and with slight indentations, the reduced area and added "feel" (contact) possibility would encourage more accurate finger action — thus minimising valve malfunction.

The basic design of brass instruments has been influenced by four factors: valve systems, bore, tuning and tone quality. Valves have already been mentioned at length and apart from a few more minor references that aspect appears to justify no further comments.

It says much for the rich diversity of design that euphoniums, for example, in brass bands can be bell-forward (American type), oval shape (continental) or upright bell models (British); likewise bells of horns, baritones, euphoniums and basses may point over the left or the right shoulder of the player, according to design and maker. Cornets made by Conn, Getzen and Vincent Bach of America are played next to British and Japanese made cornets, a permutation applicable to many bands today and relevant to other instruments and manufacturers too, as different from the situation 20 and more years ago. Improved communications, world trading facilities and growing recognition of the brass band as a cultural activity — nationally and internationally — have helped make this possible.

In recent years the bore of brass instruments has been enlarged considerably, by manufacturers in Britain and elsewhere. For example, trombones of thirty years ago and before are now referred to as "pea shooters", so small is their bore in comparison with contemporary instruments; and that change has led to a different sound, much richer and warmer than that achieved from small-bore instruments. The "F" and comparable attachments to trombones today is another design factor, affecting bore too, providing extended range and more "shift" permutations which simplify performance problems and help economise on slide movement. The latest "Sovereign" range of instruments of Boosey & Hawkes exemplifies the trend for larger bore (and bells) admirably: the "Sovereign" euphonium is virtually a small bass in size and weight in comparison with its early twentieth century counterparts, many of which were short models. Sympathy has always been due to bass players having regard to their instrument-weight problems (not forgetting the old bass player's quip "I also have to clean it!"), and anybody who has carried one of the modern EE♭ four-valve basses will appreciate those problems even more — quite apart from consideration for those who play the heavier currently made BB♭ four-valve basses . . . . . Admittedly, improved transport arrangements and cases fitted with wheels help the situation, also in some countries (particularly the United States of America) lighter plastic bell sections are being used. For smaller brass instruments too, increased bore size has been a consequential development during the past two or three decades, promoting similarly easier tone production, better tone quality and improved sound projection, also wider dynamic range. On the other hand, larger bore instruments have caused some players to lose clarity, probably because those players have not adjusted their articulation technique appropriately.

General comparison of contemporary instruments with their counterparts of, say, the 1920s indicates that valve action was longer on older instruments whose narrower bore resulted in a thinner sound if (in some cases) a quicker response. Improved design of instruments has provided a better "holding" balance, even allowing for modern instruments being heavier than earlier models; and current design improvements affecting bass mouth-pipe position illustrates that aspect particularly, besides adding to playing comfort.

Unusual instruments such as pocket cornets, doublo-

Top: Tenor Trombone B*b*, Centre:
Tenor Trombone B*b*/F, and
Bottom: Bass Trombone B*b*/F/G/E*b*

phones and echo cornets are no longer produced. Any requirement for a pocket cornet has gone, and improved playing technique plus the aid of mutes makes the other two quite unnecessary. The trombone 'F' and comparable attachments (or "plugs") already referred to are functional design attributes which can aid performers musically and technically, and the widely admired "Sovereign" double-plug bass trombone is an excellent example.

The mouthpiece is an integral part of a brass musical instrument, and mouthpiece design has progressed much during the twentieth century. Contemporary mouthpieces are generally larger than earlier productions — so providing a richer sound — and there is now far more variety with regard to rim, cup, throat and bore, meeting the more varied demands of contemporary players who are usually more willing to experiment than their forebears were. Mouthpiece types such as "Kosicup" and "Eesi-lype" were popular during the first half of this century with, of course, standard mouthpieces bearing various numbers for personal selection. American companies such as Vincent Bach and Conn added appreciably to the number available, and some players and teachers have given their name to more 'personal' products made to their specifications. It is also interesting to note the "transferable shank" idea which facilitates cornet to trumpet change. Some manufacturers supply instruments with interchangeable receivers, enabling different sized mouthpieces to be used similarly.

Increased knowledge of brass playing technique since World War II particularly has shown the importance of mouthpiece design and choice, and the commercial barons have not been slow to exploit this growing awareness! A few famous soloists and professors have given serious consideration to mouthpiece design based on experience and scientific experiment; the relationship between tone production and quality, also intonation and comfort during performance, has been carefully assessed — and with other instrumental developments has improved mouthpiece production standards. If in former times players often accepted without question the mouthpiece provided with the instrument, that is no longer the position today: a more intelligent process of selectivity has grown with the wider range of choice — and better qualified teachers within the brass band movement. There is no magic in any mouthpiece, however, and it is still "the person behind it" who determines ultimate results! It is hoped that a universally standardised system of numbering will eventually materialise to simplify choice.

Tuning has noticeably improved with the incidence of

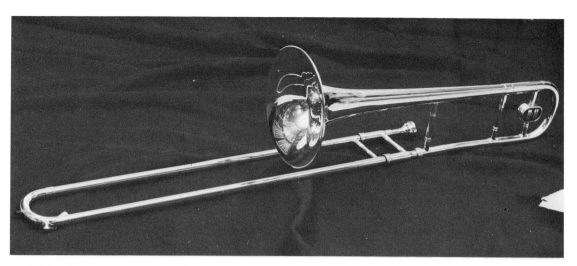

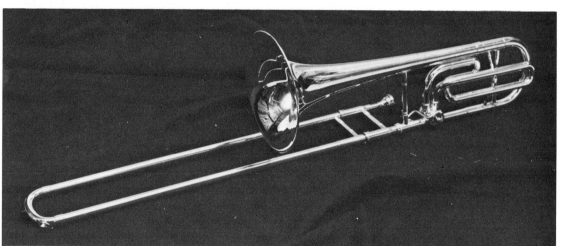

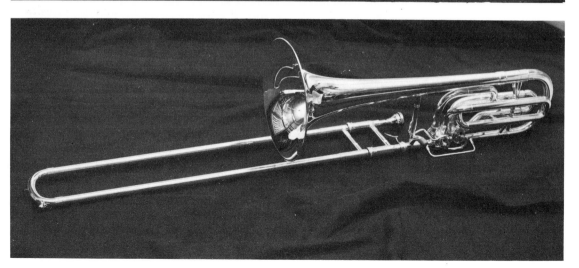

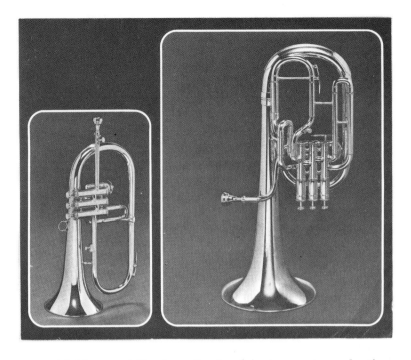

more highly specialised methods of instrument production, also sharpened critical faculties demanding better tuned instruments. Improved tuning affects tone quality because players are not required to "lip" notes in tune, and psychologically it has advantages too in performance. Besides tuning improvement effected through basic changes in construction, some modern cornets and trumpets (and a few other instruments too) have triggers added for finer tuning on certain notes.

Tone quality has improved with the metals used today; metallurgical expertise indicates that the ratio of component metals in brass, for example, affects response — and effects can differ between "smaller" and "larger" brass instruments. The overall functions of, for example, a Higham and a Thibouville-Lamy euphonium (both manufactured circa 1912) and an even earlier vintage Salvation Army short model euphonium, each played during my youth, could not compare with the Boosey "Solbron" euphonium of 1919 which was my trusted friend for something like thirty years and now resides in the Karl Burri Museum, Switzerland. But not one of those old instruments could measure up to the valve efficiency and tone production ease of my currently used Besson "New Standard" 1973 euphonium with its larger bore, and better sound projection, facts which exemplify progress in instrumental developments. Perhaps one of the most notable instruments in which development can be observed is the flugel horn; although formerly not regarded as a solo instrument and therefore neglected by composers and arrangers, its popularity in the brass band (and in jazz groups) has grown remarkably during the past few years. The larger bore and superior tuning of currently made flugel horns have influenced this change, and the instrument has become attractive with its enhanced tone colour and soloistic usefulness as well as more interesting parts in full band scoring. The Eb horn and baritone have been similarly improved with wider bore and resulting richer tone quality. Via recordings (allowing for progress in recording technique) the tonal superiority of modern instruments over their counterparts of yesteryear can be gauged clearly, one specific point being the replacement of the "G" bass trombone with the contemporary Bb/F bass trombone which helped eliminate an oft characteristic roughness from that area.

The use of mutes is much more extensive today than in previous years, a subject that constitutes an instrumental development. Formerly only cornet and trombone players used mutes but it is not unusual today to observe mutes used in horns and baritones, even basses in exceptional cases, adding colour and new tonal conceptions to the overall "band sound" as well as individual effects.

Standard International Pitch is A 440, i.e. 440 vibrations per second (also called "Low Pitch"), but up to the late 1960s most brass bands in Britain played in High Pitch, i.e. A 452.5, which caused problems over many years — not least problems of isolation from other musical media. The British Army officially adopted Low Pitch in 1928, and it was the practice of some manufacturers to mark instruments "L.P." to differentiate from those in High Pitch. The decision for British brass bands to adopt Low Pitch was ultimately made in liaison with manufacturers who ceased making High Pitch instruments with effect from 1 April 1965; and several manufacturers organised adaptation arrangements, additional slides etc., for existing High Pitch instruments where such change was possible.

Initially the idea met strong opposition from within the band movement, primarily from those whose thinking was geared to tradition rather than progress! Criticisms forecasting "loss of sound brilliance" and "worsened tuning" were silenced when the decision to change to A 440 was inevitably accepted. Change to Standard Pitch marked a very significant instrumental development, it also led to important advances in regard to brass band recognition. Brass bands could now participate in concerts together with military bands, choirs, orchestras and church organs! Only a few Commonwealth countries had High Pitch instruments like Britain, and it seems that virtually all brass bands have now adopted Standard Pitch.

One decidedly noticeable and important change during the twentieth century relates to appearance of brass bands, therefore presentation. Whereas the majority of brass band instruments up to the 1920s were not silver plated or lacquered, virtually all are treated that way today. Besides being easier to keep clean, it is more hygienic and congenial to play silver plated (or lacquered) instruments, particularly in hot conditions. Improved economic circumstances of the 1920s/30s made more funds available to bands who frequently had existing instruments silver plated, or bought instruments already plated (lacquered instruments are traditionally less popular in brass bands than silver plated instruments), and it was common for such bands to be called "Silver" Bands.

Besides the standard "frosted finish" silver plate there is now Bright Silver Plate (B.S.P.) finish available which adds to the visual attractiveness of instruments; the writer has also seen a few instruments with the inside bell gold plated. Although virtually no difference in sound quality can be detected between plated and un-plated instruments, some folk still express preference for "silver" bands to brass bands! And even *The Times* of February 13, 1976, referred to Salvation Army bands ranking with the finest "brass and silver bands" in the land. Happily, the term "silver" is gradually disappearing from band titles, also by way of record the term "prize" which, musically speaking, is irrelevant.

Up to the commencement of World War II, engraving was a feature of higher grade brass instruments; ornate designs were artistically engraved on bells, usually in the area surrounding makers' names. Instruments made by Higham of Manchester were memorable for their engraving which was often on slides as well as bells. Probably due to expense and shortage of skilled labour, engraving (or stamping) all but makers' details on bells has virtually ceased on British made instruments; and floral engraving has lessened notably on instruments made elsewhere in recent years.

Brass bandsmen of the earlier part of this century were often seen transporting their instruments uncovered in public, usually because they had no cases or instrument covers. Today it is rare, however, to see uncased instruments being publicly transported; cases (and covers) protect from dust and dirt besides guarding against dents and comparable hazards. The gradual replacement of drop-end cases by the more practical centre-opening type for horns and larger brass

Sousaphone Eb — a counterpart of the bass tuba.

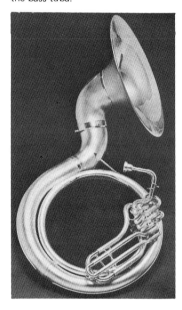

instruments also indicates growing care-consciousness.

The past decade has brought with it a marked awareness of the need for instrument hygiene, moreover dealers and manufacturers have publicised and produced special cleaning brushes and fluids for instrumental "inner cleanliness". Similarly, the unhygienic practice of expectorating on valves for lubrication purposes has largely given way to use of valve oil or water! Mouthpiece cases and mouthpiece cleaning brushes are also relatively recent innovations whose relationship with care and hygiene are obvious — and welcome developments.

The past thirty years have evidenced a marked increase in school and youth bands. Education authorities are giving more recognition to the brass band as a valid musical medium which in more than a few cases has replaced the traditional choir and orchestra, as well as supplementing those music expression forms elsewhere. Besides "feeding" adult bands with trained personnel, this development has done much to add valuable instrumental knowledge (and musicianship) to the band movement. The National Youth Brass Band and various youth brass bands formed on a county or district basis are stimulating interest generally and, with school bands, are providing good quality instruments initially for learners as well as more progressive young players who might otherwise not have such opportunities, i.e. via local bands organised outside the realms of education. Instrumental choice and selectivity of personnel for particular instruments are two aspects that have become much more specialized with the influence of highly trained teaching staff operating under the education umbrella, in addition to rising standards generally of technical and musical ability.

Two future instrumental changes seem likely. In some championship bands the soprano cornet has been replaced by an E♭ trumpet, resulting in greater ease of performance and improved sound penetrability plus enhancement of overall tonal texture. The second point affects trombones: usually only three trombones feature with any one band in accordance with normal scoring and contesting requirements; but in some bands an extra trombone has been added with considerable effect for ordinary concert work. Four-part harmony in the distinctive trombone "voice" is clearly an asset, and could become a standard idea in the future.

The increasing occurrence of divisi euphonium parts, so giving a richer harmonic mixture and wider technical resources to composers/arrangers, could conceivably lead to first and second euphonium parts as in the case of baritones.

Band formation has always been a debatable subject, and

Left: Four valve Euphonium B*b*
Right: Baritone B*b*.

there is room in that area for improvement, not least from the visual aspect. Grimethorpe Colliery Band is one of a few ensembles that have experimented successfully in recent years, even changing formation during concerts to suit specific works; frequently these changes accentuate particular instrumental sections including the percussionists, hitherto sadly neglected. Clearly, if the brass band is to retain and develop audience appeal, band formation is a subject worthy of deeper investigation, provided it is purposeful and not mere gimmickry.

Soloistically speaking the baritone and flugel horn are neglected instruments, thus new ideas in that direction would be well received.

The introduction of organ and piano soloists into brass

band programmes is another instrumental development worth cultivating; acceptance of Standard Pitch encouraged this idea and there is much scope available too with orchestras and choirs joining with brass bands for specific items. New works in concerto form featuring cornet, French horn, trombone, euphonium and bass (tuba) have in recent years added lustre and musical status to the repertoire — and brought instrumental recognition which twenty years or so ago would have been almost unthinkable (Denis Wright's delightful Cornet Concerto is the exception proving this rule).

Small ensemble works, notably since the lamentable passing of Gilbert Vinter, have been neglected. Useful repertoire extension could be achieved by introducing small ensembles such as trios and quartets, with band accompaniment; several existing operatic works could be adapted and arranged in this way, plus new compositions, which would stimulate "instrumental developments" and interest generally.

An improvement in attitudes to band membership could encourage not only basic enjoyment, social benefits and more consequential repertoire but a greater appreciation of "instrumental developments", particularly inter-change of players within bands. Ignorance and sheer prejudice instrumentally often limits, and even stifles, progress within our movement. With imagination and liaison with local orchestras, for example, our musical horizons could be enlarged considerably by occasional player-exchange. And "Instrumental Clinics" on a regional basis given by reputed players could stimulate and enlarge our instrumental knowledge immeasurably!

The percussion section has become increasingly more important during the twentieth century, and the last two decades have brought more complex scoring for, and greater demands from, percussionists. More percussion instruments are being introduced, and it seems that trend will continue into the future, with even higher musical status for percussionists.

References
The Brass Band Movement, Russell & Elliot. J.M. Dent, 1936
Musical Instruments Through the Ages, edited by Anthony Baines, Penguin Books.
The Tuba Family, Clifford Bevan, Faber.
Brass Today, edited by Frank Wright, Besson.

Acknowledgements
Boosey and Hawkes, Edgware for permission to photograph.

3. *The National Championships*

by VIOLET BRAND

THE CHALLENGE PRIZE
BRASS BAND CONTEST
DESIGNED FOR THE CRYSTAL PALACE COMPANY
BY S.J. NICKOLL, ARCHITECTS.   EXECUTED BY COX & SONS,
SOUTHAMPTON ST. STRAND.

In the early months of 1900, John Henry Iles began to organise the first National Brass Band Championship. He had gained the support of Sir Arthur Sullivan and through him the promise of the Crystal Palace as a venue. Various newspapers promised to co-operate and indeed provided silver cups to be awarded at the competition.

But the highest trophy of all and the one which inspired bandsmen over the years to even greater efforts was the famous Thousand Guinea Trophy - the Crystal Palace National Challenge Trophy. This magnificent prize was the property of the Crystal Palace authorities and had lain in the cellars there since the cessation of the choral contests a number of years earlier. It was Sir Arthur Sullivan who requested its use for the National Brass Band Championships. The first announcement of the contest appeared in the *British Bandsman* in April, 1900, although, as always, various rumours had circulated earlier.

Mr. Iles planned what he termed a stepping-stone festival — one which included a progressive series of graded contests. In this way, bands could compete at their own level, but also have the opportunity of hearing those of a higher standard. Twenty-nine bands entered for the first championships and there were three graded sections. Those entered in the top section were: Besses o' th' Barn, Black Dyke, Wyke, Hartlepool Operatic, Lee Mount, Batley Old, Wingates, Denton Original, Rushden, Kettering Rifles, Hucknall Temperance, Arael Griffin, Ferndale, Aberdare and Excelsior Temperance.

The test piece for this section was a selection of Sullivan operas, specially arranged by J. Ord Hume. To play, the bandsmen stood coatless in a square formation.

The adjudicators were chosen by Mr. Iles, and even his own staff did not know who they were, until the morning of the contest. But it would seem that his choice was approved by the audience and most competitors. The chosen four were highly respected musicians - Carl Kiefert, J.O. Shepherd, J.W. Beswick and Dr. C.W. Pearce - and as a result of their deliberations the following prizes were awarded: 1 Denton Original, 2 Black Dyke, 3 Wingates.

The comment in the *British Bandsman* following the bad behaviour of some bandsmen when the results were announced was: "We can understand the great disappointment of some of the crack bands in finding themselves out of the prizes after giving fine performances, but they should remember it does not always follow that the best band wins. It is the best performance of the day in the opinion of the judges that decides the prize list."

Opposite: The Thousand Guinea Trophy, first awarded to a brass band at the Crystal Palace Contest 1900.

Below: J. Ord Hume (1864 – 1932). Arranger of the test piece for the first Crystal Palace Championship in 1900. He was a renowned adjudicator and was invited to judge the Australian Championships.

In 1901 events took a disappointing turn for only twenty seven bands entered. But in 1902, Mr. Iles announced the first area contests which would lead to an invitation to the National Finals at the Crystal Palace. The area contests were to be held in Harrogate, Cardiff, Wolverhampton and New Brighton. The idea did not meet with unanimous approval, as the editorial statement in the *British Bandsman*, August 9, 1902, indicates.

The Postponed Semi-Finals

"Second-class bands have been only too ready to dispute the right of such combinations as Besses, Dyke, Wyke etc., to consider themselves in a class by themselves, or, at any rate, to be chosen upon their undoubtedly great reputations. Upon what else can the position of these bands be gauged? In giving such a question a fair amount of consideration, one could only conclude that a contest arranged on strict lines in every sense of the word was the only possible means of settling the matter in a way fair to all. Let those bands who consider themselves as good as the great 'cracks' already referred to, prove their opinions in honest fight, and then who shall say them nay?

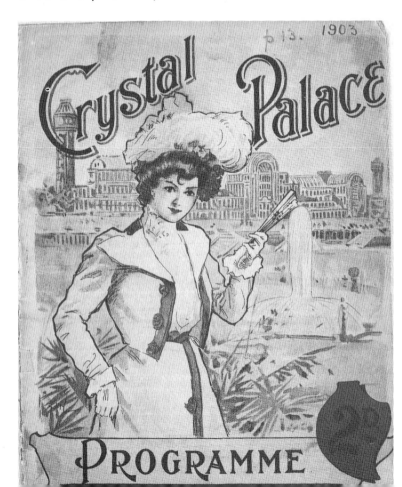

The ornate cover of the Crystal Palace programme, 1903.

"The establishment of the semi-final, so arranged to cover the various districts, was thus decided upon with the sole object of giving a chance to all rising and progressive bands to prove their mettle and win by fair fight the right to be considered among the 'cracks' of England. If young bands have no ambition and enterprise, and are not prepared to work and even make sacrifices how can they expect to rival those who have made their names famous in brass band history?

"The semi-finals at Wolverhampton and Harrogate have been abandoned, not for want of entries, but because the bands for which they were instituted did not rise to the occasion and seize the chance given them to justify themselves."

In the same issue it was reported that the area contest would go ahead at New Brighton and that the first four bands would be entitled to compete at the Crystal Palace contest. But, in Cardiff, only three bands entered.

However, there was no shortage of entries for the Grand Finals, for over ninety bands competed. Twenty one of these were in the championship section — three conducted by John Gladney and seven by Alex Owen! The test piece was an arrangement of Coleridge-Taylor's Hiawatha and the first prize was awarded to Black Dyke (John Gladney),

The line-up of bands and conductors for the Grand Championship section in 1903. The bands were competing for the Thousand Guinea Trophy.

12.0   In the Concert Hall.

GRAND CHAMPIONSHIP BRASS BAND CONTEST

FOR THE

Thousand Guinea Cup,

And Prizes as on pages 2 and 3.

Championship Section.

Adjudicators—Mr. G. T. H. SEDDON and Mr. J. O. SHEPHERD.

NAME OF BAND.	CONDUCTOR.	NAME OF BAND.	CONDUCTOR.
Besses o' th' Barn	... A. Owen	Kingston Mills ...	... A. Owen
Black Dike Mills	... J. Gladney	Lee Mount ...	... A. Owen
Cleckheaton Victoria	... A. Holden	Linthwaite ...	... E. Swift
Cleveland Steel Works	W. Holdsworth	Luton Red Cross	... A. Holden
Crooke ...	... W. Rimmer	Pemberton Old	... J. Gladney
Irwell Bank ...	... A. Owen	Rotherham Borough	... A. Owen
Irwell Springs ...	... W. Rimmer	Rushden Temperance	... A. Owen
Kettering Rifles	... A. Owen	'Tillery Collieries	... J. Griffiths
Kettering Town	... R. Ryan	Wingates Temperance	W. Rimmer
King Cross Subscription	J. Gladney	Wyke	... E. Swift

Admission to Concert Hall, One Shilling.

whilst second and third places went to Wyke (E. Swift) and Luton Red Cross (Angus Holden).

The bands competed under the following rules and regulations, which are reprinted from the *British Bandsman* of August 16, 1902.

CRYSTAL PALACE BAND CONTEST

September 27, 1902

General Rules and Regulations

(1)   This great Musical Festival and Contest is restricted to Amateur Brass Bands of not more than 24 players in each band. Any performer who, within six months of the date of close of the entries, has been engaged as a regular member of the band of any theatre or other public place of amusement, or resort, will be considered a professional, and therefore ineligible to compete. Every performer must be in a position to prove that he is in some business or profession from which he derives his chief income, apart from the playing of music.

(2)   The bands competing at this Festival will be divided into four sections:-

First Section. - For the One Thousand Guinea Cup.

Second Section - For bands wishing to be eligible to compete in the first section next year.

Third Section - Limited to bands who have not won a cash prize exceeding £15. in value.

Fourth Section - Limited to bands, who have not won a cash prize exceeding £6. in value.

(3)   All the above sections are open to bands of Great Britain and the Colonies.

(4)   All the players must be bona fide members of the band in which they are entered, and each player must have been enrolled as a member of such a band at least three months prior to the day of the contest. No member will be allowed to play with more than one band, and if found playing with two bands, both bands will be disqualified.

(5)   Every member of the band must be resident in the town or within a distance of four miles, or thereabouts, of the town from which the band is entered. Special remark must be made, and special permission obtained from the Contest Director, at the time of entry, before any member, whose residence is more than four miles distant, will be allowed to play.

(6)   Each band must play the test piece selected which will be sent free to each band competing at least six clear weeks prior to the day of Contest. No rearrange-

CRYSTAL PALACE
AND G

ELECTRIC TRAMWAYS

HIGH LEVEL S.E. & C.RY.

LOW LEVEL
L.B&S.C.RY.

FOOTBALL & POLO GROUND
14

BOATING LAKE

ANERLEY
ENTRANCE & EXIT

PENGE E

PENGE STATION
L.B&S.C.R.

1. Crystal Palace Co.'s School of Practical Engineering.
2.   ,,   ,, School of Art, Science & Literature.
3. Firework Terrace.
4. Topsy Turvy Railway.
5. Water Chute and Rapids.
6. North Tower—*Ascent by Lift.*
7. Crystal Palace Co.'s School of Physical Culture.
8. Balloon Ground.

For Plan of Inter.

OUNDS (200 Acres)
HERETO.

NORTH TOWER 6
GARDENS
ROCKHILLS
ENTRANCE
& EXIT

7
8

LAKE

12

16
CYCLE TRACK

SYDENHAM ENTRANCE & EXIT

17

21
CRICKET
GROUND

EXIT
NGE STATION. ELECTRIC TRAMWAYS
S.E.&C.R.

FOR.
tform.
g Machine.
Polo Ground.

17. Bowling Greens.
18. Swings, Roundabouts, etc.
19. Boating Lake.
20. Extinct Animals.
21. Cricket Ground.
22. Switchback.
23. Lavatories.

ilding, see next page.

---

ment of the music will be allowed.

(7) No valve trombones or drums will be allowed.

(8) Each band to send the name by which it is known, together with the names of every performer, instrument, conductor and secretary, accompanied by an entrance fee of £1 1s. for the first section and 10s/6d. for other sections. The entry fee and entry forms for first section bands containing the above particulars to be forwarded to the Contest Director, Crystal Palace, London S.E., not later than August 23, 3rd and 4th sections close on August 30.

It is particularly requested that early application be made. No performer will be allowed to play during the Contest except upon the instrument entered opposite his name in the entry form.

(9) The order of playing to be balloted for in front of the Great Orchestra, Crystal Palace, at 11.30 o'clock. All bands will be balloted for whether present or not. Any band failing to be ready within five minutes to take its place as drawn will be disqualified. Representatives from each band will be expected to be present at the ballot and elect supervision committees for each section.

(10) The Contest for first section bands will start sharp at 12 o'clock in the Concert Room as usual. The second, third and fourth sections will start playing at the same time, at stands provided at convenient places in the grounds (that is to say, in the open).

(11) The Contest Director will have power to decide any dispute that may arise in connection with the Contest, and his decision will be absolutely final. The decision of the various Adjudicators to be final, and from such decisions there will be no appeal, except where a band is disqualified for an infringement of the rules. Where a prize is withheld for a breach of the rules, such prize will be given to the next in order of merit. All cash prizes will be paid on the day of the Contest.

(12) If any band wish to lay an objection against another band the sum of one guinea must be deposited, at the same time such band must enter the protest in writing to the Contest Director, and such protest must be lodged in his hands or at the General Manager's Office within half-an-hour of the finish of the performance of the band objected to. Should the objection not be sustained the deposit will be estreated but if proved genuine the deposit money will be returned.

(13) No objection will be entertained as to a performer

Previous page: Plan of the Crystal
Palace grounds included in the
Contest Programme, 1908.

being a professional or being otherwise ineligible (except in connection with the playing of the music on the day as provided in the Rules), unless full particulars are forwarded at least one week previous to the Contest.

(14) Bands winning first prize in sections for which a Trophy is provided before receiving possession of the same must conform with the usual regulations which have been provided by the Crystal Palace Company to ensure the safe custody and return during the period of holdership by the band.

(15) In order to ensure fairness to all, no band will be allowed to rehearse on the day of the contest owing to the large number of bands competing. This rule will be rigidly enforced. Any band infringing it will be disqualified.

(16) A conductor, professional or amateur may act for more than one band, in either of the first, third and fourth sections, but will not be allowed to play in any band. In the second section only the resident bandmasters will be allowed to conduct, no man conducting more than one band.

(17) Each band of the first section must appear in uniform. For the other sections it is optional.

(18) Admission tickets to the Palace to the number of twenty-six will be forwarded to each competing band, and on no account can a bandsman enter the grounds without a ticket or payment of the usual entrance fee. Bands can obtain railway tickets at special low rates from London to the Palace by applying to the Contest Director.

(19) Any band infringing any of these rules is liable to disqualification.

(20) The Contest Director reserves the right to add to or amend either of these rules, each band being advised of such alterations or additions, at least fourteen days previous to the contest.

Yet another important step forward was taken in May, 1913, when the following announcement was made in the *British Bandsman*: "At the Crystal Palace Contest next September, a modern work, specially written for the brass band by a composer of note, will be the test-piece in the Championship section."

This was the first brass band contest at which an original work, especially written for the occasion, was used.

The piece was Percy Fletcher's 'Labour and Love', and was published by R. Smith & Co., which, by this time, was

THE FAMOUS ST. HILDA COLLIERY BAND
WORLDS CHAMPIONS
1912 - 1920 - 1921 - 1924

also owned by John Henry Iles. Percy Fletcher was himself an adjudicator at the contest and when awarding the prize to the winning band, Irwell Springs, commented "An inspiring and arresting performance, with which I was delighted in every way."

Cyril Jenkins composed 'Coriolanus' for the National Championships of 1914, but war broke out and it was 1920 before the championships were resumed.

The resumption of the National Championships after World War One was delayed for a number of reasons. In the first place the Crystal Palace had been taken over by the War Ministry and was still not released completely even by 1920. But perhaps a more important reason was that the bands themselves had suffered heavy casualties as a result of the war and needed time to reassemble and reshape.

After a number of hints and numerous speculations, the longed-for announcement was made in the *British Bandsman* of February 21, 1920: "The 15th Crystal Palace Festival would take place on September 25, 1920."

First preference for invitations to the contest was to bands who had been accepted for the abandoned 1914 contest. Numbers for 1920 were limited as space at the Crystal Palace was occupied by the War Museum and the Victory Exhibition. There was obviously much competition for the remaining places.

'Coriolanus' by Cyril Jenkins which had been written

St. Hilda Colliery Band, Crystal Palace Champions 1912, 1920, 1921, 1924 and 1926.
Back Row James Dawson, George Oliver, William Ellison, Jack Wood, Harry Bradley, Ernest Foster, Alwyn Teasdale.
Centre Row Jack Waggott, Jack Peeps, Andrew McClaren, Peter Smith, Joe Lee, Sam Craddock, Anthony Brown, Sydney Greaves, William Wood.
Front Row: Peter Hart, Albert Matthews, Tom Brennan, David Mead, James Oliver (Bandmaster), James Southern (Secretary), Harold Laycock, Jack Burton, John T. Taylor.

for 1914 was announced as the championship section test-piece, but before announcing the test pieces for the other five sections, the following comment was made: "During the period of the war, easy test pieces have been in general use. This has led to carelessness and a general slackness in playing. So in good time we issue the warning — test pieces will be more difficult than in previous years." *British Bandsman* July 10, 1920.

When announced the test pieces were: Grand Shield, 'Tannhauser'; Junior cup, 'Dinorah'; Junior Shield, 'Il Travatore'; Reed Band, 'Gems of Wagner'; Boys' Band, 'Gems of Harmony'.

It is interesting to note that drums were allowed in the boys' section.

One hundred and thirteen bands were accepted for the 1920 National Contest, but, owing to a miners' strike, a number of colliery bands were forced to withdraw at the last moment and only eighty-eight bands actually competed.

In the championship section, J.A. Greenwood conducted two bands (Black Dyke and Irwell Springs), William Halliwell three bands (Luton Red Cross, St. Hilda's and Lincoln Malleable) and George Hawkins conducted Harton Colliery and Mansfield Colliery.

Three adjudicators, Cyril Jenkins, Tom Eastwood and Walter Reynolds, decided on the following result: 1 St. Hilda's (W. Halliwell), 2 Lincoln Malleable (W. Halliwell), 3 Irwell Springs (J.A. Greenwood), 4 Luton Red Cross (W. Halliwell).

Cyril Jenkins commented: "The playing of the first six bands in order of merit was technically little short of perfection".

St. Hilda's, on their triumphant return to South Shields, were met by men from the colliery carrying the Lodge Banner and were led by Marsden Colliery Band, who had won third prize in the Junior Cup. The champion band was marched through the dense crowd of cheering supporters to a civic welcome.

St. Andrews Juniors, of Hull, who became champions in the boys' section, also received a tumultuous welcome on their return home. Huge crowds turned out to greet them and the boys were carried shoulder-high through the streets. The welcome appears to have been over-enthusiastic for two instruments were damaged and the "diminutive drummer had his drum burst".

The pattern of the contest changed slightly in 1922 when the reed section was discontinued and, for the first time, this became purely a BRASS band contest. There were only five sections in 1922, but by 1923 there were so many entries that a sixth section was added.

Another innovation took place in 1922. Up to this point, all bands stood to contest with the conductor in the centre. Now, an experiment was tried in the championship section. These bands were to sit in concert formation with the conductor in the front. In 1923 this ruling applied to all sections.

As always there was some resistance to change. When a Welsh organiser tried to emulate the National in his local contest, two bands positively refused to play sitting down!

In 1924, the Newcastle Steel Works Brass Band travelled from Australia to compete in the championship section. Even now, an expedition like that would not be undertaken lightly. The test piece was Henry Geehl's 'On the Cornish Coast' and the Australians came third with only St. Hilda's

Taken at the Crystal Palace in 1935. These happy bandsmen reflect the pleasure of a day at the National. (London News Agency photograph)

NATIONAL BAND FESTIVAL 1935
SPECIAL NUMBER

and Black Dyke ahead of them.

To commemorate the twenty fifth anniversary of the National Brass Band Championships, John Henry Iles offered a prize of one hundred guineas for the best original brass band test piece for the championship section. A young man, making his appearance on the brass band scene for the first time, with an overture, which he called 'Joan of Arc', was awarded the prize. The young man was Denis Wright. He was invited by Mr. Iles to adjudicate the championship section and thus began a long and valuable contribution to the brass band movement.

Surprisingly enough, 'Joan of Arc' became the test piece for the Grand Shield section only one year later and, once again, Denis Wright was called upon to adjudicate.

More famous names were on the lips of everyone who attended the National Championships during the thirties — Fred Mortimer, conductor of Fodens, and his three sons Alex, Harry and Rex, corner men of the band. This wonderful combination, the Fodens Motor Works Band, won the Crystal Palace Trophy in 1930, 1932, 1933, 1934 and 1936 (they were barred from entering in 1935). Small wonder that after such achievements, plus similar ones at Belle Vue, the name Mortimer became renowned throughout the brass band community.

Massed bands on the Crystal Palace platform, taken from the programme, 1934. On the right is the last ever Crystal Palace programme (1936) depicting His Majesty King Edward VIII, Patron of the Festival. In December of that year the Crystal Palace was burned down.

The first great impact of Fodens at the National, in 1930, was with 'Severn Suite', composed by Sir Edward Elgar on the invitation of John Henry Iles especially for the championship section.

On announcing it, Mr. Iles said: "Sir Edward Elgar is composing an original test piece that shall be such as to test even the cleverest brass band player in the land — and that takes some doing when the executants are acknowledged the world over as being amongst the best musicians of their time."

Commenting on the playing of Harry Mortimer, solo cornet of Fodens, one critic wrote: "Harry does not play, he sings! We sometimes hear of persons making an instrument talk, that is just what Harry does!"

The ruling which prevented Fodens from competing at the National in 1935 (bands that have won the championship three years in succession shall be barred for one year) allowed a new name to emerge — Munn & Felton's, later to become G.U.S. Footwear. The band had only been formed in 1933 and had been placed first in the second section at Crystal Palace in 1934 and then in 1935 had walked off with the Thousand Guinea Trophy under the baton of

Munn and Felton's welcomed home to Kettering following their triumph at the 1935 Crystal Palace Contest. (Photograph from the Northamptonshire Evening Telegraph).

Fodens Golden Years

Fred Mortimer conducting Foden's at the 1934 Crystal Palace Contest when the band achieved a hat-trick of wins. The test-piece was 'Comedy' (John Ireland). (London News Agency photograph)

E.R. Foden receiving the Crystal Palace Trophy from John Henry Isles.

Foden's Motor Works Band, 1938. Back Row: A. Mortimer, A. Statham, E. Spurr, F. Gowood, J Cotherill, A. Webb, A. Webb, R. Mortimer. Centre Row: W. Illingworth, J Poole, B. Stokes, H. Stubbs, D. McDean, J. Moores, H. Shergold, R. Knott, M. Cullen, H. Hardy, H. Mortimer.
Front Row: W. Pedley, W Lawton, R. Shepley, R. Moores, W. Foden, F. Mortimer, C Cook, H. Stanway, D. Thomas, E. Statham.
Top right and bottom right photographs from 'By Royal Command' by F.D. Burgess.

William Halliwell. The bandmaster at the time was Stanley Boddington. But Foden's were back in 1936, with Black Dyke taking second place.

Before the end of the year, however, the Crystal Palace, which had for so long been associated with the National Brass Band Championships, was destroyed by fire, causing a sense of personal loss to bandsmen everywhere.

A place of memories, it will soon be a memory itself. Brave old Palace! though you have stirred thousands and thousands of memories this night, and a great multitude of people will miss you, yet shall we feel that your end was such as you would have wished for

56

yourself. Truly, you went out in a blaze of light.
British Bandsman, December 5, 1936.

The burning of the Crystal Palace marked the end of an era for the National Brass Band Championships. A temporary home was found at Alexandra Palace for 1937 and 1938, but before another year had passed World War Two broke out and it was 1945 before plans for the re-emergence of the National Championships in a new form could be carried out.

Not only had the natural home of the championships been destroyed, but the years had passed for their founder and director, years in which he was powerless to restore the great occasions. By the time the war ended, John Henry Iles was over seventy and very concerned about the continuance of the national.

Relief came in the form of a national newspaper. Having attracted an audience of twenty thousand to Belle Vue in September, 1944, to hear twenty leading brass bands, the *Daily Herald* realised the size of the following for bands in this country and decided to play a more active part in organising band events. The management of the paper was therefore most receptive when John Henry Iles put to them his ideas for the restoration of the championships and requested their support.

In the *British Bandsman* of January 25, 1945, he announced that discussions with the *Daily Herald* had taken place as a result of which a series of area contests would be sponsored and organised throughout Great Britain which would lead to invitations to the restored National Championships.

John Henry Iles wearing his robes as Master of the Worshipful Company of Musicians.

"Thus a dream and desire I have had in view for many years has at last come into active being. Thanks to the broad and practical vision of the *Daily Herald* management, I am very confident nothing but complete success can result" he said.

His approaches to the *Daily Herald* met with some criticism and opposition as also did his plan for area contests. He had abandoned them once before, but still held very firmly to the view that this was the only fair way to determine which bands should appear at the finals. So this time with the backing of the *Daily Herald* he battled on.

In May, 1945, he wrote a strong article in which he declared that the proposed area contests would in no way conflict with any established association contests. He concluded: "If there is any attempt by any association to boycott any of its bands from taking part in any of these area contests it will not only be entirely out of order, but must lead to serious results. The universal rights of bands to enter the National Festival Contests have been established for nearly fifty years and I have written this leader in order that every band in the country may fully realise their complete and independent rights to act in this matter as they please."

Despite some antagonism, area contests were started in 1945 and by 1946 the eight regions (London, Lancashire, Leicester, South-West, Northern, Yorkshire, Scottish and South Wales) were firmly established.

The increased support to the areas was possibly due to the great success of the first postwar National Championships held in the autumn of 1945.

The problems posed by the lack of a suitable venue, which would house all sections under one roof, had not been completely resolved and therefore the second, third and junior sections were held at Belle Vue on September 29, whilst a week later the championship section of the National Brass Band Championships took place for the first time at the Royal Albert Hall.

The prize for the Champion Band of Great Britain was to be the *Daily Herald* National Championship Challenge Trophy plus two hundred guineas. Competing for the trophy were Scottish C.W.S., Clydebank Burgh, Black Dyke, St. Hilda's,* Brighouse, Grimethorpe, Wingates, Fairey, Blackhall Colliery, Horden Colliery, Gwaun-cae-Gurwen, Parc and Dare, Cory, Creswell, Ransome and Marles, Luton, and Hanwell.

Munn and Felton's were still reforming after the war and Foden's were excluded under the ruling which precluded bands winning the championship on three successive occasions from entering. The years in question were 1936, 1937, and 1938, and even the intervening war years did not prevent the rule from being carried out.

The Royal Albert Hall was packed and in that year the cry began "Where are all the tickets?" After the Crystal Palace no place was big enough to contain the thousands who wanted to be present to hear the champions strive for the trophy.

The test piece in 1945 was Denis Wright's 'Overture for an Epic Occasion' and to reach their decision, the adjudicators sat in a splendid new box, specially designed by the *Daily Herald* to replace the traditional tent. The box naturally attracted a good deal of attention and one hoaxer decided to exploit its modernity.

A steward found a bar attendant attempting to get into "the Box" with three glasses of whisky and a syphon of

*The name St. Hilda's was resuscitated in 1944 by a band formed, initially in Bradford. It was disbanded in 1956.

soda. He declared he had received a phone call from "the Box" ordering the drinks. The steward tried to explain that the adjudicators had no contact with the world outside throughout the contest and therefore could not have ordered the drinks. The furious attendant stormed off to find a more helpful official leaving the steward wishing he had been more quick witted and offered to take care of the drinks!

Not only had changes taken place in the organisation and venue of the championships since they were last held in 1938, but, as was to be expected, the great conductors had aged and new names appeared on the programme: Fairey Aviation Works Band, conductor Harry Mortimer; Brighouse and Rastrick, conductor Eric Ball.

In 1945 Fairey won the championship and in 1946 it was Brighouse, with Fairey as runner-up and Munn and Felton's (Stanley Boddington) in third place.

The year 1947 could be called a "Mortimer year", for Harry took the first two places with Black Dyke and Fairey, whilst his father came third with Foden's. Then followed a hat-trick for Black Dyke with Harry Mortimer conducting. In 1949 his father was ill and ordered by the doctors to rest, so Harry took Fodens as well. Until 1955 it was the names of Fairey, Black Dyke and Fodens which appeared on the Challenge Trophy.

Despite the undoubted success of the areas and the finals, all of John Henry's battles were not yet won. He was determined to "clean-up" contesting and to stamp-out the practice of "borrowed players". He felt very strongly that only bona fide members of bands should be allowed to contest. Bringing in top class corner men was to be made

Black Dyke Mills Band — National Champions 1947/48/49.

strictly against the rules. In consultation with the *Daily Herald* he drew up a set of rules, and regulations for the National Brass Band Contests, which were sponsored by the National Brass Band Club and sent out to all bands.

He continued his onslaught in the editorial columns of the *British Bandsman* and the *Daily Herald* provided the strength within its organisation to stamp out this malpractice. He applauded the creation of the *Daily Herald* National Register of Brass Bandsmen as a strong vital necessity for the establishment of fair contesting.

When life ended for John Henry Iles in May, 1951, he was convinced that his creation, the National Brass Band Championships, had passed into safe hands.

The area qualifying contests, established in 1945, had grown in prestige and acquired more and more support. They were gradually handed over to area committees, who with a secretary at the helm were responsible for their organisation under the banner of the *Daily Herald.*

Denis Wright

The year 1952 marked the formation of the National Brass Band Contesting Council, which comprised representative members of each of the area committees plus the contest manager of the *Daily Herald.*

Present at that first meeting were: Jerome Chester and E. Vaughan Morris (*Daily Herald* Contest Management); Frances Bantin (London and Home Counties); G. Halcrow (Northern Area); Tom Atkinson (North-east); Jack Whittle (North-west); D. Livingstone (Scottish); F.G. Tyrell and A.J. Williams (Wales): A.F. Bedwell (West of England); O. Pentelow (Midlands).

During the course of the meeting, Tom Atkinson was elected chairman and E. Vaughan Morris, honorary general secretary.

Eric Ball

The object of the council was to be "principally a co-ordination body for the *Daily Herald* contest" and could by discussion and review take such steps as were possible to improve standards of contesting with the basic principle of "fair for all".

Later in the year, the council agreed to invite membership from the organisers of other contests, such as Belle Vue and the Northern Ireland Brass Band League, thereby making it a more comprehensive body.

One of the functions of the council was to advise on area test pieces and also to draw up a list of approved adjudicators who would be offered a minimum national fee, plus expenses.

In 1951 the National Registry had been handed to the National Brass Band Club, which felt that a club member-

Frank Wright

ship of ten thousand would ensure that the registry could be maintained free for all members. But despite the hard work of Mr. S.A. Griffin who shouldered the responsibility for the registry, the club found it necessary to return it to the *Daily Herald* in November, 1952.

The Royal Albert Hall was still proving to be too small for the thousands who wanted to attend the National Final and in 1952 and 1953 the Empress Hall was used, but in 1954 when the decision was made to bring all sections to London for their finals, Scotland Yard stepped in. The police maintained that the borough of Fulham could not possibly cope with the proposed number of coaches and cars that these plans would entail. It was, therefore, suggested that once again, the Royal Albert Hall should be used for the championship section and all other sections should be accommodated in other halls in Kensington.

Gilbert Vinter

To help allay the disappointment of the many who would be unable to get tickets, twin festival concerts were announced. It was estimated that fifteen thousand people came to London to share in these events. By 1958, this number had risen to twenty five thousand.

Whilst it was traditional for the championship section to have a different test piece for the finals, which was announced about six weeks before the event, the second, third, and fourth sections had used again the piece on which they had contested at the areas. In 1955, this was changed and a new piece was set for all sections.

The practice of introducing music especially written or arranged for the championship finals remained and two names which figured prominently in the postwar years as composers and/or arrangers — and indeed adjudicators, were Frank Wright and Eric Ball. Later, making a great impact was Gilbert Vinter. Only his untimely death in 1969 prevented his musical influences extending further.

Feeling that men who had given much personal service to brass bands should be honoured, the organising secretary, Mr. E. Vaughan Morris, introduced a 'Spotlight on Service' ceremony to the National Finals in 1958. The spotlight fell first onto Dr. Denis Wright, founder of the National Youth Brass Band, and in subsequent years on Eric Ball and Frank Wright. A baton of honour was presented, with which the recipient conducted the assembled massed bands.

Tom F. Atkinson

A great impact was made on the contesting platform in 1956 by Major George Willcocks, who led Fairey to victory during Harry Mortimer's absence in Australia. This was followed by triumphs for Major Willcocks with Black Dyke Mills in 1959 and 1961. The championship was then won by

61

C.W.S. Manchester, who, with Alex Mortimer, thrilled everyone by their sheer beauty of performance.

Still concerned about the pressure for tickets, in 1964 Vaughan Morris investigated the possibility of using the Empire Pool, Wembley, for the finals. Although this would have provided the required number of extra seats, it was felt that the acoustics were just not good enough.

But 1964 was a momentous year in other ways, for it was announced that from the following year a National Youth Championship would be part of the national finals. All competitors would have to be under sixteen years three months at the time of entry and must not be registered with any other band. Before this could transpire the *Daily Herald* ceased publication and the control of the National Championships passed to *The People*. Mr. Vaughan Morris continued as the administrator and producer.

The regional qualifying contests of 1965 proved to be very disappointing to the organisers. Withdrawals amounted to one in five bands and most of these failed to notify their intentions prior to the event. This situation was impossible and *The People* after stating the problem made the following announcement: "In the circumstances, the Area Qualifying Finals will not take place in 1966 and onwards. This will mean that the National Registry of Brass Bands and the National Brass Band Contesting Council will cease to exist from October 16, 1965."

The national finals and the festival concerts would still be organised by *The People*, but the finals would be of invited bands.

Much disturbed comment followed this announcement and Mr. Wilfred T. Lawrence of Reading wrote: "The development is the most momentous and disastrous happening which the Brass Band Movement has had to face in its long history".

He regretted the "loss of the constant vigilance, forethought and brilliant directive influence of Vaughan Morris who practised and insisted upon one hundred per cent integrity."

Some areas decided that they would continue to run their own regional contests. Yorkshire was the first to make the decision. *The People* suggested that the same trophies could be used by the areas willing to operate their own regional championship. But the controversy and the feeling of insecurity remained.

The future of the National Registry was settled more quickly and in the *British Bandsman* of September 25, Mr. Jack Fearnley of Belle Vue made the following statement. "Mr. Vaughan Morris has generously offered to pass over to Belle Vue all the assembly of records if we would undertake the task of continuing the operation of the National Registry of Brass Bandsmen.

"Quite frankly after examining the whole position, one finds that the cost of necessary labour, printing, postage, telephone and accommodation is quite considerable. So much so, that even after one takes into account revenue accruing from the present nominal registration charges, costs will exceed £2,000 per annum.

"Belle Vue would be reluctant to attempt this without the full support of the Brass Band Associations."

The associations were invited to contact Belle Vue, making their intention known. The support proved to be sufficient and the National Registry was handed over in December.

In the meantime, another announcement had produced further shocks. Vaughan Morris was to retire. The established policy of the International Publishing Corporation was that all senior grade personnel, irrespective of identity should accept retirement at a stipulated age.

Vaughan Morris had been associated with the National Championships since 1945 and now was to be catapulted into retirement by his company. Said the *British Bandsman* October 2, 1965: "This human dynamo has never ceased to think Brass Bands — he has planned, built and worked like a tiger to bring about new thinking, together with a progressive and enterprising conception of the role brass bands should fill in a forward-looking age. As the administrator of the National Championships, he has revitalised contesting."

Even though retired, *The People* invited Vaughan Morris to continue producing the national finals and festival in a freelance capacity.

By April, 1966, it had become clear that whilst some areas would continue to organise their own regional finals, for others this was impossible and therefore Vaughan Morris offered to organise these himself. By October, 1966, he had agreed to organise seven accredited regional finals in 1967 with the help of regional committees.

The three bands placed highest in each section would receive invitations to the national finals. As a result of all this, the National Brass Band Contesting Council was reconstituted with Vaughan Morris as the organising secretary. Four test pieces were chosen which were to be used at the areas, and it was made known that adjudicators must be selected from an accredited list.

The surprises were not yet over. In December, 1966, the following announcement was made: "Throughout the long period of Odhams Press newspapers' association with the Brass Band Movement, Mr. E. Vaughan Morris has been the administrator and producer on their behalf. His services to brass bands have rightly been fully acknowledged by the movement for which he has done so much.

"The Directors of Odhams Press Newspapers Limited are therefore sure that all associated with the Movement will be glad to know that arrangements have been completed whereby responsibility for organising the Championships and Festival in their entirety, has been passed to Vaughan Morris, who recently retired from Odhams and is now free of the many other calls upon his talents and time."

The People declared that its friendly interest in the movement would remain and that its challenge trophy would continue to be awarded at the National finals.

James Abbott, president of the Scottish Amateur Band Association wrote to the *British Bandsman* in the following enthusiastic terms: "The announcement in the *British Bandsman* regarding the future of the National Brass Band Cham-

Brighouse and Rastrick Band —
World and National Champions
1968 and 1969.

64

E. Vaughan Morris, organiser of National Brass Band Championships for the *Daily Herald, The People* and from December 1966 until October 1971 under his own ownership.

Peter Wilson, who came to London in 1971 from his native Scotland to take over as organiser of the National Championships.

pionships, will come as a relief to bandsmen and band officials everywhere.

"Mr. Vaughan Morris gave the brass band business something long overdue, viz., a sound lesson in business procedure, presentation and organisation.

"He has emerged as a natural leader and is still very much needed because of his vast experience. His opinion in all matters affecting brass bands will continue to be widely sought and given with a frankness and authority that we have come to expect."

There was inevitably a period of settling down after the months of uncertainty. The National Registry was no longer part of the National Championships organisation and, of necessity, an economic charge had to be made which gave some bands cause for concern.

However, the National Championships and the regional contests progressed and developed under Vaughan Morris, causing applications for tickets to the Royal Albert Hall to be a continuing embarassment to the organiser. There were just not enough seats to satisfy all who would wish to be present. The problem became even more aggravated by the number of applications for tickets from abroad. The National Championships were becoming an international occasion.

This knowledge inspired Vaughan Morris to create the World Championship in 1969 and invite a Dutch band to join the national contest at the Royal Albert Hall. Brighouse and Rastrick, with Walter Hargreaves conducting, took the World Championship title for the first time.

The following year, 1970, the championships were divided. The National Championship to which came the regional champions became one class, whilst into the World Championship section were invited six bands on merit: Black Dyke Mills, Brighouse, C.W.S. Manchester, Fairey, Fodens and G.U.S. Footwear. To this number was added the Concorde Band from Copenhagen. This invitation marked the return to the National Championships after an absence of a few years, of Fairey and Fodens. Playing 'Benvenuto Cellini' by Berlioz, arranged by Frank Wright, Black Dyke Mills, conducted by Geoffrey Brand, emerged as the winners of this newly-shaped contest.

It was a great sadness to all present that Frank Wright was unable, through illness, to adjudicate at this event — and, in fact, he died shortly afterwards.

In the period from 1900 to 1971 the National Brass Band Championships were controlled by only two men - John Henry Iles and Vaughan Morris, each with a strong sense of purpose, knowing what was right for the progress and dev-

The scene at the Royal Albert Hall during a *Daily Herald* Brass Band Festival Concert.

elopment of fair and exciting contesting.

On August 14, 1971, the *British Bandsman* announced that Vaughan Morris was to retire as the organiser and owner of the National Brass Band Championship and after the event on October 9 the control would once again pass to the *British Bandsman* at 210 Strand. Peter Wilson had been appointed the new organising secretary and was in the process of moving from Scotland to London to take over the reins.

In November of that year, changes were heralded once again, in the structure of the National. The new management believed that the highest honour for British brass bands should be in winning the title, National Champions. The World Championship was something quite different and should be regarded as such. From October, 1972, the bands from the World Championship section would be invited to the 1972 National Finals. They were Black Dyke, Brighouse, Manchester C.W.S., Fairey, Fodens, Grimethorpe, G.U.S., and Wingates. Other bands would compete at regional level and two would go through from each area.

In 1973 the format changed again in order to regularise the situation and not give some bands a permanent bye. The only bands who would be invited to the National were those who had won the supreme title in the last four years, i.e. 1972 National Champions (Black Dyke), 1971 World Champions (G.U.S.), 1970 World Champions (Black Dyke), and the 1969 World Champions (Brighouse). All other bands would go to the regional contest if they wanted a place in the National Finals.

These decisions paved the way to the present situation where all bands, except the winner of the preceding year's National Championship compete in the regions. Usually two bands from each area go to London, but at the discretion of the regional judges, a third may be invited.

Decisions were being taken at 210 Strand, which affected the future of the National. Other decisions were taken at a more personal level. Once it had been agreed that the National Championships should be reunited with the *British Bandsman* and that from the 1973 events he would be involved in the choice of test pieces and adjudicators, Geoffrey Brand concluded that his successful contesting relationship with Black Dyke must end. As the Editor and a director of the *British Bandsman*, he could no longer contest in National events. This situation inevitably affected his conducting activities, as most British bands want their professional to be available for important contests.

During the early 1970's the cramped offices of 210 Strand were alive with discussion of bands and band events.

Peter Wilson, Organiser of the National, supervises the draw for the order of play.

They were the international meeting place for band lovers from all over the world who wanted to see their news in the *British Bandsman*, or personally make an impassioned plea for tickets to the National.

The fruits of the discussions between Peter Wilson and Geoffrey Brand were seen in announcements which appeared in the band press during 1973. On April 28, the headline — "National to Include Percussion" — caused a stir. Just a few years later it seems incredible that this should have seemed to be a revolutionary change. But the National and other band contests had been without percussion since 1900 and there were still those who resisted the change.

One correspondent wrote: "Percussion adds to the effect, but makes no improvement; on the contrary, percussion robs the brass band of those unique qualities that justify its existence."

Along with the brick-bats came the compliments — and the changes went forward despite both.

Percussion was to be phased in for two reasons. In the first place, many bands did not possess a percussion player and in the second place many lower section bands could not immediately afford the equipment. They needed due warning.

The championship section would be required to use percussion at the National Finals in 1973. In 1974 the championship and youth sections would use it at the regional events and by 1976 all bands would be phased in.

Later in 1973 it was announced that Butlins had agreed to sponsor the National Youth Championship. A new impetus and status was immediately given to these events. For the first time the youth finalists would compete on the

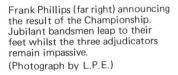

Frank Phillips (far right) announcing the result of the Championship. Jubilant bandsmen leap to their feet whilst the three adjudicators remain impassive.
(Photograph by L.P.E.)

Royal Albert Hall platform. A great experience for young players.

Percussion in the National — studies in concentration! (Photographs by Tony Pegram).

Ideas new to the National Championships were incorporated into this re-modelled contest for youth bands. No longer were their numbers confined to twenty five members. The bands could vary in size from twenty to fifty, as long as members were all under nineteen years on the day of the finals. Adjudicators were to sit in the open, as they would at a music festival and new exciting pieces for these talented young players could be commissioned with the extra funds available.

The short period from 1971 to 1975 was one of great activity in the affairs of the National but time was running

Yorkshire Imperial Metals Band,
conductor Denis Carr, winners of
the 1978 National Championship.
The Royal Albert Hall provides a
fitting background.

(Photograph by Keystone Press
Agency)

out. The lease at 210 Strand was expiring and the address
which was known throughout the brass band world would
soon cease to be a focal point.

Once more changes had to be made in the management
of the National and the *British Bandsman*. It seemed to be
important that they should remain together as being mutually supportive.

At the end of August, 1975, the ownership and editorial
responsibility of the *British Bandsman*, passed to Robert
Alexander. On October 31, the National Brass Band Championship followed. Peter Wilson remained as the organiser
and transferred with the two companies to their new home
near Heathrow Airport. R. Smith moved to Watford and
after more than seventy years 210 Strand no longer echoed
to the sound of brass band activities.

But the National remained strong and thrived. It was
sponsored by the *British Bandsman* for two more years,
when once again their paths diverged. However, 1978 marked
yet another milestone in the development of the National
Brass Band Championships. In 1977 the ownership of the
British Bandsman passed to Rosehill Instruments and Peter
Wilson became the Editor. The National Brass Band Championships remained with Robert Alexander and for the first
time, in 1978, a European Championship was held in the

Royal Albert Hall on the day following the National Championships.

Champion bands from selected European countries were invited to the event but it was Black Dyke Mills, conducted by Major Peter Parkes, riding on the crest of a wave, who were the worthy winners of the first European Brass Band Championship.

The story of the National goes on. The event which John Henry Iles created in 1900 is as strong today as ever, drawing thousands of band lovers to London every October, with twice as many turned away through lack of tickets. But it also provides, more than any other band event, the opportunity for bands to measure themselves against each other. The striving for perfection continues, thus maintaining the standard of British amateur brass bands, which is admired and respected throughout the world.

References
British Bandsman 1900 — 1978
The Brass Band Movement, Russell & Elliot, J.M. Dent, 1936.

Robert Alexander took over the National in 1975.

SEPTEMBER CHAMPIONSHIP CONTESTS.

1853
Two Selections of their own choice
1 Mossley Tem.
2 Dewsbury
3 Bramley Tem
4 Bury Borough

1854
Two Selections of their own choice
1 Leeds (By. F.)
2 Dewsbury
3 Accrington
4 Foxhill Bank
5 Milburn, Leeds
6 Bury

1855
"Orynthia" (Melling), and one Selection of their own choice
1 Accrington
2 Leeds (By. F.)
3 Mossley Tem.
4 Bramley
5 Enfield
6 Dewsbury

1856
"Stradella" Overture (Flotow) and one Selection of their own choice
1 Leeds (By. F.)
2 Leeds (Smith's)
3 Accrington
4 Foxhill
5 Batley

1857
"Il Trovatore" (Verdi) and one Selection of their own choice
1 Leeds (Smith's)
2 Dewsbury
3 Todmorden
4 Worksop

1858
"On Thee each living soul awaits and 'Achieved is the glorious work—Creation' Haydn
1 Accrington
2 Dewsbury
3 Mossley
4 Holmfirth
5 Meltham

1859
No CONTEST: Three Bands entered only:—
Black Dyke
Dewsbury
Holmfirth

1860
"Zampa" Overture (Herold) and one Selection of their own choice
1 Halifax
2 Dewsbury
3 Sherwood
4 Newark
5 Heckmondwike

1861
"Satanella" (Balfe) and one Selection of their own choice
1 Halifax
2 Dewsbury
3 Chesterfield
4 Sherwood
5 London V.A.

1862
"Muette de Portici" (Auber) and one Selection of their own choice
1 Black Dyke
2 Dewsbury
3 Chesterfield
4 Bacup Vol.
5 Compstall

1863
"Faust" (Gounod) and one Selection of their own choice
1 Black Dyke
2 Bacup
3 Silsden
4 Preston
5 Dewsbury

1864
"The Reminiscences of Auber' and one Selection of their own choice
1 Bacup
2 Stalybridge
3 Leeds Model
4 Matlock
5 Black Dyke
6 Wednesbury

1865
'Un'Ballo in Maschera' (Verdi) and one Selection of their own choice
1 Bacup
2 Dewsbury
3 Matlock
4 Stalybridge
5 Dodsworth's

1866
"L'Africaine" (Meyerbeer) and one Selection of their own choice
1 Dewsbury
2 Matlock
3 Healey Hall
4 Bacup
5 Chesterfield

1867
"Der Frei-chutz" (Weber)
1 Clay Cross
2 Bacup
3 Compstall
4 Mow Cop
5 Dodsworth's

1868
"Robert le Diable" (Meyerbeer)
1 Burnley
2 Heckmondwike
3 Black Dyke
4 Meltham
5 Matlock

1869
"Le Prophète" (Meyerbeer)
1 Bacup
2 Matlock
3 Burnley
4 Besses-o'th'-Barn
5 Linthwaite

1870
"Ernani" (Verdi)
1 Bacup
2 Matlock
3 Dewsbury
4 Besses-o'th'-Barn
5 Wednesbury

1871
"Il Barbière" (Rossini)
1 Black Dyke
2 Bury Borough
3 Bacup
4 Robin Hood
5 Burnley

1872
"Souvenir de Mozart" (Verdi)
1 Robin Hood
2 Saltaire
3 Meltham
4 Besses-o'th'-Barn
5 Bury Borough

1873
"Dinorah" (Meyerbeer)
1 Meltham
2 Robin Hood
3 Black Dyke
4 Linthwaite
5 Bury Borough

1874
"Faust" (Spohr)
1 Linthwaite
2 Meltham
3 Besses-o'th'-Barn
4 Dewsbury
5 Saltaire

1875
"Il Talismano" (Balfe)
1 Kingston
2 Meltham
3 Linthwaite
4 Stalybridge
5 Saltaire

1876
"Aida" (Verdi)
1 Meltham
2 Kingston
3 Holm Mills
4 Linthwaite
5 Golcar

1877
"Jessonda" (Spohr)
1 Meltham
2 Black Dyke
3 Holm Mills
4 Denton Original
5 Kingston

1878
"Romeo et Giulietta" (Gounod)
1 Meltham
2 Kidsgrove
3 Denton
4 Accrington
5 Holm Mills

1879
"The Last Judgment" (Spohr)
1 Black Dyke
2 Accrington
3 Barnsley
4 Saltaire
5 Boarshurst

1880
"Vespri Siciliani" (Verdi)
1 Black Dyke
2 Stalybridge
3 Nelson
4 Linthwaite
5 Trawden
6 Boarshurst

1881
"Cinq Mars" (Gounod)
1 Black Dyke
2 Meltham
3 Stalybridge
4 Boarshurst
5 Trawden
6 Barnsley

1882
"Il Seraglio" (Mozart)
1 Clayton-le-Moor
2 Linthwaite
3 Barnsley
4 Littleboro' Public
5 Stalybridge
6 Oldham Rifles

1883
"Il Giuramento (Mercadante)
1 Littleboro' Public
2 Burslem
3 Honley
4 Besses-o'th'-Barn
5 Stocksbridge

1884
"La Gazza Ladra" (Rossini)
1 Honley
2 Oldham Rifles
3 Black Dyke
4 Linthwaite
5 Littleboro'
6 Besses-o'th'-Barn

1885
"Nabucodonosor" (Verdi)
1 Kingston Mills
2 Littleboro'
3 Besses-o'th'-Barn
4 Oldham Rifles
5 Honley
6 Accrington

1886
"La Favorita" (Donizetti)
1 Kingston Mills
2 Heywood Rifles
3 Littleboro' Pub.
4 Honley
5 Stocksbridge
6 Glossop Voluntrs.

1887
"L'Etoile du Nord" (Meyerbeer)
1 Kingston Mills
2 Black Dyke
3 Besses-o'th'-Barn
4 Honley
5 Leeds Forge
6 Todmorden Old

1888
"Der Fliegende Hollander" (Wagner)
1 Wyke Te np.
2 Black Dyke
3 Todmorden
4 Wyke Old
5 Oldham Rifles
6 Rochdale Amtr.

1889
"La Reine de Saba" (Gounod)
1 Wyke Temp.
2 Kingston Mills
3 Leeds Forge
4 Stocksbridge
5 Todmorden
6 Linthwaite

1890
"Euryanthe" (Weber)
1 Batley Old
2 Leeds Forge

1891
"Das Nachlinger in Granada" (Kreutzer)
1 Black Dyke
2 Wyke Temp.

1892
"Zaar und Zimmermann" (Lortzing)
1 Besses-o'

1893
"Elaine" (Bem

1894
"The Golden Web" ng Thomas)
Barn

1895
"Hansel und Gretel" (Englebert Humperdinck's Opera)
1 Black Dyke
2 Wyke Temp.
-o'th'-Barn

1896
"Gabriella" (Pizzi)
1 Black Dyke
2 Kingston Mills
3 Batley Old
4 Lindley

1897
"Moses in Egypt" (Rossini)
1 Mossley
2 Kingston Mills
3 Batley Old
4 Pemberton Old
5 Lindley
Red Cross

189
Grand F from the Mend
1 Wyke
2 Huck
3 Lea
4 Batle
5 Kett
6 Croo

"Robi (Mac
1 Wingat
2 Black D
3 Goodsha
4 Royal Oak
5 Shaw
6 Pemberton Old

1916
"La Traviata" (Verdi)
1 Horwich Rly. Mechanics' Ins.
2 Foden's Mtr. Wk.
3 Black Dyke Mills.
4 King Cross, H'ifax
5 Wingates Temp.
6 Irwell Springs

1 h.
2 Blac.
3 Woodla.
(Donca.
4 Glazebury Cu
5 Pemberton Old
6 Foden's Mtr. Wks.

ery
nery
aegurwen
gates Temp.
'Perfection" Soap

4. The Belle Vue Championships

by VIOLET BRAND

1925
"Macbeth" (Keighley)
1 Creswell Colliery
2 Nutgrove
3 Foden's Mr. Wks.
4 Amington
5 Irwell Springs
6 Clydebank Burgh

1926
"A Midsummer Night's Dream" (Keighley)
1 Foden's Mtr.Wks.
2 Wingates Temp.
3 St. Hilda Colliery
4 Australian C'wth.
5 Glazebury
6 Hebden Bridge

19..
"Merry Wives Windsor" (Keighley)
1 Foden's Mtr.Wks.
2 Callendar's Cable
3 Milnrow Public
4 Blackpool Excelr.
5 Carlton Main Col.
6 Nelson Old

3 Nutgrove
4 Carlton Main
Frickley Colliery
5 Creswell Colliery
6 Rothwell Temp.

...astrick
2 Wingates Temp.
3 Carlisle St. Step.
4 Nutgrove
5 Milnrow Public
6 Glazebury

...psody (Granville Bantock)
1 Eccles Borough
2 Milnrow Public
3 Wingates Temp.
4 Carlisle St. Step.
5 Baxendale's Wks.
6 Glazebury

Suite—"Springtime" (Haydn Morris)
1 Besses-o'th'-Barn
2 Glazebury
3 Milnrow Public
4 Irwell Springs
5 Eccles Borough
6 Dove Holes Pub.

"The Crusaders" (Keighley)
1 Brighouse and Rastrick
2 Nelson Old
3 Metro'tan Wks.B.
4 Baxendale's Wks.
5 Luton
6 Amington

1933
"Princess Nada" (Denis Wright)
1 Brighouse and Rastrick
2 Baxendale's Wks
3 Amington
4 Luton
5 Milnrow Public
6 Dove Holes Pub.

1934
"Pageantry" (Herbert Howells)
1 Brighouse and Rastrick
2 Black Dyke Mills
3 Wingates Temp.
4 Edge Hill L.M.S.
5 Nelson Old
6 Besses-o'th'-Barn

1935
"A Northern Rhapsody" (Dr. T. Keighley)
1 Black Dyke Mills
2 Wingates Temp.
3 Abram Colliery
4 Baxendale's Wks
5 Nelson Old
6 Milnrow Public

1936
"Robin Hood" (Gechl)
1 Brighouse and Rastrick
2 Abram Colliery
3 Luton
4 Black Dyke Mills
5 Wingates Temp.
6 Metropolitan Works, Birmingham

1937
"Academic Festival Overture" (Brahms) Arr. Denis Wright
1 Besses-o'th'-Barn
2 Slaithwaite
3 Black Dyke Mills
4 Bickershaw Coll.
5 Baxendale's (Manchester) Works
6 Luton

1939
"Owain Glyndwr" (R. Maldwyn Price)
1 Shaithwaite
2 Black Dyke Mills
3 Luton
4 Bickershaw Coll.
5 Edge Hill L.M.S.
6 Brighouse and Rastrick

1940
"A Downland Suite" (John Ireland)
1 Wingates Temp.
2 Nelson
3 Brighouse and Rastrick
4 Bickershaw Coll.
5 Black Dyke Mills
6 Cadishead Public

1940
Choice at We choice Festival Overture v Robin Hood. v The Crusaders
1 Fairey Aviation
2 Carlton Main Frickley Colliery
3 City of Coventry
4 Bickershaw Col.
5 Harton Colliery.
6 I.C.I. (Alkali)

1941
"Clive of India" (Joseph Holbrooke)
1 Bickershaw Coll.
2 Creswell Colliery
3 Brighouse and Rastrick
4 J.C.I. (Alkali)
5 City of Coventry

1942
Choice of 'Lorenzo' or 'Pageantry'
1 Fairey Aviation
2 Bickershaw Coll.
3 City of Coventry
4 Brighouse and Rastrick
5 Creswell Colliery
6 Yorkshire Copper Works

1943
"Symphony No. 5" Beethovenarr D. Wright
1 Bickershaw Coll.
2 Fairey Aviation
3 Creswell Colliery
4 Brighouse and Rastrick
5 Barrow Shipyard
6 Yorkshire Copper Works

1944
"The Tempest" (Maurice Johnstone)
1 Fairey Aviation
2 Creswell Colliery
3 Bickershaw Coll.
4 Carlton Main Frickley Colliery.
5 Clydebank Burgh
6 Brighouse & Rastrick

1945
Suite; "Pride of Race" (K. A. Wright)
1 Fairey Aviation
2 Grimethorpe Col.
3 Bickershaw Col.
4 Creswell Colliery
5 Edge Hill L.M.S.
6 Park & Dare W'kmen (S. Wales)

1946
Overture "Salute to Freedom" (Eric Ball)
1 Bickershaw Colliery
2 Fairey Aviation
3 Munn & Felton's
4 Creswell Colliery
5 Barrow Shipyard
6 Grimethorpe Colliery Institute

1947
Tone Poem: "Henry V." (R. Maldwyn Price)
1 Fairey Aviation
2 Wingates Temp.
3 Creswell Colliery
4 Barrow Shipyard
5 Bickershaw Coll.
6 Black Dyke Mills.

1948
"Music for Brass" (Denis Wright)
1 C.W.S. M'chester
2 Fairey Aviation
3 Carlton Main Frickley Colliery
4 Creswell Colliery
5 Munn & Felton's
6 C.W.S. M'chester

1949
"Rhapsody in Brass" (Dean Gollin)
1 Fairey Aviation
2 Ransome&Marles'
3 Carlton Main Frickley Colliery
4 Rushden Temp.
5 Morden Colliery
6 C.W.S. M'chester

1950
"Resurgam" (Eric Ball)
1 Fairey Aviation
2 Cory Workmen's
3 City of Coventry
4 C.W.S. M'chester
5 Rushden Temp.
6 Munn & Felton's

1951
"The Conquerors" (Eric Ball)
1 Ransome&Marles'
2 Prescot Cable Wks
3 C.W.S. M'chester
4 Cory Workmen's
5 Rushden Temp.
6 Fairey Aviation

1952
Centenary "Scena Sinfonica" (Henry Geehl)
1 C.W.S. M'chester
2 Foden's Mtr. Wks.
3 Munn & Felton's
4 Prescot CableWks
5 Black Dyke Mills
6 Clayton Aniline

1953
"TheThreeMusketeers" (George W. Hespe)
1 National Band of New Zealand
2 Fairey Aviation
3 Black Dyke Mills
4 C.W.S. M'chester
5 Foden's Mtr.Wks.
6 Munn & Felton's

1954
Tournament for Brass" (Eric Ball)
1 Munn & Felton
2 Ferodo Works
3 John White
Footwear
4 Ransome&Marle's
5 C.W.S. M'chester
6 Clayton Aniline

1955
"Sinfonietta for Brass Band" (Eric Leidzen)
1 Ferodo Works
2 John White
Footwear
3 C.W.S. M'chester
4 Ferodo Works
5 Y.E.W.C.O. Wks.
6 Rushden Temp.

1956
"Tam o' Shanter's Ride" (Denis Wright)
1 Fairey Aviation
2 C.W.S. M'chester
3 Carlton Main
4 Ferodo Works
5 Besses-o' th'-Barn
6 Creswell Colliery

1961
Test Piece:
"MAIN STREET" (Eric Ball)

1 THE FAIREY BAND
2 WINGATES TEMPERANCE BAND
3 GRIMETHORPE COLLIERY INSTITUTE
4 BRIGHOUSE & RASTRICK
5 RANSOME & MARLES WORKS BAND
6 C.W.S. (MANCHESTER)

£2,000 GOLD TROPHY
This Trophy was first instituted for Annual Competition at the September Bell Vue Contest in 1924, and was on this occasion by the Australian Band, Newcastle Steel Works.

1957
"Carnival" (Helen Perkin)
1 Black Dyke Mills
2 Carlton Main Frickley Colliery
3 Foden's Motors
4 Besses o' th' Barn
5 Rushden Tem.
6 Fairey Aviation

1958
"Sunset Rhapsody" (Eric Ball)
1 Carlton Main Frickley Colliery
2 Besses o' th' Barn
3 Black Dyke Mills
4 C.W.S. M'chester
5 Morris Motors
6 Creswell Colliery

1959
"The Undaunted" (Eric Ball)
1 Besses o' Th' Barn
2 Carlton Main Frickley Colliery
3 Morris Motors
4 Fairey Aviation
5 Templemore Avenue
6 Brighouse and Rastrick

1960
"Fantasia" (Mozart-Sargent)
1 C.W.S. (Manchester)
2 The Fairey Band
3 Grimethorpe Colliery
4 Morris Motors Temperance
5 Brighouse & Rastrick
6 Luton Band

"In the days when only six, eight or ten bands competed in the Belle Vue contest, they all brought boisterous and enthusiastic supporters. Bands made the journey from neighbouring Lancashire towns in light carts. Admirers followed on foot, with their day's food tied up in a red handkerchief. They spent the day listening to bands and discussing the decisions of the unfortunate judges. Some rattled their clog-noses against the shins of their opponents and then trudged homewards feeling that they had really enjoyed themselves."

When the Belle Vue Contest celebrated its fiftieth anniversary in 1902, elderly bandsmen who played in the first contest in 1853, were invited to attend. They reminisced about those early days and their experiences (similar to that quoted above) were captured in the pages of the *British Bandsman*. Readers were reminded that the Belle Vue Contest began in the same year that Britain entered the Crimean War. John Jennison, owner of the Belle Vue Gardens, Manchester, had been prevailed upon by Enderby Jackson and James Melling to initiate a brass band contest in the grounds. The chief difficulty was to find enough competitors. Finally, eight bands attended and enthusiasts were persuaded to share the day, by taking advantage of train excursions. Enderby Jackson and his friends had induced the railways to lay on special trains to Manchester for the event. Their efforts were so successful that the commencement of the contest was seriously delayed by the late arrival of the train from Leeds. So many people were travelling that the train simply could not make it on time.

The bands played two 'own choice' test pieces and the winners were Mossley Temperance Saxhorn Band, playing on their newly acquired instruments. There were only ten players with Mossley, which was the minimum number allowed and no band present had more than eighteen.

The September brass band contest at Belle Vue, Manchester, has continued, almost without a break, through two world wars, until the present. The break came in 1859, when only three bands entered and the contest had to be cancelled. There was a great improvement in 1860 and in 1889 forty bands applied to compete—too many to be accommodated. Belle Vue set a pattern in the administration of brass band contesting, by its business-like methods; equally its presence was influential in the formation of many new bands.

A reporter observing the Belle Vue contest in 1888 wrote: "Since the establishment of these contests, twenty bands have grown up in the district, for every one previously in existence, whilst first class instruments have replaced the

Opposite: Until 1973 a news-sheet with lists of Belle Vue prizewinners, plus names of adjudicators, conductor and test pieces from 1853, was published and on sale immediately following the September Championship. The 'Stop Press' column contained the results just given. The reproduced news-sheet appeared after the 1961 Open British Championships.

The Rochdale Old Band won third prize at Belle Vue in 1893. This photograph was taken in 1900.

The Belle Vue Challenge Cup which was first won in 1889 by the Wyke Temperance Band.

miscellaneous collection that once did duty."

Two years prior to this the Belle Vue management had demonstrated its belief that brass band contesting was a growing activity, by organising a second contest for bands who had not won a prize at the September contest during the previous four years. The first contest in this series was held in July, 1886. On winning the July contest, bands were eligible to compete in September.

For both contests, Mr. Jennison established firm conditions of entry and bands had to submit the names and addresses of all players. Twenty-four were allowed, but none must be professional. The comment was made at the time that there was little chance of professionals getting a place on the platform without being discovered, as players in top bands were too well known.

Rochdale Public Band discovered to their cost, that Mr. Jennison rigidly applied his rules. They had been awarded second place to Wingates in the July contest, when an objection was raised and they were disqualified. Their explanation that neither their regular conductor, William Rimmer, nor their tutor John Gladney were available to conduct them, so they needed their euphonium player to fill the gap, thus necessitating bringing in an outside euphonium, drew sympathy, but no change of heart.

The affair brought the following comments from the Editor of the *British Bandsman*: "Many bands seem to have become imbued with the very erroneous idea that contest rules belong to the same category as pie-crust and promises — made so that they can be broken. That this was not so was demonstrated on Saturday at Belle Vue, when one band, it is alleged, played a man whose name and instrument did not appear on the entry form. Whilst we have no wish to magnify the circumstances which led to the disqualification of the erring band, we feel that Messrs. Jennison's example in insisting on a rigid adherence to their rules, might with advantage be more widely copied by other contest committees."

Unknown to Mr. Jennison, a man who was to have a lasting effect on the development of the brass band movement and the shaping of contesting, attended the Belle Vue Contest in 1898 — John Henry Iles. The event so impressed him, that when he returned to Belle Vue the following September, he was already the owner of the *British Bandsman* and had plans to become even more deeply involved. He met many bandsmen that day and in the words of one of them seemed to be a "regular tip-topper".

In the late nineteenth century, Belle Vue was the mecca of brass bandsmen. They poured into Manchester each September, encouraged by the railways, which in 1899 laid on seventy-six excursion trains for the contest. The place was alive with the sounds of brass. One visitor observed "A ride on the top of one of the Manchester express trams from Mossley Street to Belle Vue was like a musical ride. Each pub had a band practising the test piece, or waiting their turn whilst some other band was rehearsing.

"It is an insane person who says that brass band contesting is on the wane, especially after my excursion on top of that lightning — express Manchester — steam horse tram."

Then, as now, there were favourites. Black Dyke won Belle Vue for the first time in 1862 and went on to gain their first hat-trick in 1879-1881. Besses o' th' Barn won for the first time in 1892 and these two bands soon became firm rivals. In 1903 there was much criticism of the adjudicators, because they placed Black Dyke second to Pemberton Old and Besses did not appear in the prizes at all.

Criticism often turned into physical, as well as verbal abuse when the supporters felt that their favourite had been ill-favoured. As a result the Belle Vue management decided that adjudicators should no longer be required to announce their decisions from the platform and the results were written up on a board.

"Bandsmen like judges at band contests to announce

The Gold Medal, which in 1907 the Belle Vue management agreed to present to every man in the band when a hat-trick of wins was acheived.

their own decisions verbally from the platform. But it is bandsmen who caused the verbal announcement to be done away with at Belle Vue and, therefore, we have ourselves to blame and ought not to place the fault on the heads of contest promoters. They don't like to see judges insulted after they have done their best to give, what in their opinion is a right and just decision." (*British Bandsman*. April 27, 1907).

Later in 1907, Belle Vue issued a set of rules which were to be effective from the September contest, that year.

1. In the event of any band winning first prize three years in succession, every man will be awarded a gold medal and not allowed to compete the following year.
2. Every member of the band must be resident in the town, or within a distance of four miles, or thereabouts.
3. A player entered and playing at the July contest will not be allowed to play with another band at the September contest.
4. A professional may be engaged as conductor and may conduct more than one band, but will not be able to play in any band.
5. The number of competing bands will be limited to twenty.
6. The number of members in each band will be limited to twenty four.
7. No member will be allowed to play an instrument other than the one on which he is registered.
8. All players must have been members for more than three months.
9. Any member, who within six months of the date of the close of entries, has played regularly with a professional orchestra, will be considered a professional.
10. Every performer must be in a position to prove that he derives his chief income apart from playing music.
11. Preference will be given to bands who have gained a prize at the September Belle Vue contest in the past two years, or the July Contest this year.
12. The test piece must not be played in public prior to the contest.
13. Only slide trombones are allowed.

The Editor of the *British Bandsman* commented on the professional player ruling: "Many contest organisers know that this rule is broken, but prefer to ignore it. Let us be honest, and not pretend that things are something they are not. But the revolt of the amateur will come. It is to the amateurs we look to rescue contesting from the pit of mercernary aims and sordid methods. He knows that should an evil day arrive when contesting is ground under the heel of the paid player and professional musician, it is lost for ever".

The contesting conditions for Belle Vue appear to have been perfectly acceptable, but rumblings and discontent were beginning about the chosen test pieces, which were not to die away until the middle of the 1920s. Lieut. Charles Godfrey was at the centre of the complaints. He was now in his seventies and had arranged all of the Belle Vue test pieces since 1872, which by 1908 amounted to sixty pieces. He was invariably an adjudicator and this also gave rise to complaint.

But there was more than the test piece to cause comment in July, 1909. The Upper Norwood Band arrived from London and took the stage in bright, scarlet uniforms. It was not customary for bands to wear uniforms of any kind and to appear looking like an Army regimental band was asking for trouble!

Competitors from Lancashire and Yorkshire were heard to remark: "We've not come swanking in uniform, we've come to show folks how to play". It was said that it cost Upper Norwood the outrageous sum of £80 to attend Belle Vue; that included two nights in a hotel.

The September contest of 1909 marked the successful entry of a comparatively new band into the contest arena. With William Rimmer conducting, Foden's Motor Works Band won at their first attempt. Not only did they repeat their successes in 1910, but they went on to win the Crystal Palace trophy as well, conducted by William Halliwell, as William Rimmer had retired from contesting in January 1910.

Supporters of the other bands began to protest about the success of Foden's, which seemed to be based on superior players, a superior conductor and the best possible rehearsal facilities. However, Foden's would only admit to one advantage — they could afford to buy more professional training than most bands. Every bandsman worked in the firm and was treated like any other employee. There were no special facilities for rehearsals, which all took place in the men's own time. However, Foden's had a simple secret, every member took a thorough interest in rehearsals and revelled in contesting. Over the years their simple recipe for success brought nine first prizes at Belle Vue, seven of them with William Halliwell conducting.

There was disappointment amongst the audience at the 1910 September contest. Instead of the bands playing in the ballroom as usual, the event was transferred into a recently erected, large new hall. Old associations were broken and people were disorientated — they couldn't find their friends. Perhaps it would be all right when they got used to it. With this reluctant welcome, the King's Hall became the centre for the Belle Vue brass band events.

Four years later, war was declared and the National Brass Band Championships at Crystal Palace, London, were abandoned until the duration, but the Belle Vue management announced its intention of continuing its annual contests. Many bands were forced to withdraw their support as members joined the armed forces; others refused to go as a matter of principle. They were opposed to contesting "as usual" whilst the country was at war and felt that the continuance of these events would damage the image of bands in the eyes of the general public.

The number of entries dwindled and the standard of playing dropped. But what could be expected when so many bandsmen were away "competing in Flanders"? The test pieces sounded tired having been resurrected from previous contests, often pre-1900. Generally there was little enthusiasm for the event.

But, in 1918, as the war drew to a close a new interest was awakened — Besses o' th' Barn were returning to the fray. They had not contested for fourteen years due to their constant tours, when they were considered professionals and, therefore, banned from the contest scene. Due to the war, the tours ceased and the bandsmen returned to their respective trades. Thus, once more they became amateurs and Besses o' th' Barn could mount the contest stage. There were great expectations and the crowds turned out to hear them. They got a tremendous ovation, but the Besses men were somewhat surprised at their opponents' capabilities. Wingates won the contest with William Halliwell conducting, whilst Besses came third with Alex Owen.

By 1920, normality was restored and the crowds poured in by charabanc. The railways had temporarily ceased to run excursions and must have lost thousands of pounds as a result. Long before the contest started, every ticket was sold and King's Hall was packed. Besses were still very popular and their supporters were rewarded, for this time, they won.

The July and September contests continued and in May, 1922, the Belle Vue management decided to start another contest series, for lower grade bands. At the first event, twenty-three bands played and the winners were Redcar, conducted by George Hawkins.

The dissatisfaction which had existed before the war over the Belle Vue test pieces, continued into the twenties, particularly as bandsmen compared them with the original works which were being set for the Crystal Palace contest. Bands like Dyke, Foden's, Harton and St. Hilda's did not enter the Belle Vue Contest in 1923 which caused some disappointment for the audience. But bands felt they could not easily switch mentally from the old ideas of the Belle Vue test pieces to the modern idiom presented by the Crystal Palace pieces in the short time available and they found the new music more to their taste.

Besses, however, did compete at Belle Vue in September, 1923, and caused a stir by playing in concert formation, instead of standing in a square. The method had been adopted at Crystal Palace the preceding year, but even though Besses set the pace, it did not become universal practice at Belle Vue until 1928.

£2,000 Gold Challenge Trophy which was presented at Belle Vue for the first time in 1924 and won by the Newcastle Steel Works Band from Australia. It is still the trophy contested for in the British Open Championships.

In order to attract more bands in 1924, the prize money was increased and a new trophy was introduced — the £2000 Trophy, which had previously been used at a Glasgow contest. The first time it was used at Belle Vue, it was won by the Newcastle Steel Works Band from Australia and taken out of the country.

There were those who were unhappy about the success at Belle Vue of the Australian band and in order to quieten the criticism the *Australian Bandsman* published an article which was reprinted in the *British Bandsman*.

"There is a desire in certain quarters in England as well as Australia, to discount A. H. Baile's part in the Newcastle Band's big victories in England. The cry is that 'so-and-so' helped Baile put the polish on.

"Is it wrong to ask the 'helpers' why they did not put a similar finish on their own bands?

"The Newcastle Band's victory shows up the weakness of English contesting methods, where one man may conduct any number of bands at one contest. It is strikingly evident that where a chain of bands place themselves under the charge of one man, that the result must be disastrous to the majority of the chain.

"One man, many bands, is a method that makes for bad playing. Many conductors, mean numerous ideas — greater individuality, more originality, better bands."

Whilst these criticisms from the colonies led to some discussion, the English brass band scene was in no way ready to change its attitude to the role of the professional conductor and in any case, there were more pressing problems to consider. Early in 1925, rumours were flying that Belle Vue was to be sold. Reluctantly the Belle Vue management admitted that negotiations had been underway, but were broken off. What would happen to the Belle Vue Pleasure Gardens — and the brass band contests?

In splendid isolation on the front page of the *British Bandsman*, on March 7, 1925, was the headline

BELLE VUE SOLD

Inside the paper came the news that the purchasers were a syndicate of London business men headed by none other than John Henry Iles. Relief rippled through the brass bands of England.

The May and July contests were little different from the past, even though bandsmen had expected immediate miracles. But in September things began to change. For the first time in the history of Belle Vue contesting, an original

The gold medal won by Charles Badrock of the Brighouse and Rastrick Band for the hat-trick of 1932/33/34, in accordance with the Belle Vue rules published in 1907. It was proudly worn by his widow at the dinner held to celebrate the band's 1978 win at Belle Vue.

work for brass bands was set as the test piece — 'Macbeth' by Thomas Keighley. Bandsmen were delighted that at last, the Belle Vue test pieces were to be comparable to those used at the Crystal Palace.

The following July, 'Labour and Love', by Percy Fletcher, was set for the lower grade bands. This composition was the first work written especially for a brass band contest. It was used by championship section bands at Crystal Palace in 1913 and thought to be difficult to play and difficult to understand. But now, thirteen years later, "a dozen or so bands tackled the music in a manner which would have surprised those 1913 Champion Bands."

Entries to the Belle Vue contests in May, July and September, despite the industrial problems of the country, remained good throughout the twenties. The year 1929 brought a new air of excitement, when Brighouse and Rastrick won both the July and September contests. This had only been achieved once before in the history of Belle Vue, by Batley Old in 1890. Brighouse went on to prove that their success was not an isolated incident, by winning a Belle Vue hat-trick in 1932-1933-1934 and had a further win in 1936.

The period was dominated by the problem of "borrowed" players. The Belle Vue rules attempted to banish them, but it was said that one of the bands in the Belle Vue prizes in 1927, was made up of the cream of six different bands. Certain conductors were accused of taking around with them a number of soloists, whom they used like "pawns in a game of chess".

Harry Mortimer was so concerned about the issue that he wrote to the *British Bandsman* on August 4, 1928, saying that he no longer intended to be a borrowed player, as it caused too much ill-feeling.

"Friendship and goodwill of fellow bandsmen mean more to me than the £. s. d. of being borrowed," he said.

In a further attempt to eliminate the problem, Belle Vue announced that from the May contest 1930, all players would have to sign before going on to the stage. They would sign the original entry form, and then again, immediately prior to playing. This innovation met with approval, for bands could pay out as much as £70 for borrowed players, in order to win a prize of £20. "The borrowed players go home with the swag and there is no band left to play even a hymn tune," it was said.

The National Brass Band Club, formed in 1925, turned its attention to fair contesting and by 1933 had drafted a set of contest rules and regulations for national use. John Henry Iles announced that the NBBC rules would be used henceforth for both Belle Vue and the Crystal Palace.

The rules stated that bands should consist of not less than fourteen members and not more than twenty-four. Drums not to be used. All bands were to attend in uniform and should be seated in concert formation.

If a player was unable to attend for a bona fide reason, then the band would be allowed to substitute (not exceeding two) from a band of the same grade, but not competing in the same contest. If such an eventuality occurred within three days of the contest and the representatives at the draw were satisfied with the reason, then a ballot for a substitute from the competing bands would be taken before the draw for order of play.

The Club felt that as a result of these rulings there should in future be no chance of the hard-working, well-taught, village bands being robbed of a prize by a richer band hiring superior players for the day from a top-grade band. Sadly, the Club was too optimistic and there was no dramatic eradication. In 1948, it was still felt necessary to send out a "borrowed players" warning with the Belle Vue contest schedule.

Having successfully drafted contesting rules, the National Brass Band Club turned its attention to forming a national body for brass bands, a League to co-ordinate brass band activities and to clean up contesting generally. The first meeting was held at Belle Vue in July, 1933, and John Henry Iles backed his support for this proposed national band organisation, with a donation of £100 a year for five years.

Not all of those engaged in brass band activities agreed that a national organisation was necessary and after a mighty struggle, lasting a number of years, the League of Brass Band Associations foundered, like all other attempts at national unity from pre-1900 to the present day.

The year 1931 was a significant one for Belle Vue contesting, the May contest was restructured, a marching contest was introduced and Harry Mortimer's name appeared as the conductor of a prize winning band. Four classes were introduced to the May contest and it became the May Brass Band Festival, with a grading structure for bands, so that they could, if successful, move through the four May sections to the July contest and then on to the September championships.

The four sections were:

(a) for bands that had won a prize of £5 or over, but not exceeding £10 during the past two years.
(b) for bands who had won a prize below £5.
(c) for bands who had won no prize at any contest.
(d) limited to small bands of not more than twenty players and not less than sixteen.

Black Dyke Mills winning the 1935 September contest with a performance of Northern Rhapsody by Keighley. The professional conductor was William Halliwell and the bandmaster was Arthur Pearce.

One hundred bands entered this newly-shaped contest and Harry Mortimer won first prize in Section D with Leek British Legion.

The July contest was structured as a continuation of the May Festival. Section B was for bands who had won prizes over £5 and under £15 in the past two years, whilst Section A was for bands who had not been in the first three prizes at Belle Vue or Crystal Palace in 1929 and 1930. For the first time there was an apparent grading system at Belle Vue.

Another innovation in July, 1931, was the Deportment and Marching Contest. Some bands scored for playing and others for the smartness of their appearance. The event was popular and it was thought that a marching contest would have a permanent place in the Belle Vue calendar. By 1934 all bands, who entered the July contest, were expected to participate in the Marching contest. They were reminded how attractive the Australian Quickstep Contests were to the general public and how beneficial it would be to bands to think about the smartness of their appearance and deportment. Grimethorpe entered in that year and won.

To commemorate the Jubilee in 1935 John Henry staged a "monster band demonstration" at Belle Vue. Over 2000 players massed to play the patriotic march, 'England' which he conducted. Each bandmaster stood in front of his own band and synchronised his beat with John Henry's. Surely, no one who participated in that mammoth occasion will ever forget it. There were evidently many youngsters and even if those youngsters are still playing, they certainly did not participate in a similar demonstration of loyalty, to mark the Jubilee of Queen Elizabeth II.

A new name appeared in the contest lists in 1938 — Fairey Aviation Works Band. They were third in the May contest, conducted by Frank Smith and were first in the July contest, conducted by Harry Mortimer. At this time, the band was only one year old although it comprised experienced and thoroughly efficient players.

Following the contest in September, 1938, a convention took place to debate the question: "What is wrong with brass bands and brass bandsmen?" Many opinions were exchanged, some heated, but no conclusions were reached. Before the September contest of 1939 there were even more important matters occupying the minds of all British subjects. War had been declared. At the eleventh hour, a notice had been sent out to all competing bands which stated: "Owing to the exigency of War, the 87th annual September Championship Brass Band Contest has had to be abandoned. This decision was not taken until the last minute, but was ultimately enforced by the Government's proclamation to the effect that all places of entertainment must be closed forthwith."

The Belle Vue management succeeded in having the embargo lifted for 1939 and the contest was on as suddenly as it was off. The band secretaries involved endured an enormous amount of work and anxiety.

However, on September 30, nine bands of the twenty-two originally entered competed at Belle Vue. The 87th Belle Vue must have been the strangest in history. "The Belle Vue Monday suddenly became Belle Vue Saturday. There were no crowds, although in the circumstances there was a reasonable audience. All were carrying gas-masks. The contest began after lunch and ended before tea, but the wonder was, that there was any contest at all."

Once more the National Championship in London had been abandoned for the duration but the Belle Vue management were determined to keep going. Frank Parker who had been the contest organiser for almost twenty years said: "We must keep the contest going for as long as possible, in order to keep the movement alive. It will be easier to rebuild after the war if the structure remains."

The bands who were still able to function satisfactorily, supported these sentiments and in May, 1940, fifty contested. The July contest was reluctantly not held, but in September thirteen championship section bands competed. During the morning there were two air raid warnings, but the contest

Pre-war crowds thronging the entrance and grounds of Belle Vue waiting for the contest to begin.

continued and finally Bickershaw Colliery were declared the winners.

Throughout the war not only did the May and September events continue, but in 1942 a great Marching Festival was begun, which captured the imagination of bands and public alike. By 1944, over thirty bands were taking part, plus another section for A.T.C. (Air Training Corps) Bands.

Optimistically, John Henry Iles wrote "I would not be at all surprised if the marching of the bands on this occasion did not re-echo the marching of the feet of our brave lads on the way to Berlin. If the sound of victory and triumph should synchronise with this great marching day, what a scene there will be with the huge audience cheering wildly."

Such scenes were a year away, but there was cause for jubilation in 1944 in the band world for John Henry Iles was awarded the O.B.E. in the Birthday Honours List. To celebrate, he conducted the massed bands at the conclusion of the Marching Festival in a rousing performance of 'Death or Glory'.

Air Marshal Sir Leslie Gossage was present to witness the ATC Championships and was most impressed by the smartness and enthusiasm of these young bandsmen. But a brass band adjudicator was not entirely swept off his feet by the performances — "too much wind and not enough tongue, causing a strident raucous tone. Instructors should teach these 'young hopefuls' to concentrate on playing long notes to improve their sound," he said.

Dr. Denis Wright and Harry Mortimer photographed in 1942. Dr. Wright had recently been appointed Assistant Overseas Music Director and Harry had succeeded him as the BBC's Brass Bands Organiser.
(BBC copyright photograph).

Other bands were appearing in the contest lists which were as much part of wartime Britain as the ATC Bands. There were National Fire Service Bands, Home Guard Bands and Air Raid Wardens' Bands, whilst many members of the long-established bands were very young, filling the chairs of bandsmen who had joined the forces. Mothers and fathers swelled the audiences, coming to see how their youngsters would fare in the world of brass band contesting.

By now the B.B.C. had two brass band stalwarts on the staff — Dr. Denis Wright and Harry Mortimer. They persuaded the B.B.C. that it would be good for British morale to provide massed band concerts at Belle Vue, conducted by prominent orchestral conductors. Sir Adrian Boult, Malcolm Sargent, and John Barbirolli each took the stage with the massed bands of Foden's, Black Dyke, Bickershaw and Fairey between 1943 and 1945. Following one such concert the music critic of the *Manchester Guardian* wrote: "The concert yesterday afternoon at Belle Vue, Manchester, was probably as startling as it was instructive in its revelation of skill and artistry. If musical people are still uninterested, it must surely be because they are ignorant of the fact that modern composers of first-rate standing have greatly enlarged and enriched the domain of brass band music."

So successful were the Belle Vue concerts, that the B.B.C. decided to bring the same massed bands to the Royal Albert Hall and invite Sir Henry Wood and Sir Adrian Boult to conduct them. Luton and Enfield Central were invited to join the famous northern bands and City of Coventry played instead of Bickershaw, who were unable to make the journey to London. The event reminded John Henry Iles of the Absent Minded Beggar Concert in 1900, for that idea too had sprung from Belle Vue.

As a breeding ground for ideas and innovation Belle Vue had more to offer. A great patriotic display, March to Freedom, was organised by Frank Parker, directed by John Henry Iles and sponsored by the *Daily Herald* newspaper, in September 1944. Ten selected champion bands (Foden's, Besses, Bickershaw, Fairey, Brighouse, St. Hilda, Barrow Shipyard, Manchester CWS, ICI (Crewe) and Denton Original) played in massed formation with a choir of 1000 voices. Sections of the National Services, plus fifteen bands, including pipes, were also invited and the total ensemble of between 3000 and 4000 musicians, was conducted by John Henry Iles. Admission was by ticket, but all tickets were free and 30,000 people were expected to attend. As it happened, the elements were against the event and the bandsmen performed under the greatest difficulty and discomfort. Twenty thousand people came in spite of the weather and the *Daily Herald* was full of praise.

John Henry Iles took advantage of the situation and opened discussions with the newspaper about a further commitment to the cause of brass bands. His timing was perfect and by January, 1945, he was able to announce that the *Daily Herald* would, in future, organise and sponsor a series of area contests throughout the British Isles, which would link to his own National Brass Band Championships.

In May, hostilities ceased and in June, the first North West Area Contest took place at Belle Vue, organised by Frank Parker.

The National Finals of the lower sections followed in September. Belle Vue's own contests had not faced the disruption of the National events and continued smoothly. September, 1945, brought a Victory Contest and there was much speculation about the chances of Fairey. They had won in 1941, 1942 and 1944, but as they played in 1945, the vast audience knew that every man, with the exception of young Colin Clayton, had just been subjected to five innoculations

John Henry Iles, assisted by Francis Bantin, taking the draw for the 1948 September contest.

in preparation for their E.N.S.A. tour of Europe which began the next day. Would their playing be affected? Grimethorpe gave a magnificent performance with George Thompson, and Brighouse and Rastrick were appearing for the first time with Eric Ball, so there was stiff opposition. But the gods and adjudicators smiled and Fairey, conducted by Harry Mortimer, won the Belle Vue Trophy and the Victory Cup.

From the stage tributes were paid to Frank Parker, who had organised the Belle Vue contests for twenty-four years and had done splendid work for brass bands throughout the war. John Henry Iles invited the audience to stand and pay tribute to fallen band heroes and finally, to thank God for victory by singing the Doxology.

The years of peace brought inevitable changes. Giants of the past had aged, or were in ill-health. William Halliwell died in 1946 and on May 29, 1951, the death of John Henry Iles was announced, by the woman who had assisted him in all of his brass band ventures for twenty-five years, Frances Bantin. She wrote: "Everyone will agree that it has been his influence and work which have brought brass bands to their present position. When one imagines contests at Belle Vue and the Royal Albert Hall without his genial presence, words fail one."

Eric Ball conducting CWS Manchester in a winning performance.

Dr. Denis Wright in his tribute reminded readers that it was John Henry Iles who initiated original works for brass band by the finest living composers. He continued: "If we want perpetual reminder of the debt we, of the brass band world, owe to John Henry Iles, what better than that we should *listen* around us."

H. F. B. Iles, John Henry's son, known as Mr. Eric to his staff, with a background of public school and Oxford took over from his father, supported by Frances Bantin and Eric Ball, with Harry Mortimer advising on music for the Belle Vue festivals. Frank Parker died in 1953 and Jack Fearnley became the contest controller.

The Marching Contest, despite John Henry Iles' earlier optimism, did not remain part of the Belle Vue scene after the war. In the sixties Wills, the tobacco company, tried again, but British brass bands were not as enthusiastic about this form of contesting, as their Australian and New Zealand counterparts. From 1953 the May and July contests were amalgamated into the Spring Festival, with six sections — Grand Shield, Senior Cup, Senior Trophy, Junior Shield, Junior Cup and Junior Trophy. The winner of the Grand Shield automatically received an invitation to the September contest — the British Open Brass Band Championship.

New names appeared in the prize-lists in the fifties and sixties. Eric Ball was the winning conductor in 1951 and 1952, first with Ransome and Marles and then with C.W.S.

CWS Manchester, with Jack Atherton, celebrating a Belle Vue win.

Manchester. The National Band of New Zealand carried off the trophy in 1953 and in 1954, Munn & Felton's conducted by Stanley Boddington, won for the first and only time. The same could be said of Ferodo who won the following year, conducted by George Hespe. But in 1956, Fairey were back again winning first prize in what turned out to be Harry Mortimer's last appearance as a conductor on the contest platform. His B.B.C. duties prevented him from further contest activity. However, Fairey continued to dominate the Belle Vue results in the early part of the 1960s, gaining a hat-trick with Leonard Lamb conducting. Alex Mortimer with C.W.S. Manchester, George Thompson with Grimethorpe Colliery and Trevor Walmsley with Yorkshire Imperial Metals, all brought new names and exciting performances to Belle Vue. Then, for the first time for eleven years, Black Dyke conducted by Geoffrey Brand, re-emerged as the British Open Champions. Before another ten years had passed, they had won the title five times more. With Roy Newsome they completed one hat-trick in 1974 and after being barred for 1975, when Wingates won, they embarked on another with Major Peter Parkes at the helm. Who could prevent their second hat-trick in 1978? None other than their near rivals, Brighouse and Rastrick conducted by Dyke's former professional, Geoffrey Brand. The last time that the name of Brighouse and Rastrick had appeared on the Belle Vue Trophy was 1936 and the bandsmen felt that forty-two

H.F.B. Iles (Mr. Eric) who succeeded his father, John Henry, as chairman of Belle Vue.

Proud members of the Rochdale Band with the Grand Shield and a presentation cornet, following their win in the May Belle Vue Festival 1979, Frank Mallison, founder of the present band is surrounded by officials and members.

years was a long time to wait. As the September contest approaches for 1979, both Dyke and Brighouse will settle to concentrated rehearsals, each determined to win and in that determination, perfecting their art of brass band performance.

Since December 1965, Belle Vue has been the home of the National Registry of Brass Bandsmen. Changes of personnel of contesting bands are documented here and through the Registry "clean" contesting as desired by the National Brass Band Club in the thirties has come about. There was a fear in 1965 that the Registry would cease to exist, but Jack Fearnley offered to accommodate it at Belle Vue, as long as there was complete co-operation.

A new type of contest brought Belle Vue into the seventies. The Granada Television Company agreed to sponsor an Entertainment Contest, which would carry a television performance as part of the prize. With the camera and TV audiences in mind, not only were the marks given for the technical performances of the band, but also for the entertainment value of the programme and the visual impact of the bands and their conductors. The adjudicators were divided into three groups, two were enclosed in traditional brass band style and one sat in the open to react as if he were a television viewer. The series has proved to be very popular, with Stanshawe, Cory, Grimethorpe and Fairey capturing the first prizes up to the present.

But what of Belle Vue itself? Its ownership has passed

from the Iles family to a large public company. The contests are directed and controlled by Harry Mortimer, who stepped in to save them when their future was threatened, for he knew that these events represent the very roots of the brass band movement. Not only are they the oldest brass band events in the world, but from them sprang much of what is valued in the brass band fraternity today.

Acknowledgements
We would like to thank the editor of the *British Bandsman,* Peter Wilson and the managing director of Rosehill Instruments, Trevor Austin, for making available the *British Bandsman* library and facilities for research.

5. Famous Bands

by VIOLET BRAND

Bands of all grades, throughout the country, have their own loyal supporters, who provide the audience at concerts and the cheers at contests. There are, however, a handful of bands, who, by their contest successes and thrilling concert performances, create an aura around themselves, and find that they have supporters in every corner of the globe. They are the favourites at the National Championships and at Belle Vue. For them, the hall will be packed to the doors, only to empty, as their luckless successor in the draw takes the stage. This small group of famous bands does not necessarily remain constant. Form changes as players leave and conductors move on. A graph, showing the rise and fall in popularity of famous bands of the twentieth century, would closely coincide with a similar graph of their contest successes. Some reach a peak and then fall back never to regain former glory, others show a succession of peaks, and some reach a high plateau and thus maintain a constant universal following.

At the turn of the century, one of the most famous bands in the country was undoubtedly Besses o' th' Barn, with their conductor Alexander Owen. In 1892 they won the Belle Vue contest, which placed them in the position of holding every Challenge Cup in Great Britain for 1892. Never before had a brass band achieved such success. But the top prize in the new Crystal Palace National Championship eluded them until 1903. However, this was a good year to win, for early in 1904 John Henry Iles decided to take his National Champion band on a grand tour of England, Scotland and Wales.

In June, 1905, they found themselves playing to the royal family at Windsor, before embarking on a tour of

Top right: June 23, 1905 Besses o' th' Barn on Paddington Station with Alexander Owen and John Henry Iles waiting to catch the train to Windsor to play before His Majesty the King prior to embarking on their tour of France. Right: Besses in France playing in the Tuileries Gardens, conducted by Alexander Owen

92

93

Besses seeing the sights of Lyons
watched by the French crowds.

Prior to the world tour by Besses
o' th' Barn, Alexander Owen had
asked for an advance fee of £300
from the tour organiser, John
Henry Iles. John Henry agreed to
pay only £150 and the tour plans
were in danger of falling through.
To save the situation, this legal
document was drawn up whereby
Mr. Iles advanced the further £150
in return for the documents of title
to the leasehold of Besses o' th'
Barn bandroom. He was to hold
these documents as security until
the end of the tour

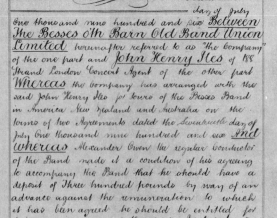

France. Prime Minister Arthur Balfour gave his official blessing to the tour and both Alexander Owen and John Henry Iles were decorated Officier de L'Instruction Publique, by the French Under-Secretary of Fine Arts. The tour was an artistic and social success.

Besses were now not only nationally, but internationally famous and John Henry Iles conceived the plan of taking them on a world tour. His principal objective was a great exhibition in Christchurch, New Zealand, but the tour was to include America, Canada, Honolulu, Fiji, New Zealand and Australia. The majority of British brass bands in the 1970s would find such a tour daunting, particularly if all travelling had to be done by sea. However, in July, 1906, Besses o' th' Barn, with conductor Alexander Owen, set sail for New York. They finally arrived home, after a series of triumphs, in December, 1907.

In their absence overseas, a newly-formed band was gradually gaining ground — Foden's Motor Works. The small Cheshire village of Elworth had for a few years boasted its own band. This was dissolved in 1902, when members demanded a fee of £4 for taking part in the local Coronation celebrations. Edwin Foden was one of the original founders

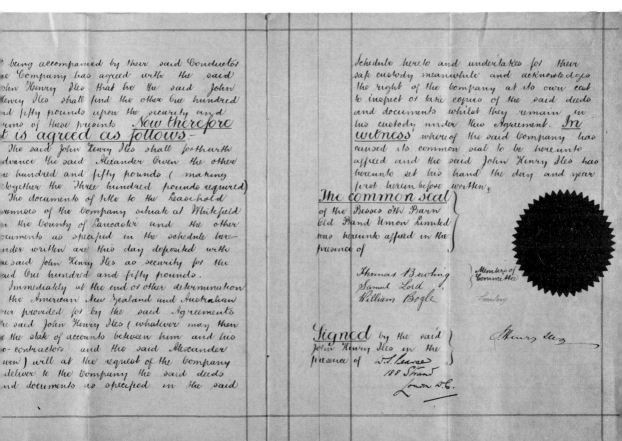

William Rimmer.

Elworth Silver Band, 1902. Taken on the occasion of the coronation of King Edward VII. They were dissolved shortly afterwards, for demanding a £4 fee for taking part in the celebrations. Out of their dissolution grew Foden's Motor Works Band.
(Photograph from 'By Royal Command' by F.D. Burgess).

of the Elworth Band and did not take kindly to its dissolution. He therefore reconstituted it, with a new set of instruments, and a new name.

Edwin Foden was not interested in the well-intentioned amateur, he wanted the best band in the world. Several of the finest players in the country were recruited, and William Rimmer was engaged as the professional coach. Contest success followed and in 1909 Foden's became the British Open Champions at Belle Vue and gained second place at the Crystal Palace.

William Rimmer decided to retire before the next contest season began, and his place as professional was taken by William Halliwell, who, in 1910, led the band to the coveted double - British Open Champions and National Champions. Black Dyke had achieved the double in 1902, Irwell Springs in 1905 and Wingates Temperance in 1906 and 1907, with William Rimmer conducting. It should, of course, be remembered, that no double was possible before 1900, as the National Championships did not exist.

Edwin Foden was justifiably proud of the band he had created and to celebrate their success in 1910, he gave 5s. each to the old people of Elworth. He died during 1911, but his band went on to become even more famous. They won Belle Vue in 1912 and 1913, but before the 1914 round of contests began, Britain was at war.

Like all bands, Foden's suffered during the war and after 1918 a major reconstruction took place.

Edwin Foden's sons were now in charge and, fortunately, they were as devoted to the band as their father had been. In 1924, W. Foden emigrated to Australia, but his brother, E.R. Foden, took over as band manager as well as band secretary. This was a fateful year for Foden's Motor Works Band. Not only were there management changes, but Fred Mortimer became the bandmaster. William Halliwell remained as professional coach until 1929, when he resigned. The musical positions in the band were then reorganised and Fred Mortimer became the full-time musical director, whilst his son, Harry, became the part-time bandmaster.

Harry Mortimer had been principal cornet of Foden's since 1924. His brother Alex was the principal euphonium, and had been the first member of the Mortimer family to join the band. Their younger brother, Rex, was also a member.

A strict disciplinarian, Fred Mortimer would not tolerate

Below. Foden's on board ship bound for South Africa in 1936. During their absence, the Crystal Palace was burned to the ground.

Bottom: Foden's 1951.

Back row: N Machin; G. Poole; W. Illingworth; W. Kitson.

Centre row: J. Thorpe; D. Heath; D. Thomas; E. Gray; C. Cook; F. Sowood; A. Webb; J. Cotterill; H. Shergold; R. Shepley; S. Garratt; R. Moores; D. Connolly.

Front row: R. Sparks; E. Spurr; S. Brough; A. Webb; F. Mortimer; W. Foden; H. Mortimer; G. McDean; H. Mather; R. Mortimer; E. Swindles.

(Photographs from 'By Royal Command' by F.D. Burgess).

slackness in playing, performance or dress. He insisted on full attendance at the twice weekly rehearsals and found the playing of a wrong note totally unacceptable. His striving for perfection led the band to even greater success.

They became the British Open Champions in 1926, 1927 and 1928 and the National Champions in 1930, 1932, 1933, 1934, 1936, 1937 and 1938. Three hat-tricks in twelve years made Foden's and the name of Mortimer renowned amongst bandsmen and lay-men alike.

During the summer months the band usually spent twelve weeks touring the seaside resorts, followed by four weeks in the London parks and then on to Scotland. Fred Mortimer would allow no lowering of standards whilst the band was on tour. He would patrol the hotel foyer during the late evening to ensure that every player was in by 11 and then, the next morning, he would check that they were all suitably dressed for breakfast.

Fred Mortimer with his sons Alex, Harry and Rex.

On one occasion, when two players had spent too long imbibing and then proceeded to talk throughout the band's park performance, Fred Mortimer had no compunction about sending them home, even though the band was catching the night boat for Ireland. Rather a band with two players short, than one with ill-behaved members.

Following the 1936 National Championships, Foden's undertook their first overseas tour. They spent five weeks in South Africa, during which time they made numerous appearances at the Empire Exhibition held in Johannesburg. Whilst they were abroad news reached them that the Crystal

Palace, scene of their triumphs, had been destroyed by fire.

When they returned, they took part in the National Championships, now housed in Alexandra Palace and won yet again. By 1938 they achieved their second National hat-trick and were barred. But war broke out before the 1939 contest and surprisingly, the bar was carried over to the first contest after the war. It was 1950 before they regained the title National Champions.

Fred Mortimer died in 1953 and later that year his son, Harry, led the band to victory at the Royal Albert Hall. Harry continued to conduct the band for the next three years and in 1956 he was appointed musical advisor to Foden's Motor Works Band, whilst his brother Rex became the musical director.

Successes over the next twenty years were more intermittent, although the glory of the name remained. The band was busy in this country and abroad, both as a solo band and as part of Harry Mortimer's Men O' Brass, with Fairey Aviation and Morris Motors.

The year 1975 might have been the one that would have ended the story of Foden's. The company was in financial difficulties and a cut-back of expenditure was necessary. Should the band go, was the question. The board decided to keep it, but there would no longer be a full-time musical director. James Scott was appointed to the part-time position and it was his task to reorganise Foden's enabling the band once again to take its rightful position in the contest field. At the 1978 British Open Championship, Foden's were not placed in the prizes, but the audience heard that here was a band to be reckoned with.

William Halliwell, who conducted Foden's to a double victory in 1910, was having considerable contest success with other bands. His name features nine times as the conductor of National Champions between 1910 - 1928 and there were no contests from 1914 to 1919.

William Halliwell.

He was invited as professional conductor to the St. Hilda Colliery Band, County Durham, in August, 1912. The band had achieved local success and had won the Grand Shield at Crystal Palace in 1909, under J.A. Greenwood. But their eyes were on the Crystal Palace 1000 Guinea Challenge Trophy and although they had competed for it in 1910, they were unplaced. So in 1911 they made changes. James Oliver, from Felling Colliery, became bandmaster. He had the reputation of being one of the foremost young teachers of the day and a most successful contesting bandmaster. The same year, James Southern joined the band as solo trombonist. It was he who persuaded William Halliwell

St. Hilda Colliery Band, 1912, after winning the Crystal Palace Championship for the first time.

to become St. Hilda's professional conductor.

On September 2, they competed at Belle Vue and came second to Foden's but on September 28, 1912, they travelled to Crystal Palace and under the baton of William Halliwell, won the 1000 Guinea Trophy. The men from South Shields had proved that they could become the National Champion Band of Great Britain. When they returned home to County Durham their reception was indescribable. So began the legend of the famous St. Hilda Colliery Band.

In 1913 they had to be content with second prize at Crystal Palace. The first place was won by Irwell Springs, also conducted by William Halliwell. Then came the war and fourteen of St. Hilda's regular members were called into the services. The band decided to continue as a playing unit and gave many charity concerts, raising over £13,000. The man responsible for organising and inspiring these events was the newly-appointed band manager, James Southern. He continued to play and was evidently a first-class trombone player, but he was already showing great skill as an organiser and entrepreneur.

After the war, nearly all of the players returned to the band and when the National Championships resumed in 1920, it was the St. Hilda Colliery Band who succeeded in carrying off the 1000 Guinea Trophy. They repeated their success in 1921.

William Halliwell confounded all northerners by winning the National Championship in 1923, with a southern band — Luton Red Cross. St. Hilda Colliery were fourth. But the following year, to the relief of all English brass band supporters, St. Hilda's, with Halliwell, were at the peak of their form. In 1924, one of Australia's finest brass bands, Newcastle Steel Works Brass Band, arrived in England to participate. They won Belle Vue and were taking back to Australia the £2000 Gold Trophy. Would they also take the Crystal Palace 1000 Guinea Trophy? In the estimation of band supporters, there was only one combination which could stop them – St. Hilda Colliery Band. The atmosphere at Crystal Palace on September 27, 1924, was electric. The test piece was Henry Geehl's 'On the Cornish Coast' and the adjudicators found St. Hilda's performance "A hugh triumph in artistic playing".

Those present felt that this was one of the most inspired performances ever heard in the history of brass bands. Even the bandmaster of the Newcastle Steel Works Band wrote a letter of congratulation, saying: "Your success was justly deserved".

St. Hilda's were now riding on the crest of a wave of popularity and were in great demand for concerts throughout the country. Some thought that they were accepting too many engagements and, following their magnificent 1924 Crystal Palace win, the band management was warned by the promoters of the National Brass Band Championships that the acceptance of unlimited engagements, was "contrary to the spirit of amateur status".

In order to remain together, the band had no choice but to ignore the warning. The cólliery was closed in 1925, first due to a local dispute, then a national stoppage and the subsequent depression. The entire band was unemployed. There was no financial support from the colliery and St. Hilda's were only able to continue on the income from prize money and engagements.

The band had their own touring charabanc which was built to carry everything that would be required during a two or three-month tour. It originally cost 2000 guineas, but was paid for in twelve months, from saved travelling

St. Hilda's Professional Band, 1928, photographed at Lord Street Municipal Gardens Bandstand, Southport. They are wearing a new uniform specially made for the band's annual Christmas 6-week engagement at Bertram Mills Circus, held at Olympia, London. The conductor is Hubert Bath.

expenses. The warning from the promoters was not immediately followed up and, in 1926, St. Hilda Colliery again won the National Championship, but their activities could no longer be ignored and they were barred from entering the 1927 Crystal Palace Contest, being considered a "professional band and ineligible to compete". The promoters quoted the ruling that each bandsman had to be prepared to prove that more than one half of his income was derived from some business other than music. The same ruling applies today, but the conditions that trapped the St. Hilda Colliery Band do not.

From 1927 the St. Hilda Band became professional, under the astute management of James Southern. The word Colliery had been deleted from the title during the General Strike, as it was felt that there could be political overtones, which would offend some members of the public and damage the name of the band.

Not all bandsmen were happy that St. Hilda's had lost its amateur status and by 1929 there had been wholesale changes in personnel including the conductor. Hubert Bath had taken the place of William Halliwell. However, in the years immediately following the decision, engagements were plentiful. There was a trip to Canada in 1931 to play at the All-Canadian International Exhibition. The band played twice daily and also accompanied the Exhibition Choir of two thousand voices. After a short tour of Canada, they travelled home, giving concerts for the passengers on the boat.

A new professional conductor, Frank Wright, arrived on the scene in 1934. He had won considerable fame in his native Australia as a cornet soloist and an adjudicator, and on his arrival in England he was invited to tour for a season as conductor of St. Hilda's.

The band existed until December, 1937, when its disbandment was announced by James Southern. He stated that there was a growing shortage of the quality engagements, which were needed to support the band and, also, his own health was failing, after twenty-seven years as manager. The last engagement of the famous St. Hilda Band was at Stanhope Show, Co. Durham, on September 12, 1937.

The decision of the St. Hilda Band to become professional in no way inhibited the contest activities of William Halliwell. Between 1926 and 1936 he won the Belle Vue Championship nine times, and in 1928 he conducted six bands in the Crystal Palace Championship. He took first prize with Black Dyke and second prize with the sister band of St. Hilda's, Harton Colliery.

Founded in 1873, Harton Colliery achieved national fame in 1919, when they won the British Open Championship at Belle Vue. The conductor was George Hawkins, a highly skilled band trainer. Shortly after their Belle Vue success Harton Colliery was joined by a brilliant local cornet player — Jack Mackintosh. For eleven years he filled with great distinction the position of solo cornet, astounding everyone with his technique. He left the band in 1930 to become the principal cornet and sub-principal trumpet of the B.B.C. Symphony Orchestra, a position he held until he retired. He was also the Professor of Trumpet and Cornet at the Royal Military School of Music, Kneller Hall, where he remained an active teacher until he reached his eighties.

Another band which has produced an abundance of famous players is Black Dyke Mills. Trombone player Jack Pinches left the brass band scene to join Jack Mackintosh in the B.B.C. Symphony Orchestra. Principal cornet player, Harold Jackson, joined the R.A.F. Central Band during the war and then was invited to become first trumpet with the newly-formed Philharmonia Orchestra in London. From Black Dyke's top chair, Willie Lang also went into the orchestral profession. He went first to the B.B.C. Northern Symphony Orchestra, and then on to the London Symphony Orchestra, whilst his successor at Black Dyke, Maurice Murphy, followed him to the B.B.C. Northern Symphony Orchestra and later to the London Symphony Orchestra. More recently, James Shepherd has achieved both national and international fame as a cornet soloist and the founder

Jack Mackintosh who was for eleven years the brilliant solo cornet player of Harton Colliery and from 1930 a renowned professional trumpet player in London for over forty years. He was professor of the cornet at the Royal Military School of Music, Kneller Hall.

James Shepherd (front left) and his Versatile Brass.
(Photograph by permission of Kirklees Printing Co., Ltd.)

of Versatile Brass, a modern brass group, which is much in demand.

Perhaps it is not surprising that a band with such an outstanding record as Black Dyke, should produce, or attract, instrumentalists of this calibre. A Belle Vue hat-trick is recorded for Black Dyke in 1879, 1880 and 1881. Almost one hundred years later, they were prevented from getting a further hat-trick by their neighbours Brighouse & Rastrick, and were barred from entering the National Championships because they had just achieved a hat-trick. For sheer consistency of standard, no band in the history of the brass band scene can compare with Black Dyke.

The roots of the band are in the small brass and reed band, founded by Peter Wharton in 1816. After a slightly chequered career, the band was in danger of disappearing, when horn player, John Foster, invited them to become associated with his Black Dyke Mill in Queensbury, Yorkshire. So, in 1855, a set of new brass instruments was purchased, a practice room was provided, the number of instrumentalists was increased to nineteen and every member was given a new uniform. Thus, the Black Dike Mills Band, sponsored by John Foster and Son Ltd. was born. The change in spelling, from Dike to Dyke, took place in 1915. All members of the band, and in fact most of the Queensbury villagers, worked at Black Dyke Mill, so from the beginning, there was this great sense of involvement both with the community and the company.

A local musician of considerable reputation, Samuel Longbottom, was appointed as the band's first professional conductor. He took them to several local contests and then, in 1860, Black Dyke Mills Band came to the first brass band contest held at the Crystal Palace, London. They won first prize and were presented with £40 in cash, a silver cup and a bass, valued at £36 15s. Two years later, they won first prize in the September Belle Vue contest, Manchester. The name of Black Dyke Mills has figured in the prizes at these two major contests almost continuously, ever since.

At the Belle Vue contest in 1873, Black Dyke, although only winning third prize, won both the euphonium and trombone instrumental prizes. This was not a unique achievement in itself, but the fact that they were both awarded to the same player, Phineas Bower, was. At the start of the test piece he was playing the euphonium, but picked up a valve trombone to play the trombone solo, later in the piece. The contest authorities were not too happy when they discovered that the adjudicators had awarded two medals to one person and tried to persuade Phineas to give one up. He bluntly refused. But, the authorities had the final say. This was the last occasion when valve trombones were allowed at the Belle Vue contest.

Phineas Bower later became the bandmaster of Black Dyke; then in 1879 Alexander Owen was invited to be the professional conductor. Successes followed and by 1881 Black Dyke had achieved their first Belle Vue hat-trick.

To mark the band's successes, in 1882 pottery jugs were produced, listing the band's achievements. Some of these jugs still exist and, in 1969, a reader wrote to the *British Bandsman* as follows: "I have cherished a souvenir for a number of years, given to me by an elderly lady, whose Grandfather was a founder member of the Black Dyke Mills Band in 1855. The souvenir is in the form of a pottery jug, white in colour, with black lettering, giving details, with prize monies, of all the contests won from 1856 to 1882. There are ninety-two contests mentioned, showing a total amount won of £2011.9.0."

Alex Owen continued to conduct the band until July, 1888, when he was succeeded by John Gladney, who was already a veteran of the contest platform. But in the 1890s, Black Dyke had a great rival, Besses o' th' Barn, who were conducted by none other than Alex Owen.

The rivalry between these two bands was stimulated in the band press, as well as on the contest platform. The *Brass Band News* carried an exchange of pointed and amusing

Alexander Owen, who was the professional conductor of Black Dyke 1879-1888.

Commemorative jug issued by Black Dyke Mills Band to show prizes won between the years 1856-1882, amounting to a total of £2,011-9 shillings. A few of these jugs are known to exist.

articles by Pondash of Black Dyke Mills and Trotter of Besses o' th' Barn. Since that day in 1891, when Jo Wood, supporting Dyke, called himself Pondash, fans of the band have been known as Pondashers.

However the exchange was not limited to supporters. The bands joined in and in the late 1800s the following acceptance to a challenge appeared:

"We, the Black Dyke Mills Band, of Queensbury, Bradford, Yorks., accept the challenge of Besses o' th' Barn Band, as previously agreed - each band to play six selections of its own choice - each band to follow on, piece for piece. Stake £50. Gate equally divided. The Champion Black Dyke Mills Band, Secretary, P. Bower. YOU WILL GET THE BIGGEST LICKING YOU EVER HAD."

It would appear that this contest never actually took place.

John Gladney had considerable success with Black Dyke, winning Belle Vue in 1891, 1895, 1896, 1899, 1902 and 1904, and Crystal Palace in 1902. But it was not contest success alone that marked this period of the band's history. In 1906 Black Dyke went on a five-month tour of Canada and the United States. They gave over two hundred concerts and travelled nearly thirteen thousand miles. By a strange coincidence, when Black Dyke went to Canada and the U.S.A. in 1972, the departure date was almost identical (Friday, June 30, 1906, and Friday, June 29, 1972) and both tours included Buffalo, U.S.A., and Toronto.

John Gladney died in 1911, but his position as professional conductor of Black Dyke had already been taken over by William Rimmer, with whom they won Belle Vue in 1908. In 1912, a regime began at Black Dyke, which was to last for thirty-six years. Arthur O. Pearce became the bandmaster, and soon became renowned for his firm handling of the band. Punctuality to the second was demanded, and if a player was missing at the hour appointed for the band coach to depart, the coach went, even though the missing player might be the principal cornet, who could actually be seen trotting down the road.

It is possible that the autocratic rule stifled Black Dyke, they only won the National Championship once (1928) between 1902 and 1947, and did little better at Belle Vue, when they did not take home the trophy from 1914 to 1935. But all bands have their fallow period and Black Dyke returned successfully after World War Two. Harry Mortimer was the professional and he conducted them to a London hat-trick in 1947, 1948 and 1949. Alex Mortimer

became the bandmaster in 1949 and it was he who conducted them successfully, yet again, in 1951.

They were still waiting to win Belle Vue and had to continue waiting until an exciting new professional came on to the scene — Major George Willcocks. He had led Fairey to success at the Royal Albert Hall in October, 1956, and Black Dyke invited him to take them to Belle Vue in September, 1957. With the test piece 'Carnival' by Helen Perkin, Black Dyke won the Belle Vue trophy again, after more than twenty years. Major Willcocks went on to win the National Championship with them in 1959 and 1961. Those performances of 'Le Roi d'Ys' (Lalo) and 'Les Franc Juges' (Berlioz) are still discussed with bated breath by all who were present. The Major's untimely death in 1961 brought great sadness to the men of Black Dyke in particular, but also to the wider brass band public who had grown to respect and admire him in those few short years.

Jack Emmott, Geoffrey Whitham, Leighton Lucas and Colonel C.H. Jaeger were all involved in conducting Black Dyke, either as bandmasters, or professionals, in the next few

The 'Journey into Freedom' win by Black Dyke Mills conducted by Geoffrey Brand at the Royal Albert Hall in 1967. Roy Newsome (Bandmaster) shares in the jubilation.
(London Press Photos).

years. But a new and exciting era began for the band in the late 1960s. Roy Newsome became the bandmaster in 1966, and Geoffrey Brand the professional conductor in 1967. With a performance, conducted by Geoffrey Brand, of 'Journey Into Freedom' by Eric Ball, at the Royal Albert Hall, on October 14, 1967, that literally made that vast audience gasp, Black Dyke made a successful bid for the top, where they have remained ever since.

In 1968 and 1972, they won Belle Vue. In 1970, they took home the World Trophy from London and, in 1972, by winning the National Championship, they once again achieved the "double" — the first time since 1902. At this stage, it was necessary for Geoffrey Brand to refrain from contesting with Black Dyke, or any other band, because of his involvement with the management of the National Brass Band Championship. Roy Newsome became the band's resident conductor in 1972 and Dyke's successes continued. By winning Belle Vue in 1973 and 1974, with Roy conducting, the band achieved a hat-trick, the first for almost one hundred years.

Major Peter Parkes was invited to become the professional conductor in 1975· and the band continued at the very peak of its form. Very few changes of personnel took place

Winning the first ever European Championship. Black Dyke, conducted by Major Peter Parkes, on the Royal Albert Hall platform. (Photograph by permission of Keystone Press Agency).

and new players seemed to integrate thoroughly into the Dyke sound. The years 1975, 1976 and 1977 placed the Black Dyke Mills Band on a pinnacle. They seemed to be invincible. They had a hat-trick at the Royal Albert Hall, so in 1978 they were not competing in the National Championships. They had won Belle Vue in 1976 and 1977, and were confident of repeating their hat-trick, but a combination of Berlioz, Brighouse and Brand, proved to be their Achilles' heel and they had to be content with second place. However, with their Yorkshire temperament and conviction that contests are for winning, Black Dyke will certainly be making yet another strong bid for Belle Vue this year.

Roy Newsome, resident conductor with Black Dyke, 1966-1978.

The first European Brass Band Championship took place at the Royal Albert Hall in 1978 and Black Dyke, together with Grimethorpe, were invited to represent English bands. The international audience were in no doubt about the winner and whatever their nationality, everyone seemed delighted that the name of Black Dyke Mills Band should be the first to appear on the new European trophy. When Major Peter Parkes and the new resident conductor, Michael Antrobus, came on to the stage to receive the prize, the applause was wholehearted.

During the last ten years, Black Dyke's musical life has not consisted simply of contests. Gramophone records, television shows, broadcasts, tours abroad and prestige concerts at music festivals, universities, the Proms and the 'Fanfare Into Europe' events, have all been part of their activity. John Foster & Son Ltd., the residents of Queensbury, and brass band enthusiasts throughout the world are justifiably proud of this great band of the 1970s.

Five miles from Queensbury is the small Yorkshire town of Brighouse, which boasts an equally famous band - Brighouse & Rastrick. Between these two bands exists a love/hate relationship, possibly unequalled anywhere in the world of brass bands.

Purple traditionally belongs to Brighouse and the colour sparks off strong reactions in the men of Dyke. When the young daughter of their professional conductor arrived at the 1968 Belle Vue contest wearing a purple dress, the Black Dyke bandsmen declared that she should go straight home and change! But, in 1978, when Brighouse won the contest, preventing Black Dyke from achieving a further hat-trick, it was John Clough, Dyke's solo euphoniumist, who stood shaking the hand of every Brighouse man, as he mounted the stage to play the lap of honour. Such is the relationship between these two great bands.

The Brighouse & Rastrick Temperance Band began

Fred Berry, in the uniform of Besses o' th' Barn Band with which he toured the world. In 1924 he became the bandmaster of Brighouse & Rastrick.

Brighouse & Rastrick 1946 National Champions, with conductor Eric Ball.

life in 1860 as a brass and reed combination. They changed to all brass in 1881 and the word Temperance was dropped from the name in 1928.

Unlike many championship section bands, Brighouse are a subscription band and receive no sponsorship of any kind. In 1860, every intending member had to sign the pledge, buy his own uniform, and pay a subscription of sixpence a week. The band remain completely independent and own a band-room they have purchased and renovated themselves. A strong local committee comprising bandsmen and supporters, determines the band's affairs and accepts the responsibility for the destiny of Brighouse & Rastrick.

The band first went to Crystal Palace in 1913 and came fifth in the championship section. In 1924, they took a daring and ambitious step, which proved to be the first rung on the ladder to national fame. They appointed Fred Berry of Wyke, as their conductor. He had been associated with bands for many years and had actually been with Besses o' th' Barn on their world tour in 1906 - 1907. Faith in Fred Berry was justified. In 1929 Brighouse & Rastrick achieved the almost impossible. They won the July and September Belle Vue contests in the same year. This had only been accomplished once before, by Batley Old in 1890.

Their 1929 success was only the beginning. William Halliwell was engaged as the professional conductor of Brighouse in 1932 and together they achieved a hat-trick, 1932, 1933, and 1934. They were barred in 1935, but returned to win again in 1936. Foden's were winning the

British Open Champions 1978.
Brighouse & Rastrick rehearsing in
their bandroom under the baton of
their professional, Geoffrey Brand.

Crystal Palace Trophy, but it was Brighouse who dominated the Belle Vue scene in the thirties.

Fred Berry relinquished his position for three years, but was persuaded to return in 1941 until he finally retired in 1949. The twenty years that he gave to Brighouse & Rastrick were enormously important in the band's development. For a very short period in the early forties, Harry Mortimer was professional conductor. But in 1944 Brighouse were looking for a replacement and had the inspired thought of inviting Eric Ball, who had recently left the Salvation Army, to take over the position. Within a very short time after the war, Eric Ball brought Brighouse back to prominence. They were fourth in the 1945 National Brass Band Championships and in 1946, to the great joy of all Brighouse supporters, and Salvation Army band enthusiasts, Eric Ball won the National with Brighouse & Rastrick.

Their success was national news and the media descended on Brighouse. Fox Movietime News made a film of the band marching in triumph from the station into the town centre for a civic reception. The film was shown in all cinemas contracted with Fox Movietime News, so that even in 1946, Brighouse were receiving star treatment.

Whilst remaining regularly in the prizes at both Belle Vue and the Royal Albert Hall, it was 1968 before Brighouse brought home a premier prize again. Walter Hargreaves became professional conductor in 1963 and his natural energy and musical enthusiasm inspired the band to greater performances. Together in 1969 they brought home to Brighouse, not only the National Championship trophy, but also a globe signifying that they were the World Champions.

But the top prize at Belle Vue eluded them and had done so since 1936. Members of the audience placed them first on several occasions during those forty years, but not the adjudicators. The year 1977 brought a new kind of fame — Brighouse were in the Top Ten. Teenagers, disc-jockeys, television and radio audiences, all knew about this Yorkshire band. Not because they had achieved outstanding success in the contest field, but because they had made a "hit" record. With their conductor Derek Broadbent, they had recorded an arrangement of 'The Floral Dance' and everyone was listening to it and buying it. The record reached number two in the charts and remained there for several weeks, with only Paul McCartney preventing it from reaching number one.

The men from Brighouse were rushed off their feet with engagements, but not swept off their feet with this popular acclaim. They stuck strictly to their calendar of traditional engagements, fitting in exotic night clubs and television shows where possible. The pop scene is rarely confronted with such sanity.

Throughout those whirlwind months critics in the band world, who didn't quite approve of the popularity of one of their finest bands, declared that Brighouse were losing their tone and precision.

In typical Yorkshire fashion, the Brighouse & Rastrick Band set out to confound their critics. They could not appear at the Royal Albert Hall in 1978, as they had missed the area contest, due to other pressures. The British Open Championship at Belle Vue was the only possibility and they had not won this for over forty years. When the test piece, 'Benvenuto Cellini', was announced, their minds were made up. Black Dyke had previously won on this piece at the Royal Albert Hall and they were the band Brighouse most needed to beat. Geoffrey Brand had conducted Dyke on that occasion and so he was their man. He accepted the challenge and on September 9, 1978, Brighouse & Rastrick once again became British Open Champions. The vast audience was delighted, Black Dyke were deprived of another hat-trick, and Brighouse had proved that as a brass band they had lost nothing.

"We are going to form a band and we are going to aim high", a reporter of the *Northamptonshire Evening Telegraph* was told in January, 1933. He was interviewing Mr. F.E. Felton and Mr. A.S. Felton of Munn & Felton's Works, Kettering. They were band enthusiasts and were determined that their factory should have one of the top-most bands in the country.

Two-and-a-half years later the paper was able to report: "Munn & Felton's Works Band, Kettering, caused one of the biggest sensations in brass band history at the famous Crystal Palace Festival on Saturday, when, making its debut in the championship section, it defeated the crack bands of Great Britain and became the country's premier brass combination. Nothing as remarkable as the Kettering band's success has ever occurred in brass band history."

Credit was given to the persistent determination and progressiveness of the brothers Felton, without which this magnificent win could never have been achieved. Tribute was also paid to the superb tuition of William Halliwell, which was a "vital factor" in the band's success.

"The band owes a big debt of gratitude to Mr. Halliwell and the players realise it", went on the reporter. He then

Below: Munn & Felton's Works Band with the Crystal Palace Trophy which they won in 1935.

G.U.S. (Footwear) Band 1971. Conductor Stanley Boddington, showing the World Champion banner and trophy.

offered praise for the work of the bandmaster — Stanley Boddington.

From 1933 to 1975, Stanley Boddington was associated with the band, first as the bandmaster and later as the musical director. During these years the brothers Felton retired from the scene and the band changed its name to G.U.S. (Footwear), but Stanley Boddington remained, maintaining the band at a consistently high standard. He conducted them in their only Belle Vue win in 1954.

Harry Mortimer became musical director in 1955, a position he held for ten years. This appointment brought further success to the band, for twenty years after their first magnificent championship win, they were once again the National Champions. In 1957, with Stanley Boddington conducting, they repeated their win, and again in 1960. But that was the last time that the name Munn & Felton's appeared on a national trophy. The firm became part of the G.U.S. group and the band adopted its name — G.U.S. (Footwear) Band. The personal sponsorship of the Felton brothers had gone forever. But Stanley Boddington continued to conduct the band into the prize list at the Royal Albert Hall. In 1964 and 1966 they were again National Champions and, in 1971, took the World Championship trophy back to Kettering.

During the sixties the G.U.S. Quartet were highly successful and won the title Champion Quartet of Great Britain in 1966, 1967 and 1968. They played music especially composed for them by Gilbert Vinter - 'Elegy & Rondo' (1966), 'Fancy's Knell' (1967) and 'Alla Burlesca' (1968). Later, these three quartets were put on to record.

Gilbert Vinter had a close relationship with the G.U.S. (Footwear) Band and was often to be found in the bandroom. He was the regular conductor of the B.B.C. Midland Light Orchestra and had recently "discovered" the brass band medium. He enjoyed it and admired it.

Stanley Boddington's work with brass bands was recognised in 1969, when he and Mrs. Boddington were invited to a Royal Garden Party, and in 1973, the G.U.S. (Footwear) Band gave a concert in Kettering to celebrate his forty years with the band. Harry Mortimer, who had been associated with him in the band's success, was the guest conductor.

In 1975 Stanley Boddington retired and Geoffrey Brand became the musical director. But times had changed for the British shoe industry and repercussions were felt within the band. Nevertheless G.U.S. continued to give prestige concerts, appearing in both the Cheltenham Festival and the Three Choirs Festival. Towards the end of 1978, the band had its own band-room once again, and Dr. Keith Wilkinson became the musical director.

Harry Mortimer has been associated with most of Britain's top-class brass bands in the last fifty years, first as a brilliant solo cornet player, and then as a conductor. He

Fairey Band 1961, in Niagara, with the Falls in the background. On the extreme left is Harry Mortimer (Professional Adviser); on the extreme right is Leonard Lamb (Bandmaster).

won both the British Open Championship and the National Brass Band Championship, nine times. Then, from 1956, he was prevented by his work at the B.B.C. from continuing his contesting activities. Like William Halliwell, his successes were not limited to one band. He contested with Fairey, Black Dyke, Foden's, Munn & Felton's, Morris Motors and Bickershaw Colliery.

It is perhaps the Fairey Band with whom he is most closely associated as a conductor in the contest field. He won the National Championship with them three times and the British Open Championship eight times.

The Fairey Aviation Works Band was formed in 1937 by a group of enthusiasts who were working in the company. They realised that if they were to enter the "big league" they would need to have a professional conductor. Harry Mortimer was invited, and in 1938 the band speedily reached the championship class, by winning the July Belle Vue contest.

Due to the nature of the work at the factory, the band was not too seriously disrupted by the war, and succeeded in winning the British Open Championship in 1941, 1942, 1944 and 1945. The National Brass Band Championships were restored in 1945 and Faireys achieved their first double, by winning that too. They next won the double in 1956 with different conductors. Harry Mortimer conducted them at Belle Vue, but was on his way to Australia before the October contest in the Royal Albert Hall could take place. He invited Major George Willcocks to take Fairey and they won.

The sheer brilliance of the Fairey sound will long be

The Lord Gregson, Band President of the Fairey Engineering Works Band, presenting Harry Mortimer with a silver salver in recognition of his 40 years association with the band. The presentation was made on 1st December 1978, and Harry Mortimer became the band's first Vice President.

associated with Harry Mortimer. The electric atmosphere he brought to the stage will live in the memories of all who were present at his performances. But perhaps behind that stage presence, the influence of his father Fred could be noticed. Harry once said: "Fred Mortimer's insistence on detail, points of balance, intonation and good ensemble has been passed on a hundred fold".

When Harry Mortimer could no longer appear on the contest platform with the Fairey Band, it was important to him that he should have a bandmaster of quality. Leonard Lamb was such a man. He conducted Fairey in a hat-trick of wins at Belle Vue in 1961, 1962 and 1963 and won the double with them in 1965. He was forced to retire from the scene through a prolonged serious illness and died in 1973, at the age of sixty-three.

Kenneth Dennison became the musical director of the Fairey Band in 1972 and Harry Mortimer became musical advisor until 1978, when he became the band's first vice-president. By this time Kenneth Dennison had moved on to the City of Coventry Band and Walter Hargreaves was appointed musical director of the newly-named Fairey Engineering Works Band.

During the band's long association with Harry Mortimer they toured Germany, Holland and Belgium. They also twice visited Canada, the first time in 1961, as part of the Men O' Brass unit and then, in 1972, in the company of Black Dyke,

C.W.S. (Manchester) and G.U.S.

Sadly, a conductor who was unable to accompany his band on the 1972 Canadian trip was Alex Mortimer. He was too ill to travel. His place, as conductor of the C.W.S. (Manchester) Band, was taken by Derek Garside, who had been the much admired principal cornet of the band for twenty-five years.

Alex Mortimer cultivated in the C.W.S. Band an ethereal quality of sound, which was quite unbelievable in a brass band. In the summers of the early sixties, Londoners would crowd into the Embankment Gardens to listen in awe at the sheer beauty of the sound. If one spoke to Alex for an extended period, one ceased to wonder at his remarkable influence on a brass band. The springs of beauty were within him and his quizzical sense of humour was a delight.

The C.W.S. Band were formed in 1901 as the C.W.S. Tobacco Factory Band and adopted their present name in 1937. They first won national acclaim in 1948, when with Eric Ball they became British Open Champions at Belle Vue. Their success was repeated in 1952. Then Alex Mortimer took over the baton in 1954 and by 1960 had created a unique sound. Together, C.W.S. and Alex, won Belle Vue in 1960, the National Championship in 1962 and 1963, and Belle Vue again in 1966. The demands on the players were great, for Alex was constantly seeking perfection. Changes took place in the band's personnel and ill-health began to overtake him. Even though he finally had to resort to a wheel-chair, Alex Mortimer continued to present a strong

The Cory Band from Pentre, South Wales, conductor Major A.H. Kenney, the first band to take the National Champion Trophy out of England.

challenge on the contest platform, until ill-health forced him to give up the baton.

The first band to take the National Championship title and trophy across the English border were the Cory Band in 1974. To the delight of Welsh enthusiasts the Challenge Trophy and the banner proclaiming Champion Band of Great Britain, were taken to Pentre, in the Rhondda Valley. Major Arthur Kenney was the proud conductor.

The band was founded as the Ton Temperance Band in 1884, but in 1895 when Sir Clifford J. Cory heard them playing at a local function, he invited them to become the band of his company — Cory Brothers Coal Company. He provided them with financial assistance and found a job in the firm for a first-class conductor. This support lasted until 1940, when the band became self-supporting.

Walter Hargreaves first compelled the English bands to regard this Welsh combination as a serious contender. He took them to second place in the Royal Albert Hall in 1948, and to second place at Belle Vue in 1950. However, it was Arthur Kenney who directed them to a hat-trick of wins in the Coal Board Championships at Blackpool in 1970, 1971 and 1972. He then went on to win the National Championship in 1974.

Alex Mortimer. Conductor of Manchester C.W.S., during a much-admired period.

The Cory Band had become B.B.C. Band of the Year in 1971, which doubtless reminded the bandsmen of February, 1965, when their conductor T.J. Powell, collapsed and died in the B.B.C. Cardiff studio, whilst the band was actually taking part in the B.B.C.'s Challenging Brass competition. Tom Powell was a highly regarded Welsh brass band conductor, who had began his life in the Salvation Army and had received a valuable musical education at the Royal Marines Band School, Portsmouth.

Cory went abroad for the first time in 1976, when they were invited to the U.S.A. to take part in the Bicentennial Celebrations. The other band on the trip was the Grimethorpe Colliery Band, from Yorkshire. These two had often been keen rivals, particularly in the Coal Board Championships, at Blackpool. But in 1976 they were united as musical ambassadors.

Grimethorpe Colliery Band was formed in 1918 and continue to receive considerable support from the colliery welfare fund. Most of the members work at the pit, which makes rehearsal time comparatively easy, particularly before a contest. George Thompson brought a sonority to Grimethorpe's sound and achieved three major contest successes with them. In 1967 and 1969 they won the British Open Championship and Belle Vue and in 1970, they became the

National Champions.

But Grimethorpe's fame in the seventies lies in a different direction from contests. With conductor Elgar Howarth, they have trodden paths no brass band had expected to follow. Doors have opened for them and audiences, to whom the sound of a brass band was distinctly foreign, have listened. In the company of Black Dyke, they appeared at a Promenade Concert in 1974. They have played in the Queen Elizabeth Hall, London, and had pieces written for them by such eminent modern composers as Harrison Birtwistle and Hans Werne Henze. Because of their association with Elgar Howarth, the music critics of The Times, Daily Telegraph and The Guardian have reported their concerts, favourably and seriously.

Predictably, Yorkshire has produced more famous bands than any other English county. The general public believes, even now, that brass bands belong to the north. The brass band public knows that this is not so. But, no one can deny that Yorkshire produces the champions. Yet again, in 1978, with neither Black Dyke nor Brighouse competing, it was a Yorkshire band, who took the title Champion Band of Great Britain at the Royal Albert Hall. The Yorkshire Imperial Metals Band, under their musical director, Denis Carr, came to London determined to win — and they did. This was the first time since the band's foundation in 1936, that they had taken home the National title. They had won the British Open Championship at Belle Vue, in 1970 and 1971, with Trevor Walmsley conducting, but until 1978 their name did not appear on the National Championship trophy.

Grimethorpe Colliery Band, conducted by George Thompson, playing at the Mineworkers' National Brass Band Competition, held annually in the Winter Gardens Blackpool.

The nearest a Scottish brass band has come to winning a British title, was in 1958 when Scottish C.W.S. came second in the National Championship. Formed in Glasgow, in 1918 the band rapidly became one of Scotland's leading brass bands. They have repeatedly won the Scottish Championship and on numerous occasions the band has represented Scotland in London.

Members of the Scottish C.W.S. Band who were runners-up at the National Championships in 1958. Bandmaster Willie Crozier is on the extreme left.

Alex Mortimer conducted them in 1960, when the test piece was 'Three Figures' by Herbert Howells. He succeeded in taking them into fifth place with 185 points, beating his own band, C.W.S. (Manchester) by one point.

As in England, there is much brass band activity amongst the young people of Scotland. In 1970, Andrew Keachie formed a band of young brass players from schools in the Kilmarnock district. When they were only two years old, the Kilmarnock Youth Band came to London to take part in the National Festival of Music for Youth and were awarded third prize. Then with the enthusiasm which marks this group and their conductor, they won the fourth section of the Scottish Championship in 1974, the third section in 1975, the second section in 1976, were placed third in the championship section in 1977 and won it in 1979. They

From Bristol-Stanshawe Band, conducted by Walter Hargreaves on the Royal Albert Hall platform. During the 1970's this newly-formed band became a formidable challenge.

changed their name to Kilmarnock Concert Band in 1978, as so many of the members had reached the great age of twenty-one. After such a brilliant short life, the Kilmarnock Concert Band is a Scottish band to notice.

It is not easy for a band to rise speedily through the grades and reach championship level, for competition is intense throughout and the standard in each section is steadily rising. Music that was written ten years ago to test the championship section bands now appears for the second section. Consequently, a new band, hoping to climb and make a national impact, needs very special qualities indeed. Such a band is Stanshawe, of Bristol.

Formed during the summer of 1968, from a group of highly experienced brass players, the Stanshawe Band were determined from the outset to achieve championship status. Members of the band had valuable business connections and they quickly acquired a set of second-hand instruments and premises for rehearsals.

During the first two years of life, the band progressed rapidly and in 1970, it was decided to approach Walter Hargreaves with an invitation to become the band's professional conductor. He accepted and phenomenal success followed. In 1971, Stanshawe won the second section of the regional qualifying contest and, later, won second prize at the London finals. These successes ensured that the band would have championship status in 1972. As if this were not enough, Stanshawe, with Walter Hargreaves, entered the 1972 Spring Belle Vue Contest and won. They had now achieved championship status in the only two contesting arenas that really count, on a national scale.

But Stanshawe did not creep into the championship section and struggle. With the talented guidance of their young resident conductor, Brian Howard, and the musical wizardry of professional, Walter Hargreaves, they became a strong challenge to bands throughout the country. They were runners-up both in the Belle Vue and London Championships, besides achieving the title Granada T.V. Band of the Year in 1974. In 1977, the B.B.C. elected them as B.B.C. Band of the Year and they were West of England Champions in 1974 and 1975.

Stanshawe, with Walter Hargreaves, won admiration and support from band enthusiasts throughout the country. It was known how difficult the task was that they had set themselves — and they had succeeded. The year 1978 brought changes. Walter Hargreaves was invited to take the Fairey Band and so relinquished his position with Stanshawe. Roy Newsome, who had recently resigned as resident conductor of Black Dyke, was invited to replace him. At about the same time, Stanshawe acquired a new sponsor — the Sun Life Assurance Society, so the future continues to look bright for this challenge to the north from the south.

Perhaps the selection of bands for this chapter could be challenged, but it is hoped that the picture presented of brass bands who have commanded the respect and support from enthusiasts for over one hundred years reflects the spirit which makes a brass band famous.

Walter Hargreaves, who in 1978 relinquished his position with Stanshawe and became Musical Director of Fairey Engineering Works Band.

References

The Brass Band Movement, Russell & Elliot, J.M. Dent,1936.
The Bandsman's Everything Within, Kenneth Cook, published by Hinrichsen.
Besses o' th' Barn Band, Joseph Hampson, published by Rogers.
By Royal Command, — The story of Foden Motor Works Band, F.T. Burgess.
British Bandsman, Weekly journal for brass bands from 1887, published by
    British Bandsman Ltd., London End, Beaconsfield, Bucks.

Acknowledgements

Robert Wray (St. Hilda's & Harton Colliery); Michael Antrobus (Black Dyke); Eddie Noble (Brighouse & Rastrick); R.G. Tucker (G.U.S.); Alan Lawton (Fairey); Stan Whiteman and Trevor Walmsley (C.W.S. Manchester); Harold Hearn (Cory); Derek Horsfall (Stanshawe).

6. Music for the Brass Band (1900-1975)

A personal view by ERIC BALL

Readers may find some difficulty in trying to imagine what life was like in areas where brass bands flourished at the beginning of this twentieth century. Villages, mining communities and even some towns were, with few exceptions, cut off from the mainstream of artistic activity. Comparatively few "working class" people could afford the luxury of attending symphony or other concerts of worthwhile music, and of course there was no radio, television, and only primitive gramophones.

Some music of value filtered into their restricted lives, of course: annual performances in church or chapel of 'Messiah' and other choral works; an organist playing the music of Bach; children learning to play the piano or violin bringing home music recommended by local music teachers; songs heard at concerts given in village halls by local worthies.

It was mainly to the artistically deprived that brass bands had brought new musical experience and even insights. Apart from hymn tunes, marches, waltzes, quadrilles, foxtrots and music for other current dance styles, there were "selections" of various kinds, sacred and secular.

Among the latter were pot-pourris of melodies from operas - mainly of the Italian school - many now forgotten. Some such were contemporary, and amongst English music set as test pieces were 'Gems from Sullivan's Operas' in 1900 (the composer died in that year); a selection from Coleridge-Taylor's 'Hiawatha' in 1902; and a selection from 'Caractacus' by Elgar in 1903.

Such selections were chosen and scored for band by skilled arrangers: J. Ord Hume, Samuel Cope, Shipley Douglas, William Rimmer, J.A. Greenwood, to name but a few. The music was, it seems, prepared with contesting in mind, and in general was tailored to suit the skill of three or four soloists, although there were a few outstanding arrangements which famous bands featured, and which might well test the full capacity of bands today.

There is a tendency in some quarters to decry the operatic selection and similar works. The writer's own experience was underlined by a world-famous orchestral conductor who, conducting massed bands, was asked why he had chosen such a selection. His reply was to ask how better to teach amateur players the art of phrasing and playing fine melodies.

Such selections were used as National Championship test pieces at the Crystal Palace until 1912; and for the Belle Vue 'September' Championships in Manchester until 1924. At local association and other contests their use continued at all levels for many more years and doubtless some are still to be heard (in 1979).

For concert programmes - especially in parks and other open-air events - selections from popular and current musical shows were, and still are a "must". Nor are these to be decried. Fine melodies by Noel Coward, Ivor Novello, Irving Berlin, George Gershwin and a host of equally talented writers of theatre and film music are not lightly to be dismissed as of little value. Where the arrangements for brass are well tailored there is great merit in playing them well.

The later tendency towards something more developed in selections is to be noted. The term "Rhapsody" came into brass band terminology early on, possibly with William Rimmer's Scottish Rhapsody 'Lord of the Isles'. The term

Gustav Holst
1928 - A Moorside Suite.

Sir Edward Elgar
1930 - Severn Suite.

generally seems to mean that the chosen melodies are inter-woven with original themes resulting in something less form-less than a "selection" or even "fantasia". Other examples are the later and well-known rhapsodies on Negro spirituals.

Apropos of this, we must take into account the influence of general contesting band music upon that of the Salvation Army, and vice versa. Early selections by Richard Slater, Frederick G. Hawkes, and particularly Arthur Goldsmith included original material, some of it quite impressive. This became a normal process for later composers - Marshall, Coles, Leidzen and many more. Authority did not admit the term "rhapsody" until much later but the idea was there and worked upon before it became generally accepted.

Of course the term has other connotations, as in Dean Goffin's "Rhapsody in Brass" and Gilbert Vinter's "Trium-phant Rhapsody". It is a useful term when all else fails!

Nearly all band music of earlier years consisted of arrangements, from the "big" selections to smaller pieces; but some original music there was, particularly marches, instrumental solos, descriptive pieces, hymn tune variations, and a great deal of easier music for probably at that time the greater majority of bands. As to the marches, there are many in the repertoire that are excellent, challenging the idea that Sousa be named "The March King" (military marches also, by Alford and others both here and in Europe, uphold this challenge).

Before leaving the subject of arrangements we must discuss the transcription of standard orchestral and other works. In earlier years operatic overtures received varied treatment and were often shortened and sometimes, one suspects, scored from pianoforte arrangements without reference to orchestral detail.

A good deal of music in the "Palm Court Orchestra" tradition was also transcribed and happily some brass bands perpetuate its pleasantries to this day. Much of it was of musical as well as of entertainment value - who would dare to underrate the lighter pieces of Elgar, Edward German, Percy Grainger and the rest? Maybe such sounds will return when the violence of much modern light music has sub-sided.

Transcription of the music of the "Masters" for brass or military band, or for any other medium, has always been a subject for debate. Earlier in this century popular virtuoso organists and pianists often included such works in their repertoire, but purists were far from convinced. The writer has some doubt as to whether most of the composers con-cerned would have objected, so long as there was care in choosing suitable music, and the arrangers were trained and experienced in the technique and art of composition. "Entering into the mind of the composer" should at least be attempted when undertaking such important work.

Why should amateur musicians not be given the opportunity of playing really fine music because they play only in brass bands? It can be for them a gateway to a new level of experience.

An interesting development was initiated by Dr. Denis Wright with his transcription of 'Themes from Symphony No. 5' (Beethoven). Here was a logical scaling down of the great work, with the main themes in their correct order; the result being a useful precis of the original. It was followed by Beethoven's No. 8 and, by another arranger, the 1st and the choral section of the 9th; and Tchaikovsky's 5th.

Some master works have been given a new lease of life through transcription for band. A notable instance is Malcolm Sargent's splendid realisation of Mozart's 'Fantasia for Mechanical Organ', a work which a famous music critic said the brass band could rightly make its own. In spite of the composer's genius, the original sound can hardly have done justice to this fine music.

The famous conductor made other effective arrangements, including music by Chopin and Sullivan.

Music for organ often sounds well transcribed for brass: the 'St. Anne' Fugue of Bach and 'Suite Gothique' of Boellmann are examples. After all, the brass band is in a sense a "pipe" organ!

By 1975 therefore, there was available to bands a varied repertoire of first-rate arrangements of worthwhile music; but their dependence upon this for programme planning still supplied the prejudiced with opportunities to discount the brass band as a medium for fine music-making, even though distinguished conductors — Henry Wood, Adrian Boult, Malcolm Sargent, Charles Groves and many others — had seemingly enjoyed conducting such music.

Orchestra, organ, pianoforte, string quartet and other chamber groups, all have their own vast repertoire; but brass bands are a much younger manifestation, emanating from a far different background. They have no baroque, classical or early romantic inheritance of their own. In this century, however, a distinctive repertoire of works specially written for the medium is evolving and in less than seventy years much has been achieved.

The first breakthrough was in 1913, when John Henry Iles, successful showman and impressario, commissioned an original work for the championship section of his Crystal

John Ireland.
1932 - A Downland Suite.
1934 - Comedy Overture.

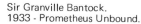

Sir Granville Bantock.
1933 - Prometheus Unbound.

127

Opposite: First page of the score of the Tone Poem : Labour and Love (P. Fletcher). The first original work for brass band which was commissioned for the 1913 Crystal Palace Championship.

Palace contest. It is likely that the suggestion came from Hubert Whitely, then editor of the music publishing firm of R Smith & Co., and of the *British Bandsman*, in both of which Iles held a controlling interest; or perhaps from Samuel Cope, composer and former editor.

Percy E. Fletcher was the composer chosen, whose works included orchestral music, songs, choral fantasias and incidental music for the theatre (at His Majesty's Theatre in London, Fletcher reigned as conductor for many years).

Wisely, he did not seek to revolutionise the accepted approach to brass band music: his tone poem 'Labour and Love', tuneful, effectively scored, was not far removed from a "selection", and included cadenzas for some solo instruments (a "must" in test pieces in those days). A descriptive programme note was printed in the full score and this useful work - still heard today - proved to be an excellent bridge between previous test pieces and the new music that was to come. His later work, 'An Epic Symphony' - fine, heroic music - was much more advanced.

It seems to have been the policy then, and for years to come, to write music for bands which could be linked with ideas poetic, literary or picturesque, and so it continues to this day, with some exceptions. Thus the repertoire is in the main still "romantic" and colourful, and one must admit that this aids amateur conductors and bandsmen a great deal in the matter of interpretation, and benefits the "ordinary listener" also. So it will happily remain for some time to come, even though a few composers for band now adventure into the neo-classical and avant garde.

Owing to war, the 1913 experiment was not followed up until 1920, when the symphonic poem 'Coriolanus' appeared. The composer was Cyril Jenkins, Welsh-born, whose works included music for chorus and orchestra and many songs. 'Coriolanus' is tuneful, dramatic, perhaps rather more astringent than 'Labour and Love'. Its form is still reminiscent of the "selection". It remains a popular work.

The year 1921 brought the famous 'Life Divine', also by Jenkins. Now there was more than a hint of symphonic development, and its technical demands were considerable — it is said that because of this the composer's first title, 'A Comedy of Errors', was thought by the publisher to be rather unwise! Nevertheless there were some splendid performances on the day.

Hubert Bath, another well-known composer of songs, chamber and orchestral music and choral works next produced what was thought to be the first Symphony for Brass Band. Entitled 'Freedom', it was even more technically

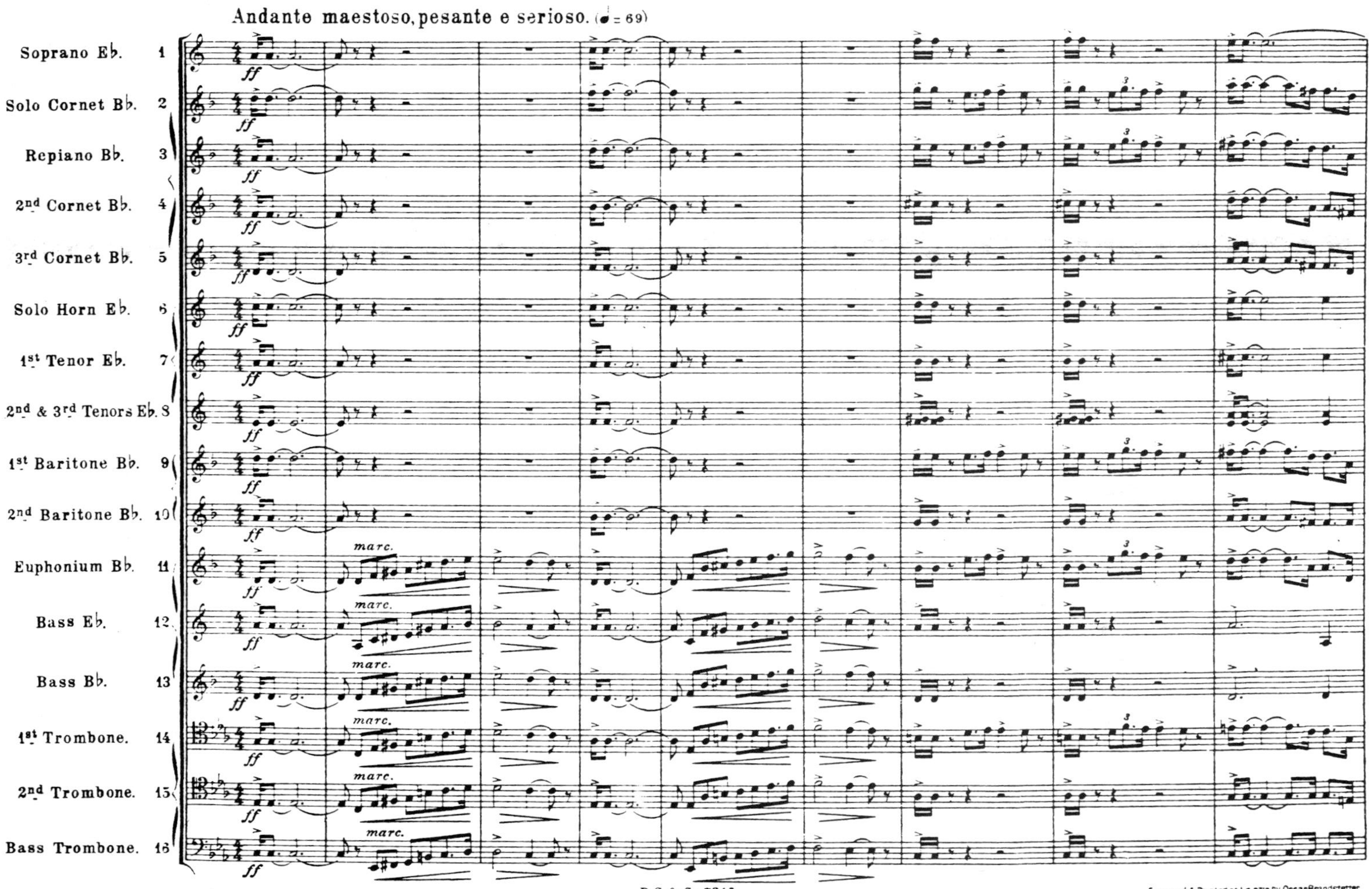

Engraved & Printed at Leipzig by Oscar Brandstetter.

Sir Arthur Bliss.
1936 - Kenilworth.

Herbert Howells.
1937 - Pageantry.

demanding, expressive, and adventurous in scoring, and it brought a new dimension of symphonic form into the repertoire. Even today it may be that its difficulties prevent it from being performed often.

The names of two composers who were to have a profound and distinctive effect on band music and musicians soon appeared - Henry Geehl and Denis Wright - the former with the splendid 'Oliver Cromwell' and 'On the Cornish Coast',and the latter with a prize-winning work 'Joan of Arc'. Wright came fully into the "movement" and as composer, arranger, conductor, initiated many new ideas. The BBC repertoire of arrangements for chorus and band owes much to him and even Handel's 'Messiah' was heard in this manner.

Henry Geehl consequently produced further works for band, some to be enjoyed in the 2nd, 3rd and 4th sections. It was rumoured that he also had a hand in the scoring of certain works by eminent contemporaries.

In 1928 the first work by a "major" composer was to appear - 'A Moorside Suite' by Gustav Holst. This was exciting news, and even more exciting was the peak reached in 1930 by the introduction of the 'Severn Suite' by Edward Elgar, "the greatest English composer since Purcell". Both demanded technical resource and musical understanding. Alas, neither composer wrote again specifically for brass band.

Granville Bantock, with 'Prometheus Unbound' and some "smaller" works, also enriched the repertoire. 'Pageantry' by Herbert Howells was another valuable breakthrough in musical style and content. Arthur Bliss, with 'Kenilworth', commenced a long association with brass bands.

It should be said that not all these works were at first received with general acclamation. Some of the old-timers were suspicious of these "new sounds"; conductors had been known to change "wrong notes" to their own satisfaction. One, it is reported, went into a music store intent on buying "senza mutes" because of the indication in one of these new-fangled pieces. The editing of these new works was very variable, and "minor" composers seem often to have been more skilled in scoring for band than certain of their more highly-rated contemporaries.

The directors of the Belle Vue September Open Championships began using original works in 1925, and in that year - and in 1926, 1927, 1928, 1932, 1935 - the organist and composer Thomas Keighley produced a series of colourful and popular works, some based on Shakespearian subjects — 'Macbeth', 'A Midsummer Night's Dream', 'The Merry

Wives of Windsor' and the popular 'Lorenzo', all valuable additions to the music of that era. Other composers introduced included Haydn Morris, R. Maldwyn Price, and in 1940 Joseph Holbrooke's 'Clive of India' was produced.

Memory records faintly that in earlier years there may have been other original works for local contests, now lost. An old recording of 'The Viking' by Weston Nicholl impressed this then young listener.

During these years - 1913 to 1940 - this evolution in brass band music applied mainly to works for championship section bands, although some were later handed down to lower sections for their encouragement and profit. However, it would be remiss of the writer to omit reference to the useful and mainly easy original fantasias of J.A. Greenwood and others. He wrote for the country and town bands he knew so well through his distinguished career as a first-rate and often severe adjudicator. He also conducted first-class bands with great success.

Such was the outlook until 1940. Belle Vue contests continued during the war years, but with no new music. The National Brass Band contests recommenced in 1945, now under the auspices of the *Daily Herald* and later Odhams Press, with an impressive reorganisation including area contests leading up to the London finals.

Gradually an enlightened attitude towards brass band music became apparent, and under the enthusiastic guidance of E. Vaughan Morris, contest organiser, and others, the policy of commissioning new works or special transcriptions for bands of all grades became a regular feature.

Great names included Vaughan Williams, Edmund Rubbra, Herbert Howells, Arthur Bliss and Gordon Jacob. Frank Wright produced some spectacular and popular transcriptions of music by Berlioz, Verdi, Lalo. Music of yesteryear was heard again - 'Oliver Cromwell' (Geehl) and the symphony 'Freedom' (Hubert Bath).

For the Belle Vue Open Championships, where Mr. H.F.B. (Eric) Iles wisely continued a similar tradition, the music of Denis Wright, Kenneth Wright, Maurice Johnstone, Helen Perkin, Dean Goffin, Erik Leidzen, also made considerable impact, enriching the repertoire.

In Scotland, and farther afield, the music of Drake Rimmer was, and is, highly thought of. 'Homage to Pharoah' and 'Quo Vadis' are typically colourful works.

One composer in particular made a directly popular appeal — Gilbert Vinter, then conductor of the BBC Midland Orchestra and a musician of vast experience and insight. His adventurous scoring, coupled with his music's considerable

An eminent quartet; Sir Arthur Bliss (Master of the Queen's Musick); Frank Wright; Dr. Denis Wright; Eric Ball.

technical demands and far from old-fashioned harmonic idiom, did much to prepare our bands for the even more "contemporary" sounds of later years.

A work which must receive special mention is Dr. Robert Simpson's 'Energy', performed by bands competing in a World Championship contest in London in 1971. In one long movement, the music gradually evolves from a quiet seminal opening to a final triumphant declaration. It set new problems for brass band conductors, performers and listeners, and has yet to be generally accepted; but those who heard the winning performances on the day would have been fully convinced of its value and its importance to the repertoire.

The many composers who wrote works specially suited to other than championship section bands deserve special mention. To write easier but no less effective music is a challenge which some do not care to take up. It is a pity that when the result is successful most "top" bands seem nevertheless to ignore it. Music is music after all, whatever its standard of difficulty.

Music written for school bands has been another interesting development. The formation of the National School Brass Band Association by the composer Kenneth Cook and others deserves special mention, especially for the valuable teaching material produced as well as for its commissioning of various works. Perhaps part of their reward is that now a few school bands can play almost anything that is put before them.

An increasing number of publishers are now interested in issuing new music for brass bands. It was not always so. Such publications were not always commercially rewarding, and we should remember with thanks those who took the risk: Boosey and Hawkes and Besson; R. Smith & Co., Paxton; Wright and Round; F. Richardson; and Hinrichsen, were among those who constantly supported our enthusiastic amateur music-making.

Our music is not confined to this country. Bands in the Commonwealth — in particular Australia and New Zealand — and in European countries, look to this country with the greatest interest, noting what is happening and what is produced here. From this we all greatly benefit.

And now it is for us to commend the chapter by Edward Gregson, a composer of the younger school, whose music and outlook is in some degree a valuable bridge between the "romantic" era of the brass band and that which appears to be even more challenging. His style and idiom have already greatly influenced our young musicians and he can perhaps best apprehend something of our "music of the future".

May I declare once more, however, that in worthwhile music there is no time, no old and new: but perhaps more than a hint of the eternal NOW?

Eric Ball
Composer

An appreciation by GEOFFREY BRAND

It is wholly in the character of the man that in writing about brass band music in the twentieth century, Eric Ball makes but scant reference to his own contribution. Yet this modest man, who has moved with and through the brass band scene for more than half a century, has been a major influence, many would say the greatest, on the style and sound with which brass bands are associated.

A glance at his list of compositions and arrangements will confirm the size of his contribution. Only by studying his music, and hearing it performed, can its quality be appreciated.

Eric Ball was born on October 31, 1903, in Bristol, ten years before the first known original work for brass band was written.

His interest in music sprang largely from a natural talent, which was stimulated by music making in his home. Later in his own words; "I had some lessons in mathematics and harmony from a private teacher who also happened to be the local church organist".

By the end of World War One Eric Ball was living nearer to London and studied the organ at churches in Staines and Dartford, as well as the piano. He has spoken appreciatively of hearing bands in the parks, and undoubtedly the repertoire being played at that time would have contained many selections of operatic airs or reminiscences of this or that composer's music. Very little original music would have been played - it didn't exist. The radio and the gramophone record were still to come, and live music-making was the only means of passing on information or knowledge.

His family had always had Salvation Army connections, and Eric Ball found his way, with some misgivings, he admits, to the Salvation Army's Music Editorial Department. Here he was near to the heart of bands and their music, albeit with Salvation Army restrictions concerning style and mood which, in those days, was a great deal more restrictive than it is now. But the exposure to music, both written and played, must have been enormously important to this sensitive musician of fine intelligence. Here, surely, was his fashioning ground for the years to come.

With access to getting his music played and published, the stream of works which, even to this time, have seemed hardly to cease, began to pour out. He wrote, naturally, for brass bands, the Salvation Army's 'Mobile Organs', and for voices also, since the evangelical message is not conveyed only through brass instruments!

Eric Ball became to many thousands of Salvationists a name associated with music of special satisfaction; he has a rare gift for writing melody, and in his own way was an innovator of different techniques, especially in achieving a new sonority from what had become, and still is, the recognised complement of instruments used in the brass band. To this day his scoring remains a model for its subtlety, whilst his care over details of balance and blend are rewarding sources of study for those who write for the band.

His work as a conductor, first with the uniquely-toned Salvationist Publishing and Supplies Band (S.P.& S.) to which some old recordings on 78 r.p.m. discs still bear witness, or later as the conductor of the International Staff Band, provided further opportunities for Eric Ball to influence countless others.

During World War Two, Eric Ball left the Salvation Army and was soon absorbed into different spheres of music making. Touring as a pianist with other artists created opportunities to widen his musical experience. He still talks of this time in his life with a twinkle in his eye!

The next significant move was when John Henry Iles, the proprietor of the *British Bandsman* and R. Smith & Co. Ltd. invited Eric Ball to become Editor of the journal and also the music publishing firm. He was to stay until 1967, a period of fifteen years.

The opportunity to work with some of the country's top bands soon followed, as well as invitations to write test pieces for major contests and other events. Again, the lists of music tell the story. It is inconceivable that any brass band library anywhere in the world today does not contain music written by Eric Ball.

By what means can one measure, or assess, the amount of influence which any one person's work has had on a form of music-making? Is it perhaps by the evidence of those who have followed or come later?

Nowadays composers from widely different backgrounds and ethnic origins are being attracted to write for the brass band. This can only be wholly good and beneficial, providing we are careful always to apply the criterion of judgement which accords with a sincere desire to preserve only that which is, according to our lights, good. Styles change; they always have, and this applies to the writing of music no less than other art forms. Yet, when the final assessment is made, it is not its style but its goodness that we need to consider.

Eric Ball's music belongs, in style and influence, to the great romantic period, of which Brahms and Elgar stand as two outstanding examples. There will, perhaps, be those in the future who turn away from the style; some already have. That is their right. There will, I hope, be none who turn from the sincerity which shines through Eric Ball's music, for in that, I believe, lies the true quality of his work.

Looking back, in 1979, we can see the essential bridge which the music of Eric Ball, together with that of others, represents.

In this book, he has paid tribute to many of those others. My concern is to ensure that the work of Eric Ball is properly placed alongside those names as one of the most important bridge builders in the development of brass band music in the twentieth century. Yet in the end, it will not be by words, mine or anyone else's, that Eric Ball will be measured, but by his music. That will remain and endure.

7. The Contemporary Repertoire

by EDWARD GREGSON

We have read of the progress of what might be called the traditional band repertoire, most of which was specifically written for the contest. In contrast to this, most of the contemporary repertoire has been written for sources other than the contest. However, even amongst the traditional contest pieces there have been a few which have caused minor sensations; for example, 'Three Figures' by Herbert Howells in 1960; Gilbert Vinter's 'Spectrum' in 1969 and then in the 1970s 'Energy' by Robert Simpson and Elgar Howarth's 'Fireworks'. All these works were received with a mixture of bewilderment and anger by at least some of the audience, players and conductors. But why? None of them were in the least "way-out"; all used conventional notation, and were written within a tonal framework, with accessible melodies and harmonic patterns. What it demonstrated was the huge gap which existed between composers on the one hand and audiences, players and conductors on the other; a gap which still exists today but which has become more severe in that the music now is 'way-out' in some cases. The result is that very few bands perform these contemporary works.

Since the mid-60s there has been a veritable explosion in the amount of new music written·for bands. There are many reasons for this explosion, one of the most pertinent being the influx of a few personalities, mainly conductors, into the band scene who have had a much more ambitious approach to the repertoire. Almost synonomous with this has been a resurgence in the popularity of bands within the so-called "serious" music world. This has led to bands appearing regularly at the major music festivals, often having a work commissioned for them in the process; it is vital to mention the role of the Arts Council of Great Britain at this point, who in the last decade or so have actively encouraged the extension of the band repertoire by making funds readily available to assist the commissioning of new works.

Let us consider for a moment the historical aspect of contemporary music for bands. It must be remembered that original music for the brass band is a relatively recent occurence (only after World War One) as Eric Ball pointed out in his chapter. It has developed along its own eclectic lines, largely ignoring contemporary idioms. The vast majority of the music between the wars is nineteenth century in concept and influence; there are few traces, if any, of the influence of major twentieth century composers such as Bartok, Stravinsky or Schoenberg upon band composers, until we reach the mid-1960s.

In the 1960s a renewed interest in the medium from "serious" composers became apparent. Martin Dalby, a Scot-

Opposite:'Cataclysm' by Paul Patterson — a page from the Score. (Reprinted by kind permission of the copyright owners, Josef Weinberger Ltd., London.)

tish composer, wrote his 'Music for a Brass Band' in 1962, whilst still a student at the RCM. This five-movement work, though quite conservative in style, nevertheless displays some interesting departures from the normal repertoire. It was two other Scottish composers, Thea Musgrave and Thomas Wilson, who soon after this made important contributions, both responding to commissions from the Scottish Amateur Music Association. This was important, because since World War Two few recognised composers had written for the medium, the notable exceptions being Vaughan Williams, Rubbra and Howells, all composers of the older generation. Thea Musgrave was an "up-to-date" composer writing in an "up-to-date" style.

Her 'Variations for Brass Band' is a short and compact work (a theme followed by five variations), and uses a more dissonant harmonic language than had hitherto been heard in the repertoire. Uninhibited by traditional scoring techniques, her textures and sonorities are strikingly different. Thomas Wilson's 'Sinfonietta' is again refreshingly new. Like the Musgrave, it is the harmonic and melodic language that is new, much of it being based on the interval of the fourth rather than the traditional third. It is highly rhythmically charged, but then bands had become accustomed to this aspect largely thanks to the music of Gilbert Vinter. No longer, however, are there lyrical tunes, immediately access-ible to the listener; there is less to "hold on to" and a greater degree of concentration is demanded by the composer. Audiences were not quite ready for this change of attitude on their behalf. But here for the first time were two composers using techniques influenced by other twentieth century composers; here was a real basis for an up-to-date band repertoire.

I have been asked to comment on my own contribution, for it was about this time that I first started writing for the medium. Whilst studying at the RAM with Alan Bush, I wrote a brass quintet for a competition (1967); this was taken up by the Philip Jones Brass Ensemble and the Hallé Brass Consort and attracted some attention. Soon afterwards, upon leaving the Academy, I was asked by Geoffrey Brand to write a number of works for R. Smith & Co., under contract. This led to a fruitful partnership during which time over a dozen works appeared, including 'Essay', the symphonic study 'The Pantagenets', 'Intrada', 'Concerto Grosso', and many more.

Stylistically the music is not severe, and is fairly access-ible from an audience's point of view. Many people have made an analogy between my music and Gilbert Vinter's. In truth, there are some aspects of similarity, mainly the mutual liking for aggressive, syncopated rhythms. Also in the way that material is built on ascending thirds in pieces like 'Entertainments' and 'The Plantagenets'. But in works such as the Horn Concerto or 'Intrada', the style is very different.

If it is possible for a composer to be objective about his own music, then I think my band music has at least given players and conductors a flavour of the contemporary idiom. The most significant contributions perhaps have been the two concertos written for orchestral instruments with band; the Horn Concerto (for Ifor James) and the more recent Tuba Concerto (for John Fletcher). It may be significant also that whereas 'Connotations' might have shocked an Albert Hall Contest audience a few years ago, in 1977 it didn't! A positive sign for sure.

But to continue the story. As I indicated earlier, towards the end of the 1960s there was an influx of personalities into the band scene. One of the direct effects of this was an intense broadening of the repertoire; one must mention Geoffrey Brand with Black Dyke and City of London Brass, Ifor James and Besses o' th' Barn, and, of course, Elgar Howarth and Grimethorpe Colliery. All three conductors were active in getting new music commissioned; their bands appeared at major festivals and managed to get extra broadcasting time as a result of this. It is difficult to assess how influential their efforts have been. I suspect that quite a few bandsmen regard their exploits as a harmless digression from the more serious business of contesting!

One work, written in 1969, deserves a mention before we look at the 1970s and that is 'Illustrations' by Phyllis Tate. This work, commissioned by the York Festival, is rarely performed today, but its five movements, each of which is prefaced by a short quotation from a different Shakespeare play, are full of interesting ideas; for example, the bitonal opening (cornets and trombones playing in two different keys at the same time) and the scherzo third movement with its tricky xylophone solo, sparse scoring, and constant changes of time.

The 1970s have seen so many new works for band that it is impossible to mention them all (please refer to the Appendix) but I shall endeavour to discuss those works which I consider to be important (you may choose to disagree!). Firstly, the work which caused a great controversy, 'Energy' by Robert Simpson. This work, the material of which is also used as the scherzo in one of his symphonies, was found difficult to comprehend by the audience because it was different. Anyone who has heard and enjoyed a symphony by Carl Nielsen, or even Sibelius, would have had no diffi-

142

Hold pitch for the length of the line

Gradually get faster

Gradually get slower

*Waggle valves as fast as possible –
tighten emboucher and slacken*

A very low note

A very high note

Repeat notes as fast as possible

*Continue pulse with /free meter or
time given in approx. seconds*

*Right hand down beat/ the number
indicates the total number of beats
per bar*

Left hand down beat

Repeat material in box until cut off

Very fast repetition staccato

But rests are ad lib

Flutter tongue

culty in grasping this music immediately, for it is all about germinal growth; that is, it is music which grows from a small idea and gathers momentum as it proceeds. There are not many melodies to remember and sing on the way and perhaps that was one of the problems. It is virtuoso, a risk for any band to play, but in essence it is not modern music; its ideas are rooted in the first part of this century.

The same cannot be said about Harrison Birtwistle's 'Grimethorpe Aria' written in 1973 (no prizes for guessing who it was written for). It is definitely music of today, painting a bleak landscape in a truly contemporary musical language. It has a sense of timelessness which is achieved in musical terms by a very slow tempo without any strong pulse feelings. Only in the middle, at the start of an intense climax, does the music burst into rhythmical life with distorted fanfare figures and syncopated accompanying chords. The flugel horn plays the main solo part in the work, unfolding a tortuous melodic line. As with 'Energy', band audiences found it difficult to accept this music, so far removed as it was from their normal repertoire; it was an understandable reaction. There are many moments in 'Grimethorpe Aria' of dense and dissonant sounds, in fact a greater degree of dissonance than had hitherto been found in any other work for band. The scoring, too, is unusual, each instrument being treated individually.

Here then was music that really was different. After 'Grimethorpe Aria' there was to be no turning back. This had a double-edged effect. Firstly, because of the publicity surrounding the work, it aroused the interest of many more composers towards the medium and since 1973 new music has come in greater abundance. Secondly, however, it had the unfortunate effect of making more of the band world hostile towards the contemporary repertoire. Catching up with the twentieth century had become too sudden.

A year later Paul Patterson ventured into brass band writing, though it must be admitted that the brass medium was nothing new to him. He studied trombone as well as composition whilst a student at the RAM, and had already written a number of brass pieces in his teens; but now as an established and increasingly successful composer, whose style had developed into a fairly avant-garde one, he had much to offer. His 'Chromascope' (commissioned by Besses o' th' Barn band and first performed at the 1974 Harrogate Festival) is not the most progressive work in his output but it is certainly progressive as far as the band repertoire is concerned. It is in two sections, the first exploring sonorities in a most original way and the second being more rhythmic and

Paul Patterson
(Photograph by Richard Brondell)

aggressive. In this section the composer asks the players to breathe through their mouthpieces, instead of playing, for several bars. He still notates rhythms for them, the effect on first hearing being novel. But this is the only unusual aspect of this work, a much bigger step being taken with his next major band piece 'Cataclysm'. This really does use many of the new notational procedures to be found in contemporary music, including a fair amount of freedom for the players. (See plate). This involves new signs and symbols to read as well as "approximate" notation (that is when the composer suggests roughly which notes should be played but the player must decide). There are also new tasks for the conductor who has to act as a general timekeeper. As in the Birtwistle there are bars of "senza tempo" where there is no pulse. In 'Cataclysm', half the time is spent on these free bars. The conductor has a number of seconds given above the bar (say 10 seconds) and he has to judge when to move on to the next bar. He has also to give left-hand beats within these bars to bring in other instruments. Altogether it makes for a fascinating experiment, every performance being different.

'Cataclysm' marked another new development in the band repertoire. It was commissioned by the National Youth Brass Band of Great Britain and perhaps now is an appropriate time to pause and reflect on the role of youth bands in the modern repertoire. Besides 'Cataclysm' the National Youth Brass Band has given first performances of a number of modern works, notably by Wilfred Josephs and Richard Steinitz. Their musical policy has been developed by Geoffrey Brand and in the last two years Arthur Butterworth (a composer himself who will be mentioned later). It is obviously vitally important for young people to have music of their day to play, and the National Youth Brass Band is a fine example of this. One must not forget the National Youth Brass Band of Scotland as well. The works by Musgrave and Wilson mentioned at the beginning of this chapter were first performed by them. In addition they have given first performances of Bryan Kelly's 'Edinburgh Dances' and my own 'Concerto Grosso'. Geoffrey Brand has been associated with them for a number of years and has continued to find new music to play.

There have been other youth bands who have also been active on the new music scene. The most notable of these must surely have been the Redbridge Youth Band whose conductor, John Ridgeon, has made a big impression on the brass scene. Whilst he was at Redbridge, John Ridgeon (who now works for the Leicestershire Education Authority as a Music Adviser) commissioned many new works for the band. One of the most exciting of these was the Concerto for Brass Quintet and Band by Derek Bourgeois (another composer who will be mentioned later). At its first performance this was played by the Philip Jones Brass Quintet with the Redbridge band. Other commissions have come from Buxton Orr and Christopher Steel (my own 'Intrada' and 'Partita' were both commissioned by the Redbridge Youth Band). No other area youth band has had such an enlightened policy towards contemporary music, but there have been quite a few who have commissioned the odd work here or there. Undoubtedly young people have far less inhibitions or prejudices concerning the performance of modern works. It is highly significant that the future generation of bandsmen will be fairly well versed in new music.

Hans Werner Henze is a German composer of international reputation. Happily he has written for the brass band. In 1975, in response to a commission from the Grimethorpe Colliery Band, he produced his splendidly entertaining 'Ragtimes and Habaneras' which is a series of eleven miniatures, brilliantly scored and slightly tongue-in-cheek. Here there is no difficulty for an audience because the music abounds in colourful tunes and rhythms, mostly overtly popular. How much of the music is a parody of the brass band itself is open to question, but parody there certainly is of other musical idioms and composers. It is thoroughly enjoyable music, slightly distorted though it is.

I have avoided discussing music written since 1965 which might be described as light, but there are two composers who have played a most important part in the development of the repertoire and who roughly come into this category. Mind you, there is light music and light music, and these two composers are no mere miniaturists. They are Joseph Horovitz and Bryan Kelly, who both wrote their first pieces for bands in the late 1960s. The works of Horovitz are well known, save for his 'Dong with a Luminous Nose' which deserves more performances. It is stylistically different from his other brass works, more dissonant and sombre (this is because it is a highly descriptive Symphonic Poem which musically portrays Edward Lear's famous poem). His 'Sinfonietta' has become a standard work, particularly amongst lower section and youth bands. He has also been active as an adjudicator and conductor.

Bryan Kelly's style is immediately accessible. It is highly melodic and rhythmic with enough harmonic invention to lift it above the mundane. His first work, the Overture 'Provence', is typical of his style. One interesting feature is that he has not scored his works himself, this task being

Arthur Butterworth.
Composer and since 1975 Music
Adviser to the National Youth
Brass Band of Great Britain

assigned to Bram Gay. 'Washington DC' is one of the most attractive marches in the repertoire and supports the view that there are still new things to be said in this form. 'Divertimento', a four-movement work of character, has deservedly become very popular.

Derek Bourgeois is a composer who thinks on a large scale. His Tuba Concerto, written a couple of years ago, is really a Symphony for Tuba and Orchestra, lasting some forty minutes. His music for brass band is no compromise. He has written two concertos, in addition to the later Concerto for Quintet and Band which has already been mentioned. The First Concerto was written in 1974 for Grimethorpe. It is in three movements, each of which has a title — 'Le Tombeau d'Arthur Benjamin', 'Monsieur Ravel turns in his Grave', 'The War March of the Ostriches'. As the titles suggest, the composer has a great sense of musical humour. Both this and the Second Concerto, written also for Grimethorpe two years later, are technically very demanding and require a lot of stamina from the players as each work is a "big blow" throughout.

The style of this very individual composer is difficult to describe. It is highly rhythmic with constant changes of metre; often the rhythms themselves are complicated and need careful working out. The music is often aggressive and powerful, with huge climaxes being built up incessantly at times. Bourgeois manages to say new things in old forms. The March from his Second Concerto is no mere miniature, or a carbon copy of the standard brass band march. It starts quietly and in a fragmented state, but gradually builds up to a tremendous climax. There is only one real theme in it, which is announced a third of the way through and then is subjected to various treatments such as being played in canon (that is when the same tune enters a few beats later on other instruments), or being inverted (turned upside down). Although his writing for brass instruments is virtuoso, he does understand them; being an ex-tuba player himself he knows not to attempt the impossible (even though there might be a few brass players with nervous breakdowns strewn along the way!)

If Derek Bourgeois represents one side of the repertoire that is both demanding for players and audience alike, then Malcolm Arnold represents a more approachable one. His music is easy to listen to, and makes few real demands on the players. Of all the music discussed in this chapter his is certainly the lightest, but also the most popular with the average band audience. This is not to say that it can easily be dismissed; Arnold has suffered much in the past from critics who dismiss his music instantly. His two 'Little Suites for Band' are delightful miniatures, full of good tunes and typical humour (for example the Galop from the 'Second Little Suite'). They are also well scored and have achieved a remarkable popularity, being two of the very few examples of works that are played by fourth section bands, youth bands and championship section bands alike. His Fantasy for Brass Band, written for the 1974 National Finals is more of a disappointment. It lacks conviction, and is rather stereotyped. It has none of Arnold's most inspired moments as can be found in some of his symphonies. I will discuss his choral work 'Song of Freedom' a little later.

Edward Gregson

Elgar Howarth is known to the wider musical public chiefly as a conductor, but to the brass world he is a man of many parts. As a player he was for many years an integral part of the Philip Jones Brass Ensemble. As an arranger, he has produced countless pieces, his most recent and largest being the Mussorgsky 'Pictures at an Exhibition', arranged for large brass ensemble. As a composer he has worn two hats; on the one hand he has produced many light novelty numbers under his famous pseudonym W. Hogarth Lear (simply an anagram of his own name) and on the other he has written substantial serious works in a fairly modern idiom. The last of these is the only one that concerns us here. His roots are in the band world and as such his compositions are mainly for the brass medium. He wrote a suite for band when he was seventeen (one of the movements is published under the name of 'Parade') and followed this in 1956 with 'Mosaic', written for a BBC Light Music Festival (interestingly enough it was disqualified on the grounds that it was too difficult for the average band — as it is now played by youth bands it just shows you how standards have progressed in a relatively short time). His three other more important works are 'Fireworks', 'Ascendit in coeli', and 'In Memoriam: R.K.'. The first of these has already been mentioned in the context of works which aroused controversy. In reality there is nothing foreboding or difficult about the piece. Written for the Belle Vue British Open Contest it is tuneful and rhythmic, with some deft touches in the scoring. One of its principal novelties is the wide array of percussion instruments asked for, including four bongo drums, four suspended cymbals, four temple blocks, three wood blocks in addition to the other usual instruments. It is really a Concerto for Band in that it singles out each section for soloistic treatment. When the narration is added it becomes a Young Person's Guide to the Brass Band. 'Ascendit in coeli' (written in memory of his father) is a much more advanced piece of writing. It uses

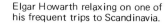

Elgar Howarth relaxing on one of his frequent trips to Scandinavia.

certain aleatoric devices (elements of music that happen by chance, or are not controlled; as in Patterson's 'Cataclysm') and there are times when the rhythms become so complex for different sections of the band that ideally two conductors are needed. His most recent work, 'In Memoriam R.K.', was written in memory of Rudolph Kempe, a conductor Howarth played under for many years and greatly admired. It is a tone poem in the tradition of Richard Strauss, the rather lush chromatic harmonies sounding very effective on the brass medium.

It must also be remembered that no discussion of the modern repertoire could be complete without drawing attention to the fact that Elgar Howarth has given first performances of many new works with Grimethorpe and has appeared at many important concerts with them. It was he who persuaded Birtwistle and Henze, as well as many other composers new to the medium, to write for the brass band.

A few other composers and compositions must be mentioned before we pass on to concertos and choral works with band. Wilfred Heaton may not be a name that is widely known, but his 'Contest Music', which was written for the 1974 National Finals but unfortunately turned down for that event, is one of the most interesting in the modern repertoire. It is tonal music, but it uses harmonic tension most effectively; its melodies are angular and taut, and the scoring has an assured touch. It is highly regrettable that this work has had so few performances, and it really ought to see the light of day as a test piece, which after all was its original purpose.

Arthur Butterworth, like Wilfred Heaton, is a composer of the North. He was born in the North, has lived only in the North and writes music that speaks of the North. A work such as his 'Path across the Moors' could only have been written by someone deeply involved with the people, nature and climate around him. In 1964 he wrote 'A Dales Suite' for school bands; an austere work but very important in the establishment of a repertoire specially for young players. He is better known for his later 'Three Impressions', which is a vivid musical portrayal of three aspects of the North of England in the industrial Revolution.

Of other important works written since 1970, mention must be made of 'Refrains and Cadenzas' by Thomas Wilson (first performed by Black Dyke, conductor Geoffrey Brand) which is more advanced than his earlier Sinfonietta, though it is rarely performed now; 'Aubade' by Michael Blake Watkins (first performance Grimethorpe conducted by Elgar Howarth) a rather difficult work to come to terms with. 'Occasion' by Howard Burrell (first performed by Besses o' th' Barn, conductor Ifor James) has an interesting scherzo with changing metres among its three movements; Graham Whettam's 'Partita' uses the well-known Coventry Carol in its slow movement; John McCabe is the latest of established composers to write for the medium, his 'Images' being commissioned by the Besses o' th' Barn Band. It is a fairly long work, much of it energetic and climactic.

From the above list it is obvious that in addition to Elgar Howarth, both Geoffrey Brand and Ifor James have been very active in promoting and performing new music. Geoffrey Brand's activities started towards the end of the 1960s, when with Black Dyke he gave a number of first performances at major concerts. He has been active in persuading many new composers to write for bands. Ifor James has also been active in this respect since the beginning of the 1970s and again has appeared at important concerts with Besses.

Concertos

One of the most interesting features in the growth of the modern repertoire has been the number of concertos written. A few years ago there was only the Denis Wright Cornet Concerto, but since 1970 a whole array of concertos for different instruments have appeared.

Firstly, for cornet Thomas Wilson wrote his 'Cartoon', an extremely difficult work, back in the 1960s. My own 'Prelude and Capriccio' was written as an intentionally virtuoso piece. Both of these were done at a recent Cheltenham Festival by James Watson with Great Universal Band conducted by Geoffrey Brand. Ernest Tomlinson wrote a rather more lightish Concerto for Maurice Murphy, and Elgar Howarth arranged the last movement of his Trumpet Concerto (with orchestra) for cornet and band, now called a Cornet Concerto.

Joseph Horovitz

Trumpet concertos have also appeared. Buxton Orr wrote a substantial and musically involved concerto for John Wilbraham; Gareth Wood wrote a less involved one for James Watson, and the most recent was one written by Chris Sansom (again for James Watson who performed it at the 1978 Scottish National Orchestra Proms with the Grimethorpe Colliery and Bo'ness and Carriden bands conducted by Elgar Howarth.

For trombone there has been Buxton Orr's concerto (for Dennis Wick), a distinctly difficult work in two movements but highly rewarding in performance; Gordon Langford's 'Rhapsody' (for Don Lusher) which is very different from the last work, being easy on the ear. Then Elgar Howarth's Concerto which he arranged from the orchestral original of 1960 and which really ought to be played more often.

Joseph Horovitz's delightful Euphonium Concerto is very melodic and idiomatically written for the instrument. It is surprising that euphonium players ignore the work and continue to play the same old traditional pieces. It is also surprising that this is the only full concerto for the instrument.

The present writer's own French Horn Concerto and Tuba Concerto were both written for particular players. In 1970 I was commissioned by the British Federation of Brass Bands to write a concerto; the Horn Concerto was the result, written for Ifor James. In 1976 Besses o' th' Barn Band asked for a Tuba Concerto, and there was no doubt who I should write it for — John Fletcher. It has recently appeared in an orchestral version, this being one of the few examples of a work originally written for band arranged for orchestra; usually it's the other way round!

Choral Music

There are few substantial works for choir and band in the repertoire. By far the biggest and most impressive is Gilbert Vinter's Cantata 'The Trumpets', written in 1964, to a BBC commission. The work, which is for bass solo, mixed choir, augmented band and percussion, owes much to the English choral tradition, and in particular to Walton's 'Belshazzar's Feast'. It is a powerfully dramatic cantata, with highly imaginative treatment of both the chorus and band. The text is from the Old Testament and the starting point or inspiration for the work came from the lines "and the Lord said unto Moses make me two trumpets of silver". It is Vinter's finest achievement.

Band and Choir in York Minster. Black Dyke Mills Band with York Celebration Choir

In 1977 another Biblical subject was the inspiration for another large-scale work, 'Samson', by Joseph Horovitz. This time a baritone soloist is called for with the usual mixed chorus and band. Again the music is highly dramatic, even if it doesn't quite reach the intensity of 'The Trumpets'. Much of the chorus writing is in block harmony, which is juxtaposed against the brass and is sufficiently uncomplicated to be manageable by most choral societies.

Of the other works, one should mention Anthony Hedges' 'Psalm 104', also Gordon Jacob's 'Psalm 103', both for choir and band, and Malcolm Arnold's 'Song of Freedom'. This latter work is for children's voices and band, and was commissioned for the 21st Anniversary of the National School Brass Band Association with the text taken from various children's poems. The words are moving, the music less so.

Summary

The years since 1965 have been exciting ones for the

modern repertoire of the brass band, which has grown out of all proportion and continues to grow. There are new works in the future promised from Ligeti (one of the leading European composers), Robin Holloway (a young composer who has already written a work for the BBC Proms) as well as another from Harrison Birtwistle who wants to write a companion piece to 'Grimethorpe Aria' (this time a fast moving Toccata).

But what does all this mean to the typical band follower and what effect has it had on players and conductors? Well, the answer is problematic for there is no sure way of assessment. It would be wrong to think that the typical brass band audience wants Birtwistle rather than Ball, any more than it would be to believe that the normal orchestral audience wants Stockhausen rather than Schubert. There has been an increasing tendency during the century to want music from the past, rather than the music of today.

It is true that many people in the band world have been alienated from contemporary music, but on the other hand it has undoubtedly raised the standards of musicianship among players and conductors. Most new scores require new types of musical understanding; the problems are different to what they used to be. Much of the traditional repertoire requires tremendous technique on the part of the players but it rarely tests musicianship to the full. The problems of tackling say 'Grimethorpe Aria' test the musicianship of players and conductor to the limit.

More than all this, however, is the fact that the new music has brought a musical respectability to brass bands. The musical world can no longer say that the brass band repertoire is trite. A few years ago, when Arthur Butterworth wrote his articles entitled "The Brass Band — A Cloth Cap Joke?" many people in the band world reacted with hostility, and yet much of what he said was true. Things have changed, albeit slowly, and there is generally a greater understanding about the function of contemporary music for bands even if everyone doesn't like it. The brass band is an amateur pursuit and always will be; as such, players are entitled to play what they want for the very reason that for them it is recreational, not professional. But ultimately all players want a musical challenge; it isn't enough only to perform music that is trivial. Modern music must be given a chance, for it is here to stay. The brass band repertoire is now fully in the twentieth century, and the significance of this may not be seen for some time yet.

8. The National Youth Brass Band of Great Britain

by MAUD WRIGHT

One cold foggy winter's night in 1950 a brass band concert by a combined band of Yorkshire school children took place in Leeds with Dr. Denis Wright as the guest conductor. A guest at the concert was Miss Ruth Railton (now Dame Ruth) who had founded the National Youth Orchestra a few years earlier. After the concert she joined Dr. Wright and the concert organisers for a meal and the conversation was naturally about the evening's performance and the need to give encouragement and help to young players. Dr. Wright happened to say: "Why don't we start something like the Youth Orchestra for young brass players?" Miss Railton's immediate response was: "Why don't you?" So there was the challenge and the birth of the idea.

With the present tremendous success and reputation of the National Youth Orchestra it is perhaps not always remembered that its origin was the inspiration of Ruth Railton who, having conceived the idea, set determinedly about the task of making it a reality with much personal sacrifice and not a great deal of co-operation. Her enthusiasm and determination were certainly examples to follow in the creation of a National Youth Brass Band.

After the meal the "band" folk continued the discussion and from this emerged the plan that, as it was to be a national band, an exploratory meeting should be held to which would be invited well-known brass band personalities as representatives of the areas in which they lived. The meeting took place in January, 1951, and the project was enthusiastically welcomed to the extent that the outline of its constitution was drawn up there and then.

Advice from Ruth Railton was greatly appreciated, particularly in terms of pitfalls she had encountered. Within a few months the organisation was set up and proved sufficiently effective to continue virtually unchanged.

Sir Malcolm Sargent agreed to be the first president. There is a governing council consisting of members all of whom are involved in band activities and who represent the whole country on a geographical basis. The council is responsible for formulating policy and is of real value in ensuring that the organisation works for the sole good of the young students and so ultimately for the band movement in general. Three members of the council act as trustees.

There is a music adviser (Dr. Wright fulfilled this role), whose responsibility is music policy, recommending possible guest conductors, ensuring that programme items are suitable and of appropriate standard, and in general making sure that the purposes for which the band exists are met. He works in close liaison with the secretary who has the major task of

Opposite: Inaugural course of the National Youth Brass Band of Great Britain held in Bradford, April 12th-19th 1952, conducted by Dr. Dennis Wright. The leader was Maurice Murphy and the third solo cornet was John Clough who is now the well-know euphonium soloist of Black Dyke Mills Band.

153

finding and negotiating for suitable locations for courses and concerts, formulating all the detailed communications, information and instructions to students and the multifarious duties of being headmaster-cum-bursar-cum-general factotum of a temporary boarding school.

John Berryman, as leader of the National Youth Brass Band of Gt. Britain. He later became the principal cornet of the G.U.S. (Footwear) Band and is now the conductor of the William Davis Construction Band.

The first secretary was Leonard Davies, a former pupil of Dr. Wright and a first-rate organiser, who volunteered for these onerous but as yet unknown duties. In the beginning the prime problem was, of course, finance and Dr. Wright himself provided the funds for the initial expenditure involved.

The first one week's course to be held at Easter, 1952, was announced. It took place in Bradford, thanks to the efforts of friends and council members in Yorkshire and to the co-operation of the local education authority. The response to the announcement was astonishing. Ninety-six people applied to attend.

It has to be remembered that at that time the "summer school" cult did not exist and also there were few residential schools and colleges available, even if we could have afforded them. Consequently early courses had to be held in ordinary day schools with classrooms turned into dormitories and common rooms, and improvisation was very much the order of the day.

A team of instrumental tutors was invited to participate

and "invited" is the operative word since with lack of funds the payment of adequate fees was out of the question. There were also willing volunteers to help look after the "house" side of the course and the general welfare and supervision of the students. It was all very much trial and error and everybody "mucked in" with whatever chores had to be done — including on some occasions washing up!

For the initial course no auditions were held so we had no idea what the standard of playing would be. The first rehearsal started with the playing of the National Anthem and it was a good sound — the practical realisation of many months of planning, organisation, detailed work and much apprehension.

So it had started, and the purpose today is as it was then — to provide opportunities for boys and girls between the ages of twelve and eighteen to make music communally under conditions unobtainable in their everyday lives. The training aims not only at helping them in their actual playing but more particularly the improving of their musicianship and the widening of their musical horizons in addition to the experience of working with leading conductors from both the band movement and the wider musical profession.

After the first course, auditions for entry to the band were held since some uniformity of standard was necessary to provide a worthwhile level of tuition. This was not, as has been said, to create a "star" band but to ensure in so far as was possible that the students were those who could benefit from the tuition and training offered. This training is intended to supplement, not take the place of, the tuition the young players receive in their own bands.

This, I think, is demonstrated by the curriculum of a course. The average number of students on a course is approximately one hundred — limited to this number for reasons of living accommodation, the size of stages usually available and to ensure a manageable sized band. Once all the students have arrived tests for each instrumental group are held to determine positions in the band. This is taken very seriously by the students and when the time comes for the first rehearsal there is a somewhat electric atmosphere while they wait for the "order of play" to be announced.

The week consists of group tuition sessions — each group of instruments coached by a specialist tutor — full band rehearsals, and other activities, giving a rest from actual playing, such as ear training, music appreciation and playing in small ensembles under the guidance of the instrumental tutors. Sometimes selected senior students study score reading and are given the opportunity to conduct. In recent

Dr. Dennis Wright. Founder of the National Youth Brass Band, with his wife, Maud, who has been the Band's Treasurer since its formation.

The 1973 NYBB in the Great Hall of Birmingham University. The leader was Linda Nicholson. The staff are seated at the back. From left to right they are Hon. secretary Stan Reakes and his wife Lydia, tutor Alf Jarvis, Jean Room, with her husband Peter (senior housemaster), tutor Peter Kitson, Violet Brand, Maud Wright, tutors Tom Atkinson and Denis Carr and Music Adviser Geoffrey Brand.

years a choir drawn from the band members has been successfully introduced, directed by an experienced choral specialist. This has proved popular with the students and is, of course, yet another aspect of music-making.

The week's work culminates in a public concert which makes a fitting end to all the work put in during the week and gives an opportunity for the students to show to their parents and the public in general what they have achieved. A wide public is reached. The students themselves come from literally all over the country and courses are held at various locations, roughly alternating between north and south so that the same students do not always have high travelling expenses. The areas have ranged from Scotland and Northern Ireland to the Channel Islands. Regrettably only one overseas visit to Denmark has been possible so far. The cost of transporting a band of this size plus all instruments, luggage and equipment is obviously considerable.

The music played is carefully chosen for its educational as well as entertainment value. The students are introduced to many works they would not meet in their normal band work. The majority of the items studied on a course are usually new to the students and it is greatly to their credit that in the course of a week they can achieve a very high standard of performance. The choir also takes part in the concert which gives them, and the audience, a change from the all brass sound.

When the possibility of a youth brass band was first contemplated the music aspect was naturally the prime consideration. It was then realised that there was a social element as well. Living communally in a boarding school atmosphere was a new experience for nearly all the students. Since although they work hard the course is also part of their holiday, every effort was made to have as few rules and regulations as possible. With the occasional exception of an over high spirited or exhibitionist character, the behaviour and discipline has been remarkable and experience has shown that often when a new student does step out of line it is indicated by the other students that such behaviour is not acceptable. The interest of meeting other young musicians from all over the country is undoubtedly stimulating and can hardly fail to help toward a sense of fellowship and a good team spirit. There are in fact many examples of such meetings leading to more permanent partnerships in that many marriages have eventually resulted from such meetings.

Now the National Youth Brass Band is over twenty-five years' old and is accepted as almost a permanent institution, but achieving this has not been easy. While the number of students attending the first course (and their parents) showed interest and enthusiasm it has to be said that there was initially considerable opposition from some sections of the band world. There was the inevitable suspicion of any innovation. We were accused of "making a good thing out of it" — they little knew how much time and money had been put into it — and some bandmasters claimed that we were out to discover promising young players and induce them to leave their present bands. A small number — "small" in relation to the number of bands throughout the country — did show interest and it is perhaps indicative that they were mostly those with a number of young players and where therefore the purpose and intention was more understood.

In the non-brass band music world there was a virtual non-reaction despite the fact that the National Youth Orchestra had been recognised and hailed as a valuable element in encouraging young musicians. The customary condescending attitude and the "cloth cap" view of brass bands was evident.

BBC Television was, however, more enlightened and the band was given a television show in 1954. The number of viewers at that time however was limited and while it proved a new experience for the students the publicity value was minimal but nevertheless welcomed.

Dr. Wright conducted the inaugural course and subsequent conductors were Harry Mortimer, Eric Ball and Leonard Davies. In 1954 criticism and correspondence appeared in the band press in protest at a military band conductor, Major Jaeger (later Colonel) having been the guest conductor. Encouraging perhaps in its way in that at least it had been noticed.

It is of interest that in giving his impressions of his first experience as guest conductor Eric Ball said he had thoroughly enjoyed the experience and was very agreeably surprised. He was particularly impressed by the musical responsiveness of the students and already there had been established a fine tradition of music making which he had found nowhere else and which was bound to be to the ultimate good of the brass band movement as a whole.

In fact suspicion and lack of understanding persisted and it is perhaps of interest that an item from the minutes of a council meeting held in 1956 reads: "In order to counteract the continued misconceptions in the band world as to the organisation of the National Youth Brass Band an open letter should be inserted in the band press which would give the names of president, vice-presidents and all councillors together with the aims and objects of the organisation, the voluntary work of the council and staff and a resumé of the first five years' activities".

There was, however, no protest when two years later the guest conductor was Sir Adrian Boult. This was a truly generous gesture on the part of Sir Adrian and while it did not necessarily change attitudes it did encourage the view that the NYBB might be a worthwhile organisation.

The attitude of the general public was for the most part not encouraging. They seemed reluctant to attend concerts — until it was too late. Clearly the attitude was "it's just a kids' band" but those who did come found otherwise and at least a return visit to the same area ensured a larger audience.

Much could be said of the trials, tribulations and vicissitudes of those early years. Much should be said of the determination and unwavering loyalty in the efforts of the council, staff and supporters who persevered.

In such circumstances realisation that such efforts have been rewarded comes slowly. One thing more than anything gave grounds for some satisfaction — the beginnings of county youth bands. While of course other influences were involved in this concept the NYBB had shown what could be done and how it could be done. Imitation is often a form of flattery and we felt we could at least take part of the credit as well as acceptance of our own existence, particularly as

Sir Adrian Boult (conductor) and George Chisholm (soloist) in discussion with members of the National Youth Brass Band during their course in 1962. The leader, nearest to the camera, was John Clay.

(BBC copyright photograph).

members of the NYBB Council and staff were being invited to serve on committees of youth band organisations.

These developments more or less coincided with the National Youth Brass Band's tenth birthday, an occasion marked by the return as guest conductor of Sir Adrian Boult, and a second television appearance. This was highly successful with Sir Adrian as conductor and George Chisholm as "link man"; an unusual but effective combination. Since then other professional conductors from non-brass band spheres have been welcomed, including Marcus Dods, Sir Vivian Dunn, Harold Gray, Bernard Keefe, Vilem Tausky and Gilbert Vinter.

While recognition is encouraging there has been the perpetual problem of finance. Students pay a fee to attend courses but to make attendance a practical proposition the fee must be kept as low as possible. The fee charged more or less pays for the actual cost of the course but it does not

In 1970, Herbert Møller from Denmark was the first conductor from overseas to direct a National Youth Brass Band course.

cover the administrative and other varied costs of running the organisation. Were fees based on the actual costs they would be beyond the means of most of the students. Admittedly some can apply to their local education authority for grants but these are not always forthcoming and some students do not qualify for them.

Over the years appeals have been made to various trusts and foundations, in general without success. It has been a chastening experience to find that benevolence is easier to achieve for an orchestra than for a brass band. An annual donation is now received from the Performing Right Society and from the Bandsmen's Memorial and Education Trust. In very recent years approaches to the Arts Council of Great Britain have been successful and have meant that the Youth Band can continue to exist, albeit somewhat precariously. The Arts Council has also on three occasions subsidised works to be specially written for the Youth Band. These have all been very "modern" in style and have demonstrated the flexibility and competence of the young players.

It is a curious fact that no direct financial help is forthcoming from bands themselves and yet, for example, a small annual donation from each band in the country would be of immeasurable help.

Finance leads directly to so many people who have been or still are connected with the National Youth Brass Band. The "turnover" in staff and officials has been small, a measure of the loyalty and goodwill on which the band has survived since they receive virtually no financial reward.

Dr. Wright remained the Music Adviser until 1967 when he invited Geoffrey Brand to replace him. This proved somewhat fortuitous since Dr. Wright died shortly afterwards. Geoffrey Brand continued until 1975 when Arthur Butterworth, the present music adviser, took over.

The original secretary, Leonard Davies, held office for twelve years and was succeeded by Mr. D.S. Reakes who also held office for twelve years before handing over to the present secretary, Mr. W.J. England.

Tutors and house staff continue to devote two weeks of their holidays every year to assist on courses. Whilst it is not possible to name everybody, particular mention must be made of Tom Atkinson, well known for his work with young musicians in Yorkshire, one of those who attended the inaugural meeting when the Youth Band was only an idea, and who attended every course as bass tutor from the beginning until his death in 1974.

On the death of Sir Malcolm Sargent, Harry Mortimer became president after being a member of the council and enthusiastic supporter since the band's inception.

And a most vital element; the parents. Without them there would have been no Youth Band. We shall always be grateful to those parents of our first students who showed such willingness to allow their children to try something new, and to all subsequent parents for their interest and support, their willingness to travel sometimes long distances to visit the course and attend concerts.

Many thousands of students have passed through the Youth Band and for those who simply carry on their music as a hobby as well as those who are now household names as leading orchestral players, conductors and teachers, we hope the Youth Band in its way made some contribution to the development of their music making and enjoyment in it. The fact that some present day students are children of former students is perhaps an indication that all the effort has been worthwhile.

9. The National Youth Brass Band of Scotland

by BRADLEY CATTO

The National Youth Brass Band of Scotland this year celebrates the twenty-first anniversary of its formation. It was in 1958 that the Scottish Amateur Music Association, an organisation responsible over the years for the instigation and development of many facets of music-making in Scotland, decided that the time was ripe for a National Youth Band.

The first Director was the late Drake Rimmer, and tutors originally came from Kneller Hall Army School of Music. Among them was the late Colonel Sam Rhodes, a musical giant feared and respected by many an army bandsman, but who in his later years and until 1973 gave incomparable help to the cornet section. David Merchant, Music Adviser for Fife, became Director and in 1960 Dr. Denis Wright was invited to conduct. Then Cedric Thorpe Davie, President of the Association, and a well-known composer in his own right, took over the following year. It was not till 1964, however, that the first regular conductor was appointed. This was Bryden Thomson, an Ayrshire product, and perhaps even better known in the symphony orchestra scene. His term of office ended in 1970 after a tour of Germany with the Band. 1971 saw changes both in Director and Conductor. Bradley Catto, Music Adviser to Central Region, succeeded David Merchant, and Geoffrey Brand, already renowned in the world of brass, replaced Bryden Thomson. This partnership has flourished, and the Band has now expanded to a size of eighty members. So great has the demand for places become that the Association decided to form a Reserve Section in 1978. This rehearses on the same course as the NYBBS under Nigel Boddice, principal trumpet player of the BBC Scottish Symphony Orchestra, and himself a highly successful brass band conductor.

Financial restrictions are such that the Band can meet only once each year for a week's course, held in the month of July. Over the years this has been held in many parts of Scotland; St. Andrews, Aberdeen, Perth, Forfar, Alloa, Kirkcudbright, Arbroath, Paisley, Edinburgh, Dumfries, Stirling, Falkirk and Dundee. It was in 1974 that the Band gave the one and only performance on 'enemy' soil. When resident in Dumfries an invitation was accepted from the Carlisle Band, and a performance was given in the Town Hall, enthusiastically received by an appreciative audience.

Personnel must be under twenty-one years, and have to pass a strict individual audition which consists of playing scales and arpeggios from memory, a sight-reading test, and performing an own choice piece of suitable standard. Members come from all parts of Scotland, from the Orkneys to the Borders, and from Ayrshire to Dundee. In addition, exiles from as far as Manchester, London and Swansea manage to find their way back for the annual course. Family ties are strong, and it is not uncommon to find two, and on one occasion three from the same home. Apart from Geoffrey Brand and Nigel Boddice, there is a team of tutors who are well known in Scottish brass band circles both as performers and conductors. All of them are also employed as instructors in schools.

Apart from the tour of Germany already mentioned, and from several broadcasts, the band's proudest moment must have been in June, 1976, when an invitation was accepted from the Scottish National Orchestra to share the platform at the Kelvin Hall, Glasgow, as part of the Promenade Concert Season. Under Geoffrey Brand the Band tackled a most

demanding programme, which included the two commissions: Suite No. 1 by Malcolm Arnold and The Suite of Edinburgh Dances by Bryan Kelly, as well as the overture: Comedy by John Ireland and the Edward Gregson French Horn Concerto, with Frank Lloyd, Principal Horn of the Scottish National Orchestra, as soloist. An audience of 3,000 gave the Band a rousing and highly deserved ovation.

The greatest contribution made by the Association, and undoubtedly one of the outstanding landmarks in 20th Century Brass Band Music, has been the commissioning of works for the NYBBS from well-known composers. The Association felt the need for development in serious music for brass bands, with the result that since 1958 the Band has had an impressive and unequalled record of works written specially for it. There have been sixteen commissions in all, and these are listed separately. Many of these works have since become standard repertoire with brass bands throughout the country, and some have become test pieces for the National Championships. The Association has been much indebted to the Carnegie UK Trust, and the Scottish Arts Council for financial assistance in the commissioning of these works.

Since 1971 the policy of the Director has been that only original brass band music should be performed by the Band. Transcriptions and special arrangements are not permitted. Whilst acknowledging that such excellent transcriptions have been made, it is felt that youngsters should be given the opportunity at least once a year of being introduced to music they might not meet with normally in their local bands. Also, there are so many fine such compositions coming forward, that the need for transcriptions or arrangements, which could be classified as second-hand music from another medium, is no longer necessary, as it might well have been a quarter of a century ago.

What of the future? In the present economic struggle it is regretted that more financial aid is not forthcoming from official sources. What is the alternative? Obviously the modern popular concept of sponsorship by a well-known company is attractive and appealing. Although attempts to secure such support have so far been unsuccessful, it is hoped that the high ideals of the Band and its office-bearers will be recognised by industrial concerns as a worthwhile cultural venture.

10. The National School Brass Band Association

by CHARLES SWEBY

There is an obvious reason for the success of brass bands in schools. Within a year the pupils who become members of them are able to achieve a standard of performance on a brass instrument which might take twice as long in the case of woodwind, and still longer when stringed instruments are involved. A well taught school brass band can give quite satisfactory performances of comparatively difficult music once it has a nucleus of players with two or three years' experience. There is, of course, no special merit in playing music which is not easy, for it is not necessarily good music; but once the need to look for an easy score is past, the scope for teaching music through the brass band is enhanced. This should not be assumed to mean that brass bands are a more important means of teaching music than any other; circumstances may easily make it more appropriate.

During the latter years of the decade which ended in 1950 a small number of school brass bands became aware of each other's existence. Some inter-school concerts were arranged, and some of their teachers became convinced that it would be beneficial if they met to discover the extent of the development of brass bands in schools, and to discuss mutual problems. A particular difficulty which had to be faced at that time was the dearth of music possessing aesthetic value but which was not too difficult for these young pioneer bands to play well enough to give them and their audiences satisfaction and enjoyment. There was also a natural desire to discover the prevailing standards of performance achieved by the school bands, to consider whether some co-operation might help to improve these, and the extent to which the stronger might help the weaker and the experienced bands the tyros.

The necessary lead was given by Lance Caisley and Kenneth Cook who became greatly impressed by the results of their inquiries into the existing state of bands in schools. They agreed whilst boating in Christchurch Harbour during the summer of 1952 that there was a need for an organisation which would aim to further the development of this form of music making, and decided upon steps which should be taken to launch it.

Lance Caisley, joint founder of the N.S.B.B.A. and for many years editor of the Association's magazine *The Trumpeter*.

Within six months the National School Brass Band Association had been formed and had acquired a membership of twenty bands and a number of individual supporting members. Encouraged by this promising start, Mr. Caisley and Mr. Cook organised a conference at Trinity College of Music which duly took place in April, 1953. It was attended by an impressive number of people including some of the country's most eminent musicians from many spheres of musical activity. Bodies represented included the Ministry of Education, several education authorities and some music colleges. In retrospect it seems that much of the subsequent success of the association lies in this combined interest of bandsmen and musicians with other backgrounds but similar basic incentives. Several of the leading musicians who were present at the conference became founder members of the Advisory Council of the association which was by now properly constituted. Their influence, particularly during its formative years, was of very great value. Indeed, the Advisory Council continues to be a source of encouragement, and, although only two of the original council members are alive today, their helpful interest still inspires those who belong to the N.S.B.B.A.

A founder member of the Advisory Council was Max

Hinrichsen, who undertook to do his best to remedy the deficiencies in and lack of suitable music for school bands through the facilities of his firm. His offer to publish music in conjunction with a newly-formed association which had as yet but twenty bands in membership was generous, courageous and far-seeing. The appearance of the first of the Hinrichsen Journals for Young Bands showed that one of the main aims of the association was being met, and there was a rapid growth in its membership. Of even greater significance was the publication in 1954 of Music through the Brass Band which was written jointly by Lance Caisley and Kenneth Cook. The title of this book emphasises a priority in fundamental outlook which has lived on into the present — *music* through the brass band. This was followed by more journals of music, specially composed or arranged. The quality of the music in these early efforts to provide it may in more enlightened days appear uneven, but at the time of its publication, it satisfied a very real need both within and outside the membership of the N.S.B.B.A. Indeed, it is still widely used by newly-formed bands, and some of the arrangements, such as that of 'The Earl of Salisbury's Pavane' and of a Gabrieli canzona, can still sound as lovely and as stirring as they did twenty-five years ago.

Journals continue to be published under the name of Hinrichsen in conjunction with the association, and the latest volumes have but recently appeared. School, and other bands of today, may find in them music of many styles and periods, original and arranged, and geared to the needs of bands at different stages of development. A considerable amount of it is comparatively sophisticated. It is comforting to think that the attention which in more recent times has been given by composers, arrangers and publishers to the production of music suited to the needs of younger and other less skilled brass players may have roots in the early attempts of the N.S.B.B.A. to meet them. Whether or not this is the case, we cannot have too much good music. It is inevitable that some of what is now available may seem to many musicians to have at least one laudable quality — its easiness. The importance of providing young instrumentalists with a clearly printed part is sometimes overlooked. One recalls the question of a famous trumpeter who, after giving an excellent lecture at a N.S.B.B.A. teachers' course, joined the third cornets during a session which dealt with conducting techniques. Addressing an equally well-known conductor he asked. "Why should I find it harder to see brass band music than that I use when I am playing with an orchestra?"

In recent years the N.S.B.B.A. has been able as the result

Kenneth Cook, who, with Lance Caisley, founded the National School Brass Band Association.

of its own special efforts to commission music by Malcolm Arnold for school band and choir, and, with the help of the Arts Council of Great Britain and industrial sponsorship, several other notable works. Some of these have proved to be of value beyond the sphere of school bands, and due acknowledgement of the part played by the N.S.B.B.A. in obtaining them has been made in the scores by the publishers.

The effort to improve standards of performance has been approached at two levels, through teachers and through their pupils. Courses for teachers, mainly residential and lasting from a weekend to a week, have been organised in widely scattered centres throughout the country. They have proved popular and helpful, and have endeavoured to meet the different needs of qualified teachers who wish to know more about brass bands and proficient bandsmen who seek to learn something of the art of teaching their skills to young people. Courses for school bands have also been arranged in various parts of the country, and these are obviously most successful when planned on a local basis. Later courses of this kind became known as brass clinics, a type of course which proved to be valuable enough to attract sponsorship. The association may take justifiable pleasure and pride in having been pioneers in organising what may be called specialised general courses — specialised because of the experienced teaching provided, and general because they are open to pupils whatever their standard of playing.

The festivals of the association, whether national or locally organised, help to further the aim to improve standards of performance. Festivals organised on a national basis have taken place in many parts of the country from Kent to Lancashire and from Cornwall to County Durham. The music selected for the massed bands to play is intended to increase the skill of the participating bands and to widen their knowledge of repertoire. The extent to which this has improved can best be realised by comparing the programmes of the festivals in the early days with those of recent years. These programmes are, naturally, also a means of assessing the improved standards of the playing. The festivals include items which are performed by individual bands chosen because it is felt that their performances will encourage other bands to attempt to achieve a similar standard. For a number of years it has been possible to include at least one very good band in each festival. No competitive element has any place in N.S.B.B.A. festivals. Their objective is to offer to the young musicians involved the pleasure of a day of music making in different surroundings together with the thrill of rehearsing and giving a concert under the baton of one of the country's

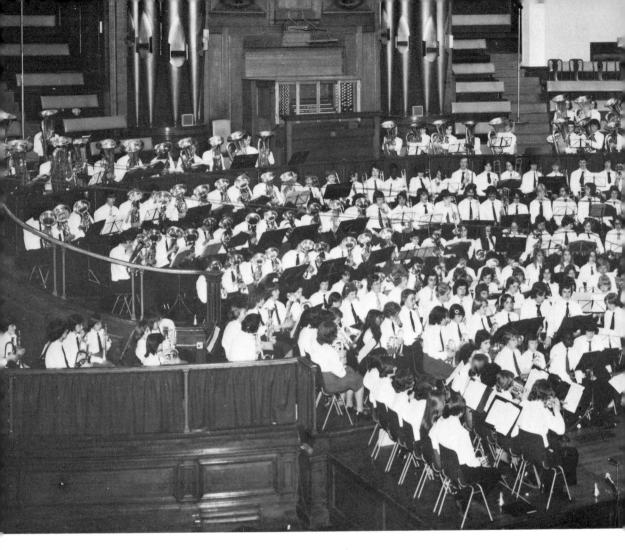

leading conductors. At first one festival took place each year, but as the membership passed two hundred bands, two annual national festivals have been organised.

Locally arranged festivals follow the same basic scheme as those of the larger festivals, often including an invitation to a good band which can demonstrate a high standard from further afield. Inter-school visits still take place between member bands. Whatever form festivals take, they inevitably become social as well as musical occasions.

Another way of enabling members to keep in touch with one another is through the pages of the magazine of the association, *The Trumpeter*. This title may seem somewhat incongruous, but it is a good one. It is published once in each school term and is sent gratis to all members. Others may obtain copies for a modest charge. An important section of *The Trumpeter* is that devoted to reviews of new music, for

Harry Mortimer rehearsing in the Westminster Central Hall, London, for the 1976 N.S.B.B.A. Festival.

this is obviously related to the fundamental wish to increase and improve the available repertoire. The music is not only assessed as the result of studying the score — for the association feels strongly that a full score is necessary for all conductors, particularly during the teaching stages and when younger players are involved. It is also played by a mature school band so that the reactions of the pupils can be assessed. In these days of sophisticated youngsters, their opinions are worthy of consideration. Music which is felt to be of value to school bands is graded so that it may be included in due course in the N.S.B.B.A. Graded Music List.

This list has proved to be among the most useful publications undertaken by the association. At present it is being reviewed and revised in preparation for a third edition. The second edition now in use included some music felt to be out of place in it, and it needs to have recently published music added to it. The music list is sent free to school members, and, like *The Trumpeter*, it is made generally available at a reasonable price. A methodical teacher who has added the titles of new pieces to his list as they have been announced in *The Trumpeter* could possess a quite comprehensive catalogue from which to select music for his band. When the revised edition of the music list is published it will be an addition to a series of Brass Brochures which are issued free to school members and which may be obtained by any other interested persons. Through these booklets the association is attempting to provide information on a wide variety of topics which it is felt will be helpful to teachers. Excellent examples are brochures by Patrick Rivers on the arranging of music for brass bands or ensembles, and by Geoffrey Brand on the basic training of a school brass band. Obviously, these and other brochures are useful outside the sphere of school brass bands.

A most encouraging development in recent years has been the increasing interest in brass bands in junior schools. This has caused the N.S.B.B.A. to organise several festivals for junior school bands, and to be present at one of these is to have shared a rejuvenating and exhilarating experience. So often does one hear "Junior school bands are now playing as well as senior school bands did twenty years ago" that it has almost become a cliché. Whether or not this claim is justifiable, certainly the enthusiasm of these very young musicians, some of whom seem smaller than their instruments, is very promising. Their talents are being developed at an impressionable age, and they are more fortunate than were the seniors of more than twenty years back in the music available to them.

Whatever the age range of a school band, the question ultimately asked is whether or not its members will be able to continue to play when they leave school. It is no more certain that there is a secondary school band within the catchment area of a junior school than it is that there is an adult band which will wish to recruit those leaving a senior school. In the former case, there is a reasonable chance that a place will be found for all the younger players, but it is, of course, impossible for adult bands to accept all the brass players who leave school, there are too many of them. And, unfortunately, a few bands may not appeal for various reasons to a young person. The complaint which is made occasionally that ex-school brass players (and other instrumentalists) do not continue to play need not be taken so seriously as sometimes it appears to be. If the instrumental work has been used as a means for teaching music in the fullest possible sense, it will have provided a life-long interest. Some school leavers will become professional musicians; some will continue to play as amateurs. All should possess the knowledge and enthusiasm which makes up the discerning concert-goer and even home listener.

The overall title which is to be given to this collection of essays suggests that one may attempt to look forward towards the end of the twentieth century. During the last five years or so, the average age of the committee of the National School Brass Band Association has been lowered. It is an inevitable fact of life that new blood, especially young new blood, will endeavour to improve the future life of the body to which it has been introduced. This transfusion has taken place at a time when the future needed to be faced because it had become obvious that a great deal of what the association had set out to accomplish has been achieved. A solid foundation upon which those who wish to introduce brass bands into their schools has been prepared, and the future needs of school bands are currently a regular item in the committee's agendas. Changes are likely to be made to activities which have become traditional in the calendar of the association, and new ideas ought to be such that tradition is not broken for the sake of change. One factor which has to be faced is the effect of financial limitations imposed at the present time. For instance, it may become necessary to arrange events like festivals with an eye on the cost of transporting bands to them.

The increasing number of wind bands in schools, some of which are already members of the association, suggests that a need may exist for an association able to do for these bands what has been done for brass bands. Present needs of bands which use brass and woodwind are not dissimilar to those of school brass bands nearly thirty years ago. This is a controversial topic which leads to lively discussion. There are those who are convinced that brass bands are worthy of the full attention of the N.S.B.B.A. Others consider that an association which has reiterated the opinion that brass bands should not isolate themselves from the full world of music, nor be isolated from it, ought to take a wider view. Both sides are aware that the association possesses the necessary expertise within its Advisory Council and its committee. One member of the council has already composed and arranged music which, like many simplified brass band scores, may be adapted to suit the needs of incomplete wind bands of differing instrumentation. A case could be made that the brass band with several clarinets in the cornet section is in need of advice! So far, no successful effort has been made to proffer this, and an existing organisation may be in a position to undertake the work this would involve. It is agreed that the line should be drawn at instruments which are blown.

The penultimate paragraph is meant to show that the N.S.B.B.A., which has more than once been described as one of the more effective of the organisations which attempt to cater for the needs of school music and musicians, intends to retain this good opinion. A mixture of experience and youthful enterprise on both its council and committee, fortified by the adoption of a readily adaptable new constitution, augers well for the future of the National School Brass Band Association. What has been accomplished may well prove to be but a beginning.

11. Discography
by TIM MUTUM

If you are not fortunate enough to be able to attend concerts of brass band music on a regular basis then listening to the music of the brass band through the medium of the gramophone record is probably the next best thing. Records do not have the same atmosphere as the concert hall but they do offer an excellent opportunity to listen, for enjoyment (and also to learn), to some of the best bands, musicians and conductors in the business.

The first sounds to emanate from a gramophone (now more popularly referred to as stereo or hi-fi) were a far cry from the quality of today. It is doubtful, however, whether any brass bands were recorded on cylinder, although regimental or concert bands like the National Military and house bands such as the London Regimental did record on Edison Bell. It is difficult to be precise about the date of issue of the first brass band recordings. They were on 78 rpm. records, two sided and ten inches in diameter which, in some cases, were later extended to twelve inches.

Record companies at that time did not print the year of publication on the label and some of the information on dates has been acquired from the record catalogues of that time which still exist. The seventy-eight era lasted from about 1903–4 to the late 1950s; CWS (Manchester) recorded 'The Shaggy Dog' and 'The Enchanted Garden' in about 1956. During that period numerous brass bands were recorded and hundreds of 78 rpm records released. The recordings tended to be marches, hymn tunes and lighter numbers which were well suited to the short length of playing time on each side of the record. Many fine test pieces were recorded, however, and records also exist of the Crystal Palace concerts.

One of the earliest seventy-eights was recorded by the Black Dyke Mills Band in 1904. The piece recorded was 'Pluie D'or' by Waldteufal on a twelve inch, single sided record (Record No. Monarch 011). Other records made in the same year were selections from 'Ruy Blas', 'Hiawatha', 'L'Africaine' and 'The Songs of Scotland', as well as gems from Sullivan's operas. Besses o' th' Barn were certainly recording from 1906 and recorded at least seven records up to the outbreak of World War One. Most of the records featured hymn tunes. The Salvation Army Processional, as it was called, also recorded for Zonophone prior to 1908.

Many of the bands recording at that time are, sadly, no longer in existence. It is fortunate, therefore, that many of their recordings are with collectors throughout the country. The 1920s saw a flood of issues by some of these now defunct bands. The St. Hilda Colliery Prize Band, the Wigston Temperance Prize Band, the Carlisle St. Stephen Band and the Horwich RMI Band all recorded for labels such as Regal and Zonophone. During this period, St. Hilda's became a professional brass band known as the St. Hilda Professional Band. Their choice of music at times probably did not befit their professional status or, at least, the titles suggest a certain air of frivolity. There were the 'Tyneside Tunes', 'The Flying Squad' and 'The Slippery Slide' to name but three.

However, as mentioned earlier, the original works existing at that time were not ignored and it was the practice, as it is today, for the winning band at the Crystal Palace Championships to record (in the majority of cases) the chosen test piece. For example, Carlisle St. Stephen recorded 'The White Rider' (two records) by Denis Wright in 1927 and 'Victory' (two records) in 1929. The many famous marches of Rimmer and Ord Hume were not overlooked either and popular ones such as 'Slaidburn' and 'The Victor's Return' found their way on to seventy-eights in the late 1920s.

The 1930s were described as "the golden years" for the Foden's Motor Works Band and many recordings were made during the period leading up to World War Two. These included 'A Downland Suite' in 1931 (probably) and 'Kenilworth' in 1937, as well as pieces such as 'The Teddy Bears' Picnic' and 'The Whistler and his Dog' which were recorded in 1937 and 1935 respectively.

There were two other interesting features of the thirties. One was the considerable number of issues of massed band records from the Leicester Festival and the Grand Massed Bands from the Crystal Palace (conducted by James Oliver). Much of the music, again, tended to be marches, classical selections and lighter numbers. Secondly, the names of Jack Mackintosh and Harry Mortimer were frequently seen on record labels both as soloists and duettists. William Oughton was another name featured with Jack Mackintosh. Jack and Harry recorded many famous pieces such as 'Mac and Mort'; Harry also recorded many solos with the Foden's Band.

During the war, at least in the early years, Foden's, Black Dyke (conducted by Arthur O. Pearce), Bickershaw Colliery and the Fairey Aviation Works Band (conducted by Harry Mortimer) all made recordings on Parlophone, Columbia, Rex and other similar record labels. In 1945–6 Fairey recorded 'Overture for an Epic Occasion' written by D. Wright for the National, but with a title that speaks for itself.

After the war, new names appeared. Morris Motors recorded for Columbia in 1946 and in 1953 the National Band of New Zealand were recording for HMV. The CWS (Manchester) Band, conducted by Eric Ball, recorded 'Scena Sinfonica' by Henry Geehl on Columbia in either late 1952 or early 1953.

And so with the advent of the Long Playing Record (LP) in the 1950s, the great era of the seventy-eight finished. They are still much sought after and many people collect them and seek to compile catalogues. It is doubtful whether anyone will ever know exactly how many seventy-eights were made. Suffice it to say that some great bands and musicians made wonderful music which will last, hopefully, for posterity. There are too many bands and personalities to be able to mention them all, but some that immediately spring to mind and are not included above are the Callenders Senior Band, the Wingates Temperance, Frank Biffo's Brass Quintette (who recorded for Columbia in 1936 and 1937) and the

Harton Colliery Band. A whole book could probably be written solely on seventy-eights, but it is hoped that these few paragraphs will, at least, give the reader some idea of the fascinating world of brass band seventy-eights.

The LP record is generally twelve inches in diameter although, for many years, ten inch and seven inch were also made. From the brass bands' point of view, it was not until the late 1950s that record companies signed contracts with them for LP records. Two big record companies signed up bands on long-term contracts and one independent company began issuing ten inch and seven inch records. The 'big two' were Fontana and Columbia (controlled by Phonogram and EMI respectively). Fontana signed up the CWS (Manchester) Band conducted by Alex Mortimer; the band was referred to as The Famous CWS (Manchester) Band and they made over a dozen LP records for Fontana over a period of ten or so years. These records are no longer available but, like many of the seventy-eights, they are collectors' items because they were the first LP records; they were a series and they featured recordings of many fine works, e.g. 'Oliver Cromwell', 'Rhapsody in Brass' and 'Journey into Freedom'. Two of the many featured soloists were Derek Garside and Lyndon Baglin. Columbia contracted the GUS (Footwear) Band conducted by Stanley Boddington. They initially recorded a series from about 1957 of ten records under the title Championship Bandstand with Harry Mortimer sharing some of the conducting. This contract continued with the issue of records right through until 1976.

Paxton Records were the third company to record brass bands and over a period, ending in the late 1960s, they recorded most of the top bands on ten inch LP or seven inch EP (Extended Play) records. Again, these records are no longer available and, to some extent, they are collectors' items. Their recordings were broken down into two fields — the EPs tended to feature lighter, shorter numbers and, occasionally, test pieces and the LPs featured test pieces and longer works. Fairey, Foden's, CWS (Manchester), Creswell Colliery, Crossley Carpet Works Band and the Ferodo Works Band made the majority of the LP records, plus Harry Mortimer and his All Star Brass and the Black Dyke Mills Band.

Special mention must be made of Black Dyke because they recorded what is probably the most famous Paxton record. In 1959 the band had won the National Championship playing 'Le Roi D'ys', conducted by Major Willcocks. As was Paxton's practice during the late 1950s and early 1960s, the test piece was put on record and became one of the most famous recordings of this work; it featured Maurice Murphy on cornet and Geoffrey Whitham on euphonium. Harry Mortimer's All Star Brass made many records for Paxton, but they also recorded for another big company, Decca. They recorded regularly for this company on both EP and, later on, LP records under the title of Harry Mortimer and his All Star Brass, Men o' Brass and, sometimes, Cathedral Brass. They subsequently transferred to EMI and a release in 1978 was appropriately titled 'Harry Mortimer — A Lifetime of Music'.

Around 1966 the record companies started to record brass bands in a far bigger way than they had since the LP record was first introduced. EMI had a budget label called Music for Pleasure and started a series entitled Listen to the Band. The first recordings were made by the Scottish (CWS) and Wingates Temperance Bands, followed by a re-release of Championship Bandstand No 1 featuring the GUS (Footwear) Band. At about the same time Pye Records began releasing band records on their Golden Guinea label and many of the recordings released were sub-labelled Top Brass Series. Amongst the early bands recorded were the Brighouse and Rastrick, the Crossley Carpet Works Band and the Markham Main Colliery Band. Pye subsequently introduced band records on their budget label Marble Arch. If one had to isolate any particularly outstanding recordings, the Black Dyke Mills Band (again!) recorded some remarkably good LP records on Pye, notably 'The Champions' (featuring an outstanding performance by John Clough playing the euphonium solo, 'Grandfather's Clock', and also including the 1967 National piece, 'Journey into Freedom') and 'Champions Again', which was one of the first records to feature four original works.

Other companies soon released albums and, throughout the late 1960s and early 1970s, there was a flood of LP record issues. Surprisingly enough, some of the seventy-eight era and early LP recorded bands did not fare so well and newer bands found themselves earning good fees from recording contracts. Established bands such as Brighouse, Black Dyke, Fairey and Grimethorpe had regular releases, but other bands coming into the limelight were Stanshawe, City of Coventry, Royal Doulton, Hammonds Sauce Works Band and Cory.

Record companies, on the whole, however, did not appear to want long term contracts such as those which CWS and GUS had enjoyed in the past. Decca did, however, appear on the band scene again in 1972 with their Sounds of Brass series and for two years part of the prize for winning the

The GUS (Footwear) Band with Harry Mortimer and Stanley Boddington taken at a recording session at EMI's Abbey Road Studio

National Championships was a recording contract with them on Sounds of Brass — Cory, Brighouse and the Tredegar Junior Band benefited from this innovation. RCA have, perhaps, taken the biggest plunge in recent years. Not renowned for brass band releases, in 1974 they entered the market in a serious way (although they had recorded Fairey on a budget label) with what was described as "one of the most important records released", an album by the City of London Brass. Black Dyke have since signed a contract, and two albums per year, at least, are released; RCA subsequently signed up the Grimethorpe Colliery Band.

As well as Decca, RCA and Pye, EMI continued to release albums mainly by Men o' Brass, although middle price recordings of Cory, Hammonds and Parc and Dare have also been released. Polydor also issued two short series of LP records entitled 'Carnival' and 'Fanfare'. Grosvenor Records, who are a considerably smaller company than EMI etc., also regularly release brass band LP records. At first, some important works were included, e.g. a movement from the 'Buxton Orr Trombone Concerto' but, sadly, insufficient copies were, it appears, sold and later releases have tended to be more middle-of-the-road in approach. Nevertheless, these recordings are valuable additions to the brass band recording catalogues.

Other areas besides pure brass have been explored; band and choir, quartet and solo albums have been released, although these have been few and far between. One of the most important choral works to be recorded was Gilbert Vinter's Cantata 'The Trumpets' for bass solo, mixed chorus, brass and percussion which has been recorded twice, once by Men o' Brass and on the other occasion by Black Dyke. The City of London Brass have recorded Malcolm Arnold's 'Song of Freedom' and, sadly, of the three recordings at the time of writing, only the latter is currently available. Various albums of Christmas carols and other band and choir items have been released from time to time.

Solo and quartet albums are distinct rarities. A company called Kennedy Recording released an album entitled 'Solo Brass' featuring James Shepherd on cornet and Keith Swallow on piano. The Saydisc Recording Company based near Gloucester made a very ambitious album featuring Lyndon Baglin, the difference with this album being that much of the accompaniment was provided by a harp and two flutes, used to great effect. Two quartet albums have been released as far as it is known; one of which featured the famous GUS Quartet who won the British Quartet Championship in 1966, 1967 and 1968 featuring three Gilbert Vinter compositions. On the ensemble front, the James Shepherd Versatile Brass have made a significant impact with the release of six recordings, including one using the direct cut technique.

Various private labels specialising in brass band recordings have come to light from time to time. Possibly the most successful has been the Virtuosi Recording Company who formed a Virtuosi Band, consisting of twenty-eight hand-picked players, and have made nine records over the past five years. A more recent company intent on recording in a

Three record sleeves from Decca's 'Sounds of Brass' series, Decca Record Co. Ltd.

modern style, in terms of music, has been 210 Records which is a division of R. Smith and Company Ltd the famous music publishing company. It is too early to say how successful this venture will be.

Who has made the most LP records? Well, like seventy-eights, it is very difficult to be precise. The following gives an indication (excluding massed band and compilation issues): the Black Dyke Mills Band — twenty-nine, the GUS (Footware) Band (now Great Universal) — twenty-one, the Grimethorpe Colliery Band — eighteen, the CWS (Manchester) Band — fifteen and the Brighouse and Rastrick Band — fifteen.

It must be stressed that these figures are not guaranteed to be one hundred per cent accurate, because bands make private LP records etc, and they relate to 12 inch LP records only.

As in the days of the seventy-eights, recordings have been made of the Festival Concerts which follow the National Championships. It is thought that this practice was started in 1967 by Pye, and Decca and RCA have all contributed to the recording of this important concert in the brass band calendar.

The last few years have seen brass band recordings breaking into a new area, and an unusual one at that. In 1972 a solo singer, Peter Skellern, wrote and recorded a song entitled 'You're a Lady' and chose a brass band to provide the accompaniment. The band in question was the Hanwell Band from London. This popular music record was extremely successful and reached a very high position in the British Popular Music Charts. In 1978 a few bars of 'Punchinello' introduced a song by Bryan and Michael entitled 'Matchstalk Men and Matchstalk Cats and Dogs' and eight members of the Tintwistle Band provided the accompaniment. However, it was in 1977 that the brass band really stormed the popular music market. In autumn, 1976, the Brighouse and Rastrick Band recorded, as a single, a Cornish tune entitled 'The Floral Dance'. It was released by Transatlantic Records in the spring of 1977, made no real impact and was subsequently withdrawn. In the autumn of 1977 it was re-released (by Logo Records who had taken over Transatlantic) and was played extensively on BBC Radio 2. It subsequently became an enormous success reaching No 2 in the Popular Music Charts, a position it held for several weeks over the Christmas and New Year. Sales exceeded 700,000 copies and a Silver Disc was awarded. An LP record was subsequently released and within a short period 70,000 copies had been sold, with a further Silver Disc awarded to the delighted "Briggus" Band. This eventually reached No 12 in the Popular Music LP Record Charts.

Checkmate. A recent release on the Two-Ten record label. The record title is derived from the name of the test piece with which the Band of Yorkshire Imperial Metals won the 1978 National Championship at the Royal Albert Hall.

The Brighouse and Rastrick Band are captured here as they play The Floral Dance during a BBC transmission of Top of the Pops, conducted by Derek Broadbent.

In general terms, however, the brass band, as a recording medium, has failed to attract the attention of record companies in the same way as have other mediums in the music world, e.g. orchestras, jazz bands, pop groups etc. Brass bands have not been accepted as a serious recording medium. Records are released on mid-price, middle-of-the-road labels and not on the more accepted classical labels. Very few records enter the classical section of books such as the Gramophone Classical Record Catalogue, yet several band records feature only two works to a side by composers of some repute such as Edward Gregson, Eric Ball and Gilbert Vinter. Exceptions to this, however, have been records by Grimethorpe, Black Dyke and GUS which were released on classical labels by Decca, RCA and EMI respectively. Grimethorpe subsequently had a very contemporary record, 'The Grimethorpe Special', released on Decca's Headline label. For reasons best known to reviewers of records and record companies releases such as that by Besses o' th' Barn entitled English Brass and featuring works by John Ireland and Gustav Holst did not receive the attention they deserved from the critics.

Brass bands will continue to make records and record companies will, hopefully, develop the medium's musical value. One thing, however, is for certain — without the gramophone record a lot of people would not have had the opportunity to listen to one of the greatest amateur music making activities in the United Kingdom.

12. *Salvation Army Bands and their music*

by ERIC BALL

The International Staff Band of the Salvation Army (left) with the Melbourne Staff Band, playing in the grounds of Buckingham Palace during the centenery celebrations, July 1978.

The Victorian era seems to have been a period of surprising contrasts. The growth of the British Empire, the glorification of military power, the exploitation of the poor and defenceless were offset by a rising tide of liberal thought, by the growth of the "Nonconformist Conscience" of the free churches, and by many other reform movements and charities.

A hundred years ago the Salvation Army's appeal to the spiritually and artistically deprived was made more effective by the fact that new converts were encouraged to become personally involved in the work and worship of the organis-

ation. No sitting passively listening to a choir! If you could sing a song, or compose one — however inartistic — play an instrument, make a speech, you were expected to bring your talent to the service of God. So, though in a more sophisticated manner, it is today!

At the same time the growing popularity of the brass band, with its cornets, saxhorns, trombones, tubas, meant that those who were called "The Working Class" — most of whom were very poor and underprivileged less than a hundred years ago — could find a comparatively easy way of making music together. These were the people the Army attracted, and anyone who played instruments of any kind — brass, woodwind, concertinas, banjos, accordions, aeolian harps, anything — were encouraged to bring them to the indoor and open-air meetings in order to "make a joyful noise unto the Lord" and attract the attention of the public — which they certainly did!

It was natural that in some cases the players would wish to form organised groups, and the brass band seemed to be the most useful type of ensemble. After all, what is an army of soldiers without a band?

But if the Salvation Army was to be a disciplined force, there would have to be some regulation for the forming of bands and the music they would play.

It is doubtful if at first there was envisaged a particular long-term principle or policy. Army music-making was a natural growth, and any regulations governing it were made by Headquarters in what was thought to be the best interests of the movement as a whole, and could be altered when necessary from time to time.

General Bramwell Booth was said to have described the Army Band as a "peripatetic organ" — an organ which walks! The church organ must stay indoors, but the Army's organ can go out to the people. Its main functions, even today, are

The Fry family from Salisbury - recognised as being the first Salvation Army Band

186

to accompany congregational singing and to lead the soldiers on the march. It has adequate music for these purposes. Added to this, just as an organist will sometimes play a "voluntary" in church, so may the band when necessary.

It seems that the bands and their repertoire have developed from such basic needs, and of course they have evolved often to a high degree of artistry and even inspiration. This was inevitable, although it has often been challenged.

A poor, ignorant early-day convert would naturally wish to see his children and grandchildren better equipped mentally and in every way: they would become "middle class" and eminently respectable, and their appreciation of music, art and literature would evolve. General Bramwell Booth is said to have envisaged the Salvation Army as "a nation within the nations," with its own art, literature and music. So, indeed, it has to a great degree become.

It is doubtful if any Army leaders evolved a particular philosophy about the effect of music upon people's minds and hearts. What has happened is that it came to be a tradition that all instrumental music should contain tunes based on religious songs and hymns. By this means there was a reference point — even in playing and interpreting the music — to Christian ideas, about Salvation, Holiness, and other doctrinal concepts. Listeners could be told about the music they were to hear, and its implications.

Some of the Meditations in the repertoire — a form of

Consett Band 1879. The first corps band of the Salvation Army.

Richard Slater who is acknowledged as the 'Father of Salvation Army Music'

Ealing Salvation Army Band, 1890.

The International Staff Band c.
1910, with bandmaster Col.
George Mitchell.

188

musical composition evolved particularly by Salvationist composers — and later certain tone poems, are among the best composed works in the repertoire, but can still be understood by "ordinary" listeners in the congregations.

We have written of the poor unprivileged of the early days, but of course educated and sensitive people were also attracted to the Army. Some of the Founder's family were most effective song-writers and musicians. Then came Richard Slater — the Father of Salvation Army music, and an experienced musician and Wagnerite — and later his protegees, Frederick G. Hawkes and Arthur Goldsmith. Most of the music for bands came from these writers who were also members of the Music Editorial Department at Headquarters.

Gradually new names began to appear: Bramwell Coles, and George Marshall. In the 1920s F.G. Hawkes had full charge of the musical output, and he has been rightly described as the architect of The Salvation Army music. Under his indefatigable control, two new band journals were regularly produced, plus that already in service, thus providing a constant supply of new works for bands of all grades there were albums of music for soloists, quartets, etc., and all this besides large quantities of vocal music.

It was the privilege of the writer to work under the direction of this remarkable man, who put aside his own efforts as a composer in order to make a place for others of a younger school. Into the department came Albert Jakeway and Philip Catelinet, helping to make up a team of new ideas and humour, but fully under F.G.H.'s control.

Since then this important and influential department has been staffed by many who were to make their mark. Donald Osgood was there, Bramwell Coles became the head, as later did Albert Jakeway and Charles Skinner, all producing valuable additions to the repertoire as well as carrying out the arduous and never-ceasing editorial work.

Captain (later to become General) Wilfred Kitching, pictured here around 1920 with two band lads.

Present-day incumbents are Ray Steadman-Allen and Leslie Condon, both producing challenging new works, worthy additions to an extensive repertoire of brass band music which concert and contesting bands might well envy. There are those who would aver that S.A. music has in some measure been in advance of most of that produced in the "outside world" for many years.

Other writers have given terms of service in the Music Editorial Department, but it is also in a real sense a centre towards which composers the world over converge in spirit — and in hope of publication!

The list of Salvationist composers grows beyond counting. From Scandinavia, in the early days, the erudite Klaus

An unusual photograph from the past. The Pittsburgh Temple All Girls Band of 1923 with its Bandmaster Capt. W.E. Bearchell. This band carried out many engagements and once played for Commander Evangeline Booth in Columbus, Ohio.

Erik Leidzen (centre) pictured here at Star Lake, New Jersey, around 1950, with Col. Bramwell Coles (right) and Lt. Col. W.E. Bearchell, Bandmaster of the New York Staff Band.

Ostby and later, via the U.S.A., Erik Leidzen, Emil Soderstrom and others. Many from Australia and New Zealand include Dean Goffin, whose 'Rhapsody in Brass' has enriched the contesting repertoire. Vaughan Williams and other professional musicians like Thomas Rive and Wilfred Heaton have added their quota, and newer names are coming forward all the time: in the U.S.A., James Curnow, William Himes, the two Broughtons (their grandfather had led the way); in Denmark, Erik Silfverberg; and an increasing host in other countries.

Jazz idioms — formerly forbidden — are now allowed; with harmonic sequences that would have caused Hawkes to tear his hair and reach for a book of musical theory. As the man said: "We used to play wrong notes accidentally: now they write them in!"

In these days the Salvation Army boasts bands which could challenge the best in the contesting field. They are not type-cast; the personnel varies in numbers; the style varies from town to town, from country to country. Bands from Australia, New Zealand, the U.S.A., Scandinavia, Holland and Switzerland visit Britain, invariably giving us something to think about!

For most of this century the International Staff Band, attached to Headquarters in London, has been expected to set high standards in technique, presentation and spiritual impact. Former conductors George Mitchell and George Fuller are still remembered and talked of. Latterly Bernard Adams evoked from the band a standard never before attained — Vaughan Williams admired its "classical" style. Now, under the direction of Ray Bowes, the band continues the tradition of trying out new works, providing music at many and varied functions, and giving concerts.

Staff bands in Toronto, Melbourne, New York, Chicago and Amsterdam carry out similar duties.

Many local Corps Bands, past and present, have attained high levels of music-making and service. In the past these were often led by father-figures like A.W. Punchard of Chalk Farm, H.W. Twitchen of Regent Hall, London, Sidney Cox of Exeter, and many others.

Today's conductors have different problems, musical and spiritual, with which to cope, but they are still guided by tradition, wise regulations, and aided by the dedication of the bandsmen and women to an over-riding ideal.

These men and women are true amateurs — playing for the love of it, seeking high-standards, receiving no financial reward, even buying their own uniforms and subscribing to the work of the Army.

There are losses of course. Many Salvation Army bandsmen have transferred to contesting bands, although some retain their spiritual links with the organisation. Some become professional musicians and uphold high standards. The contesting movement and The Salvation Army have benefitted mutually from the exchange of ideas, and we can but hope that the highest ideals of both will be consistently upheld. It

There are Salvation Army bands in Finland, too. These bandsmen are marching through the streets of Helsinki.

Lt. Col. Ray Steadman-Allen, head of the International music board.

is of interest to note that many contesting performers and administrators freely admit to a background of Salvation Army experience.

It is a long time since rough, untutored men and women tried to play brass instruments, in the spirit of Blow and Believe; we must hope that the faith and believing are still there, and that Salvation Army bands and composers will continue to enjoy the confidence of those who believe their spiritual work to be of the greatest importance.

And in closing, we wonder why their counterparts — bands attached to churches, chapels and missions, seem to have almost died out? Did they miss the mark somewhere?

Acknowledgement

We should like to thank The Salvation Army Editorial Department, International Headquarters, London, for photographs used in this chapter.

The Hong Kong Staff Band (Bandmaster Capt. G. Becker) performing during a Christmas engagement in Hong Kong.

Staff Bands of the Army

The International Staff Band is the premier band of the Salvation Army and is based at the Army's International Headquarters in Queen Victoria Street, London. The band was formed in December 1891 under the leadership of Staff Captain F.W. Fry and gained official recognition on September 23, 1893. The band first toured abroad in 1892 when it supported General William Booth's campaign in Holland. Since then it has performed in many parts of the world including Australia, USA, Canada and many European countries.
More recently, the ISB toured Switzerland in 1973 and Holland in 1977. The present bandmaster is Lt. Col. Ray Bowes.

New York Staff Band (Bandmaster Derek Smith)

Chicago Staff Band (Bandmaster Brigadier Ronald Rowland)

Amsterdam Staff Band during its tour of Switzerland in 1976

Melbourne (Australia) Staff Band (Bandmaster Colin Woods) captured here during a recent television transmission.

13. The International Scene

by VIOLET and GEOFFREY BRAND

Brass bands are a uniquely British form of amateur music-making, but they are not restricted to the United Kingdom. They were one of our nineteenth century exports to Australasia, when the early settlers carried their enthusiasm for brass with them. More recently, the Europeans have become interested and in Scandinavia, Holland, Belgium and Switzerland, British style brass bands are a way of life for thousands.

Organised brass band activity in New Zealand is almost as old as it is in England. In 1980, the New Zealanders will celebrate one hundred years of national brass band contesting in Christchurch, scene of the first major contest. National contesting is not confined to one day, or even one weekend, as in England, but continues for five days. The New Zealanders take the word 'championships' in the widest possible sense and include everything — solos (senior and junior), quartets, ensembles, full band "own choice", hymn tune and set test piece (in four sections), plus a street parade, quickstep and marching display championship. For the chief adjudicator, sometimes a visitor from Australia or England, this is a marathon.

Lieutenant J. Ord Hume was the guest adjudicator from England in 1924 and at the conclusion of the events he made the following comments: "They expect a good deal from the various adjudicators and they are not slow in giving their opinions upon any judge in whom their faith is not too strong. Unlike the Old Country, they will listen most attentively to a detailed criticism of the various performers. They are intelligent listeners. Every possible point of vantage is carefully noted, and in fact it is remarkable indeed and truly creditable to the bandsmen that they take so wide an interest in their competitive work. Any advice from the adjudicator, no matter whether mild or strong, is cordially received and freely debated upon."

Ord Hume's comments on the attentiveness of the audience and its expectation of a lengthy analysis of performances are just as true today. An English observer, used to the restlessness for results at contests in this country, was agreeably surprised at the 1978 New Zealand Championships, when a member of the audience was heard to say: "Fine adjudicator" after he had sat for twenty minutes listening to the criticism — before he had even heard the results!

The main band events take the form of pre-1900 contesting in England, in that every band has to present an "own choice" piece, as well as playing the set test piece. There is, therefore, a winner for each of these events, plus an overall champion band, which has the highest aggregate of marks, but which might have won neither event.

Bandsmen boarding a TWA Boeing 707 en route to Niagara Falls, Canada, on Friday, June 30, 1972. Black Dyke, CWS (Manchester) Fairey & G.U.S. travelled on the plane with guest conductors Eric Ball, Geoffrey Brand and Harry Mortimer.

Perhaps the section which is most spectacular, and finds no place in the English brass band scene, is the display marching. The deportment, the precision and the imagination of the displays compel the admiration, not only of brass band enthusiasts, but the general public.

Brass band affairs are controlled by a strong, democratically elected, New Zealand Brass Band Association, which was formed in 1931 by an amalgamation of the North and South Island Band Associations. It is the unification of brass band affairs, unlike the fragmentation in the United Kingdom, which makes the concentration of national contesting events possible, but the activities controlled by the NZBBA are not confined to the contest field. The National Youth Brass Band and the National Band of New Zealand come under its jurisdiction.

The National Youth Brass Band of New Zealand who held their 1959 course at Lincoln College, near Christchurch. Mr. R.E. Belgrave, President of the N.Z.B.B.A. could well be termed the band's founder.

The National Youth Brass Band grew from residential courses, organised for the young brass bandsmen of New Zealand. Dr. Denis Wright learned of these on his adjudication visit in 1951 and commented on their educational value. He was embarking on a similar project in England and was, therefore, much in sympathy with the idea.

Approximately every four years, the National Band of New Zealand is formed by audition for a world-tour. The tour lasts for several months and not only are bandsmen unpaid during this time, but every man is required to make a financial contribution to his own expenses. It is not unknown for a bandsman to take out a second mortgage on his house to provide the necessary funds. Despite this, there is great competition for a place in the National Band. Individual members are proud of their selection and their local bands share in the pride. A great feeling of comradeship exists

198

between National Bandsmen, like membership of an exclusive club.

The first composite band, known as the Hinemoa Band, came to England from New Zealand in 1903. Sponsored by the Union Jack Club, the tour was organised by John Henry Iles. It was not a complete success, but patterns were set for future tours. Maori dancers toured with the band in 1903 and have remained a very popular part of the programme on each succeeding tour. The silver fern leaf was adopted as the motif and remains so.

Hinemoa, the composite New Zealand band which toured England in 1903 under the sponsorship of the Union Jack Club and the organisation of John Henry Iles.

In 1953 the first National Band of New Zealand toured the U.K. The coach shown was the property of Foden's, who placed it at the disposal of the New Zealanders throughout their stay.

Fifty years elapsed between the visit of Hinemoa and the tour of the first National Band of New Zealand. Foden's Motor Works Band were very generous and loaned the New Zealanders their band coach, for travelling in Britain. Visits to the Edinburgh Festival Contest and to the British Open Champions, at Belle Vue, Manchester, were very successful. The National Band of New Zealand came to England in August, 1978, and received much acclaim for their concert before a packed audience in the Westminster Central Hall, London. During the day, they had delighted the many tourists to Westminster Abbey by playing in the nave. Earlier in the week they had entertained the crowd at the Oval Cricket Ground during the Test Match between England and New Zealand.

But the life-blood of the New Zealand brass band movement is the enthusiasm and hard work of the many bands in towns and villages throughout the two islands. This perhaps can be epitomised in the story of the Hastings Citizens Band. Founded in 1886, the band needed a new band-room in 1977 — and discovered one. Unfortunately, it was on the wrong site. The band's own site was on the opposite side of the town. It was decided to hire a transporter and transfer the band-room intact! Curtains, carpets, kitchen fittings all remained, merely the roof came off to save damaging telephone wires in transit. Praying that there would be no rain,

Hastings Citizens Band (New Zealand) escorting its band-room to a new site at 7a.m. one March morning in 1977.
(Photograph — Hawke's Bay Herald Tribune)

the band played its band-room off the old site and on to the new one, at daybreak on March 31, 1977.

Despite the size of the country the pattern of brass band activity in Australia is very like that of New Zealand. There is a strong, democratically elected national body, the National Band Council of Australia, which deals directly with the Music Board of the Australian Council (equivalent of the Arts Council of Great Britain) on behalf of all Australian bands. The National Band Council determines contesting policy, but the organisation of national events is in the hands of local committees, as the annual events take place in different states each year. Financially this eases the cost of travelling for bands, otherwise if the bands from Perth had always to contest in Melbourne or Sydney they would be either permantly insolvent or would never participate in national events.

Contesting in Australia has changed very little in the twentieth century, and comments made by a reporter with the Besses o' th' Barn Band on their 1907 tour, could still apply today.

"The winner is declared on an aggregate of marks — test piece, selection and march. The contest itself does not differ much from our own except in detail, but their marching is something to be remembered. The committee contrived to put the best marching bands in Australia to compete while we were there. We have never seen anything like it in band-

The march diagram and instructions for the Display Marching Contest of the 1977 Australian National Brass Band Championships, held at Wagga Wagga.

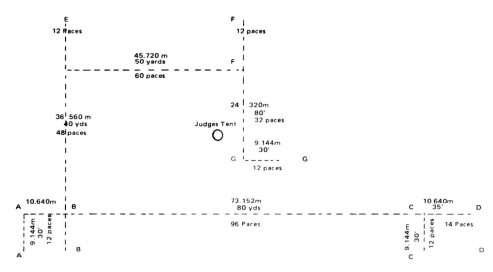

Band will fall in, in marching formation at point AA and prepare to move off playing the Quickstep March and march to point DD. On arriving at point DD Band will counter-march from front to rear to point CC, then counter-march from flank to flank, right turn and march to point AA. On arriving at point AA Band will counter-march from front to rear to point BB, then counter-march from flank to flank and continue marching to point E, right turn and march to point FF, right wheel and march to point GG, halt and continue to play march to the end of strain. Any band halting before or moving past point GG will be penalised one point for each pace.
NOTE: When Band turns right to counter-march from flank to flank at point BB, Drum Major and Drummers will turn left. When leading file is in line with left flank side-drummer, they will move off with Band and complete the diagram. Band means front rank.

201

ing. They have to march at the pace of 120 yards to the minute, playing all the while. They are judged on the exact space stepped. Then at the sound of a whistle, they have to turn left wheel, march about another 60 to 80 yards right wheel, come to a point indicated and counter-march, each player twisting and turning in bewildering fashion and yet in perfect order. Sometimes drums behind, next in front, until one gasps and wonders how they do it."

Even at the beginning of the century the Australians were inviting adjudicators out from England to judge the main musical events, which at that time took place in Ballarat, Victoria. But in 1910, there was an outcry in the *Australian Bandsman.*

"I should not be surprised to find that after this year we shall have seen the last of the English judges in Australia. Why bring them out at enormous cost if they are no better than Australian and New Zealand judges? At first we thought they were. Now we know they're not."

Whatever caused that outburst in 1910, the writer was quite wrong in his assumption. They had not seen the last of English judges. Geoffrey Brand adjudicated the Australian

Hawthorn City Band, the 1979 Australian champions, taking part in the Display Marching Contest on the banks of the Swan River, Perth. The band is executing a square right turn towards the President of the Australian National Band council, Fred Hodgkinson, who stands ready to take the salute. Marching adjudicator, Syd Court, brother of Sir Charles Court, Premier of Western Australia, can be seen in the back-ground.

National Brass Band Championships in Wagga Wagga, N.S.W., in 1977. Roy Newsome adjudicated at Melbourne, Victoria, in 1978 and Geoffrey Brand returned in 1979 to adjudicate at Perth, Western Australia. Dr. Denis Wright, Eric Ball, Harry Mortimer and Walter Hargreaves have all paid postwar visits to Australia as teachers and adjudicators.

The brass band traffic between Australia and England is not entirely one way. In 1934 Frank Wright, an outstanding Australian cornet soloist, a fine adjudicator and a conductor, arrived in England. Almost immediately he was invited to participate in brass band events at the highest level. He adjudicated the championship section at the Crystal Palace shortly after he arrived and was then invited to tour as the conductor of St. Hilda's. He remained a highly respected and much sought after adjudicator for almost forty years. His brass band arrangements of classical works are frequently used as top section test pieces, but they are not just played at contests and then left to gather dust in the cupboard, they remain popular items in the concert repertoire.

His death in 1970 left a gap in British brass band circles, and Australians can be justly proud of this man who made such an impact on this side of the world.

Between Australia and New Zealand there is a regular flow, not only of adjudicators, but also of bands and soloists to participate in contests. State events are sometimes as attractive as the National Contests because of the timing. The Australian National Brass Band Championships always take place at Easter, whilst the New Zealanders compete for National titles in early May. Every Australian state has its own, very active, brass band association which promotes annual contests for full bands, soloists and quartets. These events can stimulate a new spurt of activity before both

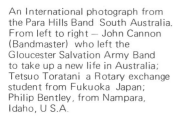

An International photograph from the Para Hills Band South Australia. From left to right — John Cannon (Bandmaster) who left the Gloucester Salvation Army Band to take up a new life in Australia; Tetsuo Toratani a Rotary exchange student from Fukuoka Japan; Philip Bentley, from Nampara, Idaho, U.S.A.

203

Frank Wright, an outstanding cornet soloist, who left Australia in 1934 and until his death in 1970, was highly regarded in U.K. brass band circles as an adjudicator and arranger.

countries slow down for their lengthy Christmas/summer holidays, or can rejuvenate interest immediately after.

In 1978 the National Band Council of Australia appointed a full time liaison officer to be responsible for the co-ordination of band activities, courses and educational programme throughout Australia. New Zealand has followed with a similar appointment. In the United Kingdom we are a very long way from such unity.

Surprisingly, those who emigrated from Britain to Canada did not carry the enthusiasm for band activity with them, like the early settlers to Australia and New Zealand. Consequently the band pattern in Canada has closely followed that of the U.S.A. The wind band predominates. However, this is not to say that there are no pockets of interest particularly in Salvation Army circles. It was to satisfy this enthusiasm that four top class British bands were flown to Canada in 1972 to perform massed band concerts in Niagara and to tour extensively in the region as individual units. The bands were Black Dyke Mills, CWS (Manchester), G.U.S. and Fairey. Each took their resident conductor but three guest conductors, Eric Ball, Geoffrey Brand and Harry Mortimer, accompanied the bands. A plane load of supporters travelled to Niagara to share the excitement. A number of them were elderly band enthusiasts who had never set foot outside England before. Enthusiasts crossed the Atlantic from Europe and there were even visitors from Australia and New Zealand. The tour was a great social and musical success, but unfortunately not a financial one, so that plans to repeat the operation two years later were abandoned.

The pattern of English-style brass band music-making in Europe, is interesting. France, Italy, Spain are definitely not involved, although a group of Spaniards attended the National and European events at the Royal Albert Hall in October, 1978. So who knows? In Germany there is a small, but avid group of listeners and performers, whilst in Belgium through the enthusiasm of a small number of families there are a few English type brass bands and a National Youth Band of Belgium has been established. The Youth Band is based on the pattern of the National Youth Brass Band of Great Britain, the enthusiasts having spent many hours listening to, talking about, and observing the residential courses of the N.Y.B.B. It is felt that brass band music, unrelated to religion and politics, has more chance of succeeding with the youth of Belgium, than with their elders.

Across the border, in Holland, English style brass bands are firmly established. Before World War Two, music publisher Pete Molenaar had established strong links with the British

scene, through John Henry Iles. He was elated at the liberation and determined to continue the work already begun. There are now numerous brass bands in Holland, contests are held regularly, visits from English brass bands might be called constant and hundreds of Dutch brass band enthusiasts fly into London each October to participate in the Royal Albert Hall events.

The first British-style brass band in Luxembourg was founded in June 1973. In the middle of the photograph is the conductor M. Fred Harles and on his left is M. Gust Reimen, director of the school of music from which most of the band came.

So great is the influx of European visitors that a reader of the *British Bandsman* recently (December 30, 1978) felt compelled to put pen to paper and protest at the number of visitors from the continent to "our National event." But, the director of the Royal Dutch Federation of Brass Bands felt equally compelled to reply: "Don't forget that the National is the top event in brass band music, just as in former times British football was top in the world of soccer. Therefore, we come from abroad with our musicians, composers, publishers and instrument salesmen. We meet and invite British bands to come to us. We pay them for coming. British companies sell instruments, music and records in Europe.

"While it is your National, it is also an international event for people who like good brass band music."

As well as the Dutch, the Swiss like good brass band music and organised trips from Switzerland to London in October have been a regular event for a number of years. Equally, English bands are annually invited to enthral the Swiss with their music, who in turn overwhelm the brass bandsmen with their hospitality.

Switzerland is a country of cultural and language differences, so that the formation of a Swiss Brass Band Association in 1977 was a considerable achievement. The association hopes to assist young and small brass bands to achieve higher standards and wants to establish more communication between British and Swiss bands. The first National Brass Band Contest held under the auspices of the new association was on November 25, 1978, in Zurich and one of the adjudicators was Roy Newsome.

Following the event Roy wrote in the *International Bandsman* on the choice of adjudicators, Albert Benz, Jean Balissat and himself: "The philosophy behind the choice of adjudicator is to get as wide as possible a view on the musical quality of the performance. Mr. Benz is for the German speaking part of Switzerland and Mr. Balissat for the French speaking part (each with its own style and tradition) and of course I was the British representative, as all the bands taking part in this particular competition are to some extent influenced by the British style of brass band playing."

Like the Belgians, the Swiss also have a National Youth Brass Band and often invite not only a conductor from England for the course, but also outstanding instrumentalists who perform and instruct.

Perhaps in each of the European countries with a brass band development, there has been a pioneer, or group of pioneers. Certainly the pioneer in Denmark was Herbert Møller and his guide and mentor was Dr. Denis Wright. The change to British brass band instrumentation began to take place in the 1950s, when a group of thinking, musically interested young Danes were inspired by Herbert Møller to form brass bands and acquaint themselves with the repertoire. Contesting for the Danes is a continuing topic of discussion. Many will claim to be non-competitive. Nevertheless, bi-annual National Brass Band Championships are held and in 1978 the events lasted two days. Geoffrey Brand was one of the adjudicators (the other two were distinguished Danish

The first National Brass Band Championship of Belgium took place on November 11, 1978. This photograph of Sone Vole Brass Band, from Kapellen, Antwerp was taken on that occasion, with Louis Cuypers conducting.

musicians) and his comments on the own choice section of the contest are quite illuminating. "The own choice section produced highly interesting performances. Danish bands know the British repertoire quite intimately, especially the more serious items from it. They are not as influenced in their choice by tradition as one sometimes feels with British bands. Recently written music was prevalent. Of special interest were some of the items written by Danish composers. Gone is the day when brass band music was only written by British composers."

Twenty-five minutes by hydrofoil across the water from Copenhagen, is Malmo, in southern Sweden. This is the home of several brass bands, including Limhamms. Formed by Bertil Hansson, who had a Salvation Army background and a burning desire to establish British style brass bands in Sweden, the band was originally named LKU and was attached to a church in Limhamms. English conductors have regularly been invited to work with the band and members are frequent visitors to England always with the desire of learning more. They had previously visited Scotland for the Edinburgh Festival Band Contest in the company of the Concorde Band from Copenhagen, Denmark, but it was not

Limhamms Band, Malmo, with their conductor Jan Eskil Anderson, achieved their ambition in 1978 when they travelled from Sweden to perform on English soil.

Above: Representing Sweden at the
first European Brass Band
Championships, held at the Royal
Albert Hall, London, in October
1978, was Solna Brass, conductor
Lars Gunnar Bjorklund. They
gained third place on an aggregate
of points.
(Keystone Press Agency Ltd.)

Right: In northern Denmark, young
brass players not only enjoy the
challenge of British brass band
music, but easily cope with the
language during a rehearsal conducted by a visitor from England.

until 1978 that they achieved their ambition of coming to England and playing on English soil, with their conductor Jan Eskil Andersson.

Further north, in Stockholm, is Solna Brass. This is a group of brass bandsmen who established themselves in 1970 under the direction of Per Ohlsson to perform the best in the brass band repertoire. Many of the members belonged to the Salvation Army, so there were no restrictions — Salvation Army and non Salvation Army music was included. Since its formation, Solna has toured Norway and England and in 1978 represented Sweden in the first European Brass Band Championships held in the Royal Albert Hall. They gained third place, based on an aggregate of points for playing a set piece, plus an own choice.

Norway is developing, particularly with young musicians, the British style brass band and, in 1974, City of London Brass was invited, not just to give concerts, but to teach groups of young Norwegian brass players. Subsequently, a member of the band took up residence in Norway to swell the numbers of those teaching brass the British way.

Luxembourg, the Faroe Islands, Iceland and Japan, all have brass bands. They all look to the United Kingdom for stimulation and inspiration. Either they invite English brass band trainers to work with their groups, or they come to England to listen and learn. It is gratifying that whilst in so

Brass Band Speicher was the first British style brass band in Switzerland. It was founded in the early 1950s by its present conductor Ernst Graf, who had lived in Northern Ireland for about twenty years.

The National Youth Band of
Switzerland was founded in 1976
by Markus S. Bach who used the
National Youth Brass Band of
Great Britain as a model. This
photograph was taken at the 1978
course when the conductors were
Albert Benz and Markus Bach. The
tutors were Jean-Michel Chappot
and from England, Graham Walker
and Barrie Perrins (a contributor to
this book)

In 1968 the first brass band was
formed in Germany -- Musik korps
der freivillingen Feuerwehr
Hamburg-Sasel, attached to the
Auxiliary Fire Brigade of Sasel, a
suburb of Hamburg. The man
inspired to form this group was
Armin Forst a great brass band enthusiast who received considerable
help from Herbert Moller of
Denmark.

many fields British has ceased to be best, in the world of brass bands it is universally ackowledged that British bands are still supreme.

This panoramic view of the brass band scene is intentionally superficial. No doubt, given time, each country will produce its own in-depth survey, but for now, it is important to record that this form of amateur music-making is long-established in parts of the Commonwealth and is proving to be an esteemed export to Europe and beyond.

References

The British Bandsman, published by British Bandsman Ltd
The International Bandsman, published by British Bandsman Ltd
The Music of the People – the story of the Band Movement in New Zealand
– by S.P. Newcomb, published by G.R. Mowat, New Zealand.

Gordon Higginbottom of Versatile Brass coaching a member of the 1979 National Youth Brass Band of Switzerland, during the summer course, which took place on the banks of Lake Thun, surrounded by the Alps.

Photograph by P. Hegmaier.

Markus Bach, founder of the National Youth Brass Band of Switzerland, conducting a rehearsal on their 1979 summer course.

Photograph by P. Hegmaier.

14. A hobby
for life

by VIOLET BRAND

In a century which has seen the change from active participation in entertainment to passive watching whilst others perform, the brass band has survived remarkably well. Not only has it survived in its traditional form, but it has begun to push out the frontiers socially, musically and geographically without the help of the mass media and the false boom created by the advertising gimmicks of big business.

At a time when group and self-discipline are unfashionable, when taking is more in vogue than giving and when there is an acknowledged generation gap, the brass band should predictably have faded away. But there are thousands in this country who willingly submit themselves to the rigours of both private and group practice, who wish to raise money for their band, and happily play in the same unit as father and possibly grandfather.

What is the twentieth century attraction of brass bands?

In some parts of the country, it is certainly tradition. Father teaches son, or maybe father's band has a junior section and it is the most natural thing in the world for the young boy of seven or eight to want to play a brass instrument. Father shuts himself away to practise and goes out regularly twice a week to rehearsal. There are contests and concerts to attend. Sometimes father comes home with a silver cup that he has won and the family joins in the general celebrations. When old enough, the children go along to band events too. There are the very special days at Belle Vue, Manchester, when "all the fun of the fair" can be incorporated with a band contest.

Then in the young boy's life, comes the day when he is the contestant, and mother and father, uncles and aunts, grandparents and cousins are all in the audience listening to him playing his solo, or the band performing its test piece.

As we enter the 1980s it may not be just the son of the household who is taking up father's hobby. Girls are very much part of the brass band scene and it might be that mother is a brass instrumentalist too. She could have even met father in a brass band, for romances flourish in school and youth bands.

Brass bands in the mid-twentieth century have not stuck to their traditional social and geographical boundaries. Changes have taken place largely through education. A new awareness of the value of teaching brass band instruments in schools has arisen. The primary value is seen to be the speed with which a brass ensemble can create musical performances, but a secondary and more enduring value is the provision of a lifetime hobby plus the satisfying of the com-

Ninety-two year old Edward Tadd, who joined Chichester City Band at the age of 16 years, was still a playing member seventy-six years later. He is seen here with his son, Eric, who joined the band, aged 12½ years and is still playing fifty-five years later. Their combined playing years total one hundred and twenty-nine. (Photograph — Portsmouth and Sunderland Newspapers)

petitive spirit in teenagers. It has further been realised that the school brass band member gains in confidence, wider social contacts and travel. There is a great deal of fraternisation between school bands and visits abroad are frequent.

There are, then, young people who are playing brass instruments and joining brass bands from families and regions where no tradition has previously existed. Parents are being introduced to this British form of amateur music-making which they may previously have associated only with factories and mines, or the bandstand on Sunday afternoon. For them the school band provides an insight to an unfamiliar world. They may spend hours travelling across the country to hear their band perform on concert or contest platform. They may find themselves organising money-raising events, so that the school band can go abroad.

The Woodward family of the City of Leicester Band. Linda, the mother, plays horn; her twelve year old daughter Nichola plays cornet; her nine year old son Paul plays drums, while eleven year old Andrew plays baritone. Her husband David is on trombone and her father Bernard plays the bass.

Their involvement may not stop when their child leaves school as he may want to join the local band, if one exists. If it does not, they may be induced to join the organising committee of a completely new band. The lifetime hobby, which the music staff at school so confidently initiated their child into, might become their hobby too.

Parents who encourage their child to join the school-band at eleven, may not realise that they will still be following the fortunes of his band twelve or fifteen years later, perhaps for ever. It has been known for fathers to become so involved that they have left the ranks of the supporters to become learners and later to join the band as playing members.

The brass band is a particularly valuable outlet for the

teenager. He submits to discipline in his musical performances and conforms in his appearance so as to be an acceptable member of the band. He cannot "do his own thing" within the unit. He can pit himself against others and use up his aggressive feelings in a perfectly acceptable way on the contest platform. He learns to become a good loser as well as a good winner. He knows also that he is part of a progressive musical organisation. He need not feel frustrated on the bottom rung of the ladder. If he practises and has the ability, there is always a top class band available for him. He can become so engrossed in his personal practice and band commitments that he has no time for the anti-social pursuits of the bored teenager. When a high-ranking official at the Home Office was asked about the possibility of forming brass bands in prisons, he commented that there were very few brass instrumentalists confined within prison walls, as they were "usually too busy to get into trouble."

Three generations of the Chalk family are with Wilton & District Band. Percy plays bass, Dennis is the conductor and Jonathan is on trombone.

It is not just the young who benefit from this hobby. Their grandfathers, probably of pensionable age, may have decided to retire as players, but still find themselves involved as librarians, tea-makers, or draw-takers on contest day.

One Hertfordshire town has even formed a band for pensioners. It was discovered that a number of former bandsmen would love to "have a blow", and even though their teeth had gone, their eyesight was blurred and some were physically disabled, those afternoon sessions of making music on brass instruments and talking about band affairs, were just the therapy they needed. There were even the highlights of performing at Derby and Joan clubs and old people's homes.

The whole family may benefit from brass band connections. If a move to another part of the country, or even abroad, is necessary, strangeness will soon evaporate when contact is made with a band in the new area. Friendships will be established for playing members and supporters. Apart from playing with a new unit, the familiar pattern of regional and national contests will be the same. The same friends will be milling around, the same music will be performed and the adjudicators' faces will be familiar. The traditions of brass band contesting are national and a strong community sense permeates the whole of the brass band scene.

Even when going on holiday, many brass bandsmen actively seek out the local band in the seaside town of their choice and are delighted to join in the local activities during their stay. Families seem to enjoy the opportunity to make new friends and repeat the experience year after year. The *British Bandsman* annually carries a Summer Service column, where bands in holiday centres invite visitors and holiday-makers request information from unknown areas.

For some bandsmen their first trip abroad has been with a band. Many brass bands are invited to Europe to participate in music festivals, beer festivals and town twinning celebrations. Some arrange exchange visits with continental bands and long-lasting relationships are forged. Usually the bandsmen stay with families in their host town. Rarely do they stay in hotels. This has financial advantages and also has social advantages. There is no better way to understand a country and its people than to share their homes. Language barriers never seem to be insuperable when bands are the common interest.

Likewise, bands from the continent visit England and share experiences of the British brass band scene with their hosts. This is a great thrill, for many of them feel that they are reaching the roots of their hobby.

Annually, in October, brass band enthusiasts from the continent, from Canada, U.S.A., Australia and New Zealand descend on London in plane loads to share the excitement of the National Brass Band Championships at the Royal Albert Hall. This is a truly international occasion and is used by many British bandsmen to renew the friendships made on trips abroad.

Since World War Two the development of an international flavour to the British brass band scene has been one of the significant social changes, along with the interest being taken by education authorities. There have been other changes of equal significance.

James Rippin of Upminster, Essex proves that brass banding is a hobby for life. On the left he is seen in 1913 with his tenor horn, accompanied by his father and his cousin. On the right, sixty-three years later, James Rippin is still proudly holding his tenor horn.

216

It is less likely now, than at anytime in the past, that a bandsman's job and position in the band are in any way related. In the Black Dyke Mills Band there are fewer than half-a-dozen members working for the sponsoring firm and the same could be said for most of the bands bearing the name of a famous company or group. Bandsmen found it was disadvantageous to their business prospects to be in the firm as a cornet player, rather than, say, a cost accountant. Very few bands rehearse during business hours, even before major contests, as it is impossible for the men to get away from places of employment. By the same token, few brass bands spend summer weeks playing in seaside bandstands, or going on prolonged tours abroad. If they do undertake tours it is because bandsmen and families have agreed that the band tour should take precedence over an annual holiday.

The exception to the new employment conditions which bandsmen find themselves in, lies with the coal board bands. A significant number of their members work in the colliery or in associated industries.

A brass band romance. Murray and Josie played in the same band, Clacton-on-Sea, and were also members of the National Youth Brass Band. They are now married and have two young aspiring bandsmen of their own.

With the radical changes which have taken place in education circles and employment it is inevitable that brass bands will have a far wider social appeal than in prewar days. The dentist, the accountant, the solicitor and the research scientist will be just as enthusiastic about their banding as the miner, the factory worker and the lorry-driver, and within the band it will be their expertise on their instrument which counts, not their occupation, or social position.

In former years the professionally qualified son of a bandsman, who had perhaps also learned a brass instrument, would have buried this part of his life with shame. But more and more not only are these men continuing their banding in whichever part of the country they happen to be living, but they are even taking it up again after a lapse of several years, enjoying the social life and musical experiences it brings. Many of them too accept administrative responsibility within their own bands and in local and national associations.

We have reached the time when any child, at any school, in any part of the country, of either sex, is likely to confront its parents with the statement "I want to join a brass band". What is more, that child is likely to retain his active participation in brass band activities throughout his life right into retirement.

Surely this is a hobby for life.

Appendices

The Editors of
'Brass Bands in the 20th Century'
Violet and Geoffrey Brand

GEOFFREY BRAND

Geoffrey Brand was born into a Salvation Army family in Gloucester. He won an Open Scholarship to the Royal Academy of Music, London, and following national service in a military band, entered in 1947 until 1950. The trumpet and conducting were his principal studies.

He became a professional trumpet player, working regularly with the Royal Philharmonic, Philharmonia, and Covent Garden Orchestras. In 1955 he joined the BBC as a music producer; he also frequently conducted and adjudicated in this country and abroad and in 1967 left the BBC to concentrate on these activities.

He became the professional conductor of the Black Dyke Mills Band, winning major contesting awards and giving important first performances. From 1967 to 1975 he was Music Adviser to the National Youth Brass Band of Great Britain and editor of the *British Bandsman*.

Currently he is the conductor of the National Youth Brass Band of Scotland and professional adviser to the Brighouse and Rastrick Band. He has made numerous records for all the major companies and contributes regularly to radio and television programmes. He travels widely throughout Europe as a conductor and adjudicator. In 1975, 1977 and 1979 he adjudicated at the National Brass Band Championships of Australia and in 1972 and 1978 the National Brass Band Championships of New Zealand.

Geoffrey Brand is an examiner for Trinity College of Music, London.

VIOLET BRAND

Born into a Salvation Army family in Canterbury, Violet Brand has always been surrounded by brass band enthusiasts. She was educated at Simon Langton Girls' School.

In 1947, while a student at Avery Hill Teachers' Training College, London, she met Geoffrey Brand. They were married in 1950 and have two children — Michael, now a BBC producer, and Gillian, a medical social worker.

In 1959 Violet Brand returned to teaching and worked with children with learning difficulties. Her particular specialisation is with dyslexic children and adults.

From 1967 to 1975 she worked at 210, Strand editing the *British Bandsman*. During this time she learned a great deal about the brass band scene and became fascinated by the history of the brass band movement. She has travelled extensively with Geoffrey, meeting brass bandsmen all over the world. She particularly enjoys his work with young people and for eight years she was on the house staff of the National Youth Brass Band of Great Britain.

Since 1976 she has worked for the Adult Literacy Scheme at the Harrow College of Further Education.

Meet the contributors...

EDWARD GREGSON was born at Sunderland, County Durham, in 1945. At the age of eighteen he entered the Royal Academy of Music, London, where he studied piano and composition with Alan Bush. Whilst at the Academy he won five prizes for composition and had many works performed there. Now he devotes his time to composition, teaching and conducting.

Edward Gregson's brass music has received international recognition; his compositions are played at concerts throughout the world, and are regularly broadcast and recorded. Among his major contributions to the brass repertoire are a Horn Concerto (written for Ifor James), a Tuba Concerto (written for John Fletcher), and a Brass Quintet (written for the Philip Jones Brass Ensemble). In addition he has written orchestral music, chamber music, piano music and music for the theatre.

He is at present a Senior Lecturer in Music at the University of London Goldsmiths' College.

MAUD WRIGHT was born in 1915 and educated in Glasgow. In 1932 she joined an Insurance Company and studied for Associateship of the Chartered Insurance Institute. Subsequently she decided against insurance as a career and joined the BBC in Glasgow in 1938 working first on Children's Hour and later on the administrative side dealing with contracts and copyright. In 1942 she transferred to BBC External Services in London to do similar work in the fast growing overseas broadcasting service.

She first became interested in bands when helping Dr. Denis Wright with correspondence for his non-BBC band activities and assisted in the formation of the National Youth Brass Band. She is still a member of the Council and Treasurer for the Band.

In 1955, she married but continued with BBC work, moving to wider administrative and personnel posts, first as Assistant Administrative Officer for the European Service and later Senior Personnel Officer for the BBC's Administrative Directorate.

She is a member of the Institute of Personnel Management, and although now retired, serves part time as a Panel Member on Industrial Tribunal hearings.

CHARLES SWEBY, M.B.E., L.R.A.M. learned to play piano, organ and viola. An accident and operation limited opportunities to exploit a traditional musical education which was to be useful when he became a school music teacher. His interest in brass bands was that of many musicians with a similar traditional background.

His conversion began when he read "Music through the Brass Band" and discussed it with Ernest Hall during a teachers' refresher course in 1956. He founded a school band, joined the N.S.B.B.A., and was its secretary for fourteen years. He was awarded the M.B.E. in 1977 and became chairman of the association.

ERIC BALL was born in Bristol, on October 31, 1903. He acquired his musical education through the church and the Salvation Army. He became a Salvation Army Officer and worked with the Salvation Army Music Editorial Department and conducted the Salvationist Publishing Supplies Band for a number of years.

He left the Salvation Army during the second World War and subsequently conducted contesting bands. In 1952 he became editor of the British Bandsman and Music editor of R. Smith & Co. He held these positions until 1967. Throughout his life, Eric Ball has composed music for the brass band and is renowned for his work throughout the world.

BRADLEY CATTO is 51 years of age and was born and educated in Dundee. After Army service, mainly in the Middle East, his music studies gained him the L.R.A.M. and A.R.C.M. diplomas. He entered the teaching profession in 1954 and was ten years a principal teacher in Dundee before being apponted Music Organiser to Clackmannanshire in 1965. In 1975 he was appointed Adviser in Music to the Central Region. He has served on the executive committee for the Scottish Amateur Music Association since 1967, when he was made Director of the Training School for Young Brass Players. In 1971 he took over as Director of the National Youth Brass Band of Scotland.

TIM MUTUM, A.I.C.S. was born in Bury St Edmunds, Suffolk in 1955 but has spent most of his life in Ipswich and is married to a local girl.
Professionally he is a Chartered Secretary working in local government.

He started to learn to play the piano at the age of seven and the euphonium when he was eleven. He is very keen on brass bands and is a founder member of a local Ipswich Band, but has also played in several other bands in the area. He developed an excessive enthusiasm for brass band records and has a large collection of LP's and 78's.

He has contributed record reviews to the weekly paper *British Mouthpiece* for a year and is currently record critic for the monthly journal *Brass Band News.*

BARRIE PERRINS has been principal euphonium of The Hendon Band, London, since 1960 and National Champion Euphonium Soloist of Great Britain on four occasions. He has also twice been runner-up for the title of Champion Soloist of Great Britain. He has successfully participated in approximately 150 solo competitions (including sonata and concerto events) and often lectures on brass instruments for societies and educational establishments. An instructor-soloist at band camps in Europe, he frequently plays as guest soloist in Britain, Belgium, Switzerland and the Netherlands; he toured the USA in 1962 and has featured on British and foreign radio and television programmes. A regular contributor to music journals in Britain and abroad, nearly 400 articles, book/music/record reviews by him have been published. An adjudicator at the 1976 Swiss National Solo Championships, he was awarded the Insignia of Honour that year for service to the Brass Band Movement. Although he has choral and orchestral (violin and tuba) experience, he prefers the musical variety and purpose of the brass band. He also has an interest in musicology and music therapy. By profession Mr. Perrins is a legal assistant with a Local Authority.

The Contemporary Repertoire

Malcolm Arnold	Little Suite No.1	
	Little Suite No.2	
	Fantasy	
	Song of Freedom	
George Benjamin	Altitude	
Harrison Birtwistle	Grimethorpe Aria	
Derek Bourgeois	1st Concerto	
	2nd Concerto	
	Concerto for Brass Quintet and Band	
	Serenade	
Howard Burrell	Occasion	
Arthur Butterworth	A Dales Suite	
	Path Across the Moors	
	Three Impressions	
Frank Cordell	Spirals	
Martin Dalby	Music for a Brass Band	
David Dorward	Contest for Brass	
David Graham Ellis	Diamond Piece	
Jim Ellis	Formants of the Steeples and the Mountains	
John Maxwell Geddes	Fanfare	
Edward Gregson	Horn Concerto	
	Tuba Concerto	
	Connotations	
	Intrada	
	Concerto Grosso	
	Essay	
Wilfred Heaton	Contest Music	
Anthony Hedges	Psalm 150	
Hans Werner Henze	Ragtimes and Habaneras	
Joseph Horovitz	Euphonium Concerto	
	Sinfonietta	
	Samson	
	The Dong with a Luminous Nose	
Elgar Howarth	Fireworks	
	Ascendit in coeli	

	Cornet Concerto
	Trombone Concerto
	Mosaic
	In Memoriam-R.K.
John Howerd	The Two Regions
Wilfred Josephs	Concerto for Brass Band
Bryan Kelly	Provence
	Washington DC
	Divertimento
Philip Lane	A Spring Overture
David Lumsdaine	Evensong
John McCabe	Images
William Matthias	Vivat Regina
Thea Musgrave	Variations
Buxton Orr	Trumpet Concerto
	Trombone Concerto
Paul Patterson	Chromascope
	Countdown
	Cataclysm
Anthony Payne	Fire on Whaleness
Kenneth Platts	Little Suite
Chris Sansom	Trumpet Concerto
Robert Simpson	Energy
Philip Sparke	Concert Prelude
Christopher Steel	Suite 'Odyssey'
Richard Steinitz	Tableau of the Animals
Phyllis Tate	Illustrations
Gilbert Vinter	Spectrum
	Cantata 'The Trumpets'
Gareth Walters	Processional
Michael Blake Watkins	AUbade
Graham Whettam	Partita
Graham Williams	Paean
Thomas Wilson	Sinfonietta
	Refrains and Cadenzas
	Cartoon
Gareth Wood	Trumpet Concerto
	Coliseum

List of commissions for the National Youth Brass Band of Scotland by the Scottish Amateur Music Association

Year	Title	Composer
1962	Variations on a Theme of Lully	Cedric Thorpe Davie
1963	Little Suite No. I	Malcolm Arnold
1963	Second Suite for Brass Band	Gordon Jacob
1964	Suite for Brass Band	Alan Rawsthorne
1965	Music for a Brass Band	Martin Dalby
1966	Contest for Brass Band	David Dorward
1966	Dance Scenes for Brass Band	David Dorward
1966	Variations for Brass Band	Thea Musgrave
1967	Sinfonietta	Thomas Wilson
1968	The Ballad of St. John's Town	Cedric Thorpe Davie
1968	Commission I	Bryden Thomson
1968	March : The NYBBS	Bryden Thomson
1969	Divertimento	Bryan Kelly
1972	Concerto Grosso	Edward Gregson
1973	A Suite of Edinburgh Dances	Bryan Kelly
1978	Culloden Moor	Gareth Wood

Music for Brass Bands by Eric Ball...

ORIGINAL WORKS
Akhnaton
American Sketches
A Psalm For All Nations
Call of the Sea
Celebration
Contest Day
Devon Fantasy
Divertimento
English Country Scenes
Everybody's Child
Festival Music
Four Preludes
Fowey River
High Peak
Holiday Overture
Holiday Suite
Homeward
Impromptu
Indian Summer
In Switzerland
Journey into Freedom
Kensington Concerto
Main Street
Morning Rhapsody
Oasis
Peniel
Petite Suite de Ballet
Princess and the Poet
Resurgam
Rhapsody on American
    Gospel Songs
Rhapsody on Negro
    Spirituals
Rhapsody on Negro
    Spirituals (No.2)

Rhapsody on Negro
    Spirituals (No.3)
Salute to Freedom
Sinfonietta – 'The
    Wayfarer'
St. Michael's Mount
Sunset Rhapsody
Swiss Festival Overture
Thanksgiving
The Ancient Temple
The Conquerors
The English Maiden
The Undaunted
The Young in Heart
Three Songs Without
    Words
Tournament for Brass
Youth Salutes a Master

MARCHES
October Festival
Rosslyn
Royal Salute
Sure and Steadfast
Torch of Freedom

SOLOS
Conchita (cornet)
Legend (trombone and
    piano)
Mountain Melody (horn)
September Fantasy
    (horn)

ENSEMBLES
Friendly Giants (quartet)

In This Hour of Softened
    Splendour (quartet)
Quartet for Tubas
Quid Pro Quo (double
    trio)

ARRANGEMENTS
All in the April Evening
    (Roberton)
Amen Chorus from
    'Messiah' (Handel)
Andaluza (Granados)
Cossack Patrol (Knipper)
Dances from 'Checkmate'
    (Bliss)
Egmont Overture
    (Beethoven)
Fascination (Marchetti)
Favourite Hymn Tunes
    (13)
Fugue in Eb 'St. Ann'
    (J.S. Bach)
Galantia (Scull)
Golliwog's Cake Walk
    (Debussy)
Harry Lauder's Songs
Jesu, Comfort of My
    Heart (J.S. Bach)
Orb and Sceptre (Walton)
Prelude to 'The Dream of
    Gerontius' (Elgar)
Rhondda Rhapsody
    (Jones)

Suite Gothique
    (Boellman)
The Homeland (Sullivan)
The Long Day Closes
    (Sullivan)
Themes from Symphony
    No.1 (Beethoven)
Themes from Symphony
    No.9 (choral section)
    (Beethoven)
Themes from Symphony
    No.5 (Tchaikovsky)
The Wizard of Oz
    (Arden)
Two Preludes (Chopin)
Waltz Memories of
    Schubert
We Wish You a Merry
    Christmas (Scull)
Worthy is the Lamb from
    'Messiah' (Handel)

SOLOS
Andantino (Stradella)
Berceuse de Jocelyn
    (Godard)
The One-note Bugler
    (Scull)
To a Wild Rose
    (McDowell)

BAND AND CHOIR
A Christchurch Cantata
For All Mankind
Hail to the Lord's
    Anointed

...and his Salvation Army Music

A Carol Fantasy
Adoration
An Appeal
A Soldier's Experience
A Soul's Awakening
A Soul's Triumph
A Warning Message
A Warrior's Testimony
Break Forth Into Joy
Centennial Review
Challenge and Response
Constant Trust
Devoted Service
Exodus
Forward to the Fight
Glory Songs
Good News
Hanover
Hold Thou My Hand
In the Power of the Spirit
In the Ranks
Invitation and Warning
Joy of the Redeemed
Lessons from Nature

Love Divine
Meditation on a Theme
    by Spohr
More Than Conquerors
Night of Wonder
O'er Mountain and
    Valley
O God, Our Help
On Service Overseas
O Remember Calvary
Our Saviour's Praise
Peace With God
Perfect Trust
Pilgrim Way –
    Meditation
Psalm 150
Sanctuary
Saviour and Friend
Songs for Pilgrims
Songs in Exile
Song of Courage
Songs of the Fight
Songs of the Morning
Songs of the Valiant

Sound Out the
    Proclamation
The Awakeners
The Day of Victory
The Eternal Presence
The Good Old Way
The King of Kings
The Kingdom
    Triumphant
The Old Wells
The Pilgrim Way – Suite
The Saviour's Invitation
The Triumph of Peace
The Victory of Love
The Warrior's Reward
The Whole Armour of
    God
Through Storm to Safety
True Life
Trust in God
War Songs No.1
War Songs No.2
We Will Fight

MARCHES
Fight On
Hoist the Flag
In the Light
Pledge for Service
Star Lake
Star Lake No.2
The Golden Stair
The Gospel Feast
Torchbearers
Wondrous Love

SOLOS
Clear Skies
Glory to His Name
In the Army
Song of Faith
Swiss Melodies
The Challenge

ENSEMBLES
Jewels (quartet)
Love Eternal (quartet)
Never Give Up (double
    quartet)

British 'Open' Championship Results

Year	Placing		Conductor	Test Piece
1853	1.	Mossley Temperance Saxhorn	William Taylor	Own choice
	2.	Dewsbury		
	3.	Bramley Temperance		
1854	1.	Leeds Railway Foundry	Richard Smith	Own choice
	2.	Dewsbury		
	3.	Accrington		
1855	1.	Accrington	Radcliffe Barnes	'Orynthia' (Melling)
	2.	Leeds Railway Foundry		plus own choice
	3.	Mossley Temperance Saxhorn		
1856	1.	Leeds Railway Foundry	Richard Smith	'Stradella' Overture (Flotow)
	2.	Leeds (Smith's)		plus own choice
	3.	Accrington		
1857	1.	Leeds (Smith's)	Richard Smith	'Il Trovatore' (Verdi)
	2.	Dewsbury		plus own choice
	3.	Todmorden		
1858	1.	Accrington	Radcliffe Barnes	'On Thee each living soul awaits'
	2.	Dewsbury		and 'Achieved is the glorious work'
	3.	Mossley Temperance		from *The Creation* (Haydn)
1859	NO CONTEST			
1860	1.	Halifax (4th West Yorkshire Rifle Volunteers)		'Zampa' Overture (Herold) plus own choice
	2.	Dewsbury		
	3.	Sherwood		
1861	1.	Halifax (4th West Yorkshire Rifle Volunteers)		'Satanella' (Balfe) plus own choice
	2.	Dewsbury Rifle Corps		
	3.	Chesterfield		
1862	1.	Black Dyke Mills	Samuel Longbottom	'Muette de Portici' (Auber)
	2.	Dewsbury		plus own choice
	3.	Chesterfield		
1863	1.	Black Dyke Mills	Samuel Longbottom	'Faust' (Gounod)
	2.	Bacup 4th Lancashire Rifle Volunteers		plus own choice
	3.	Craven Amateur, Silsden, nr. Leeds		
1864	1.	Bacup	John Lord	'The Reminiscences of Auber'
	2.	Stalybridge Old		plus own choice
	3.	Leeds Model		
1865	1.	Bacup	John Lord	'Un Ballo in Maschera' (Verdi)
	2.	Dewsbury		plus own choice
	3.	Matlock		
1866	1.	Dewsbury Old	John Peel	'L'Africaine' (Meyerbeer)
	2.	Matlock Bridge		plus own choice
	3.	Healey Hall		
1867	1.	Clay Cross, 3rd Batt Rifle Volunteers	John Naylor	'Der Freischutz' (Weber)
	2.	Bacup		
	3.	Compstall Bridge		
1868	1.	Burnley 17th Lancashire Rifle Volunteers		'Robert le Diable' (Meyerbeer)
	2.	Heckmondwike		
	3.	Black Dyke Mills		

1869	1. Bacup 2. Matlock 3. Burnley	John Lord	'Le Prophète' (Meyerbeer)
1870	1. Bacup 2. Matlock 3. Dewsbury	John Lord	'Ernani' (Verdi)
1871	1. Black Dyke Mills 2. Bury Borough 3. Bacup	Samuel Longbottom	'Il Barbiere' (Rossini)
1872	1. Robin Hood Rifles 2. Saltaire 3. Meltham Mills	H. Leverton	'Souvenir de Mozart'
1873	1. Meltham Mills 2. Robin Hood 3. Black Dyke	John Gladney	'Dinorah' (Meyerbeer)
1874	1. Linthwaite 2. Meltham Mills 3. Besses o' th' Barn	Edwin Swift	'Faust' (Spohr)
1875	1. Kingston Mills 2. Meltham Mills 3. Linthwaite	John Gladney	'Il Talismano' (Balfe)
1876	1. Meltham Mills 2. Kingston Mills 3. Holm Mills	John Gladney	'Aida' (Verdi)
1877	1. Meltham Mills 2. Black Dyke Mills 3. Holm Mills	John Gladney	'Jessonda' (Spohr)
1878	1. Meltham Mills 2. Kidsgrove 3. Denton Original	John Gladney	'Romeo e Giulietta' (Gounod)
1879	1. Black Dyke Mills 2. Accrington 3. Barnsley	J. Fawcett	'The Last Judgement' (Spohr)
1880	1. Black Dyke Mills 2. Stalybridge 3. Nelson	Alex Owen	'Vespri Siciliani' (Verdi)
1881	1. Black Dyke Mills 2. Meltham Mills 3. Stalybridge	Alex Owen	'Cinq Mars' (Gounod)
1882	1. Clayton-le-Moor 2. Linthwaite 3. Barnsley	Alex Owen	'Il Seraglio' (Mozart)
1883	1. Littleborough Public 2. Burslem 3. Honley	Edwin Swift	'Il Giuramento' (Mercadante)
1884	1. Honley 2. Oldham Rifles 3. Black Dyke Mills	John Gladney	'La Gazza Ladra' (Rossini)
1885	1. Kingston Mills 2. Littleborough Public 3. Besses o' th' Barn	John Gladney	'Nabucco' (Verdi)
1886	1. Kingston Mills 2. Heywood Rifles 3. Littleborough Public	John Gladney	'La Favorita' (Donizetti)

1887	1. Kingston Mills 2. Black Dyke Mills 3. Besses o' th' Barn	John Gladney	'L'Etoile du Nord' (Meyerbeer)
1888	1. Wyke Temperance 2. Black Dyke Mills 3. Todmorden Old	Edwin Swift	'Der Fliegende Holländer' (Wagner)
1889	1. Wyke Temperance 2. Kingston Mills 3. Leeds Forge	Edwin Swift	'La Reine de Saba' (Gounod)
1890	1. Batley Old 2. Leeds Forge 3. Wyke Temperance	John Gladney	'Euryanthe' (Weber)
1891	1. Black Dyke Mills 2. Wyke Temperance 3. Dewsbury Old	John Gladney	'Das Nachtlager in Granada' (Kreutzer)
1892	1. Besses o' th' Barn 2. Kingston Mills 3. Lindley	Alex Owen	'Zaar und Zimmermann' (Lortzing)
1893	1. Kington Mills 2. Cornholme 3. Rochdale Old	John Gladney	'Elaine' (Bemberg)
1894	1. Besses o' th' Barn 2. Kingston Mills 3. Black Dyke Mills	Alex Owen	'The Golden Web' (Goring Thomas)
1895	1. Black Dyke Mills 2. Wyke Temperance 3. Besses o' th' Barn	John Gladney	'Hansel und Gretel' (Humperdinck)
1896	1. Black Dyke Mills 2. Kingston Mills 3. Batley Old	John Gladney	'Gabriella' (Pizzi)
1897	1. Mossley 2. Kingston Mills 3. Batley Old	Alex Owen	'Moses in Egypt' (Rossini)
1898	1. Wyke Temperance 2. Hucknall Temperance 3. Lea Mills	Edwin Swift	Grand Fantasia from the works of Mendelssohn
1899	1. Black Dyke Mills 2. Hucknall Temperance 3. Lee Mount	John Gladney	'Aroldo' (Verdi)
1900	1. Lindley 2. Black Dyke 3. Pemberton Old	John Gladney	'La Gioconda' (Ponchielli)
1901	1. Kingston Mills 2. Lindley 3. Crooke	John Gladney	'Mirella' (Gounod)
1902	1. Black Dyke Mills 2. Pemberton Old 3. Besses o' th' Barn	John Gladney	'L'Ebreo' (Appoloni)
1903	1. Pemberton Old 2. Black Dyke Mills 3. Irwell Springs	John Gladney	'Caractacus' (Elgar)
1904	1. Black Dyke Mills 2. Pemberton Old 3. Lindley	John Gladney	'Semiramide' (Rossini)

1905	1. Irwell Springs 2. Black Dyke Mills 3. Lindley	William Rimmer	'Cosi Fan Tutte' (Mozart)
1906	1. Wingates Temperance 2. Goodshaw 3. Richdale Public	William Rimmer	'Les Huguenots' (Meyerbeer)
1907	1. Wingates Temperance 2. Black Dyke Mills 3. Goodshaw	William Rimmer	'Robin Hood' (MacFarren)
1908	1. Black Dyke Mills 2. Rushden Temperance 3. Perfection Soap Works	William Rimmer	'A Souvenir of Grieg'
1909	1. Foden's Motor Works 2. Black Dyke Mills 3. Perfection Soap Works	William Rimmer	'Il Bravo' (Marliani)
1910	1. Foden's Motor Works 2. Shaw 3. Perfection Soap Works	William Halliwell	'Acis and Galatea' (Handel)
1911	1. Hebden Bridge 2. Foden's Motor Works 3. Perfection Soap Works	William Halliwell	'Eugene Onegin' (Tchaikovsky)
1912	1. Foden's Motor Works 2. St Hilda Colliery 3. Shaw	William Halliwell	'Les Diamants de la Couronne' (Auber)
1913	1. Foden's Motor Works 2. Shaw 3. Irwell Springs	William Halliwell	'A Souvenir of Gounod'
1914	1. Black Dyke Mills 2. Wingates Temperance 3. Foden's Motor Works	J. A. Greenwood	'Joseph und seine Bruder' (Mehul)
1915	1. Foden's Motor Works 2. Horwich Railway Mechanics Institute (RMI) 3. Kings Cross, Halifax	William Halliwell	'Il Furioso' (Donizetti)
1916	1. Horwich RMI 2. Foden's Motor Works 3. Black Dyke Mills	J. A. Greenwood	'La Traviata' (Verdi)
1917	1. Horwich RMI 2. Black Dyke Mills 3. Woodlands Village	J. A. Greenwood	'Le Pre aux Clercs' (Herold)
1918	1. Wingates Temperance 2. Irwell Springs 3. Besses o'th'Barn	William Halliwell	'Il Bravo' (Marliani)
1919	1. Harton Colliery 2. Wingates Temperance 3. St Hilda Colliery	G. Hawkins	'The Lily of Killarney' (Benedict)
1920	1. Besses o'th'Barn 2. Wingates Temperance 3. Yorkshire Main Colliery	W. Wood	'I Lombardi' (Verdi)
1921	1. Wingates Temperance 2. Barrow Shipyard 3. Black Dyke Mills	William Halliwell	'Maritana (Vincent Wallace)
1922	1. South Elmsall and Frickley Colliery 2. Black Dyke Mills 3. Besses o'th'Barn	Noel Thorpe	'Lohengrin' (Wagner)

1923	1. Wingates Temperance 2. Creswell Colliery 3. Besses o'th'Barn	William Halliwell	'Dinorah' (Meyerbeer)
1924	1. Australia (Newcastle Steel Works) 2. Creswell Colliery 3. Harton Colliery	A. H. Bailie	'Selection from Liszt'
1925	1. Creswell Colliery 2. Nutgrove 3. Foden's Motor Works	J. A. Greenwood	'Macbeth' (Keighley)
1926	1. Foden's Motor Works 2. Wingates Temperance 3. St Hilda Colliery	William Halliwell	'A Midsummer Night's Dream' (Keighley)
1927	1. Foden's Motor Works 2. Callender's Cable Works 3. Milnrow Public	William Halliwell	'Merry Wives of Windsor' (Keighley)
1928	1. Foden's Motor Works 2. Callender's Cable Works 3. Nutgrove	William Halliwell	'Lorenzo' (Keighley)
1929	1. Brighouse and Rastrick 2. Wingates Temperance 3. Carlisle St Stephens	F. Berry	'Pathétique' (Beethoven)
1930	1. Eccles Borough 2. Milnrow Public 3. Wingates Temperance	J. Dow	'Oriental Rhapsody' (Granville Bantock)
1931	1. Besses o'th'Barn 2. Glazebury 3. Milnrow Public	William Halliwell	Suite: 'Springtime' (Haydn Morris)
1932	1. Brighouse and Rastrick 2. Nelson Old 3. Metropolitan Works	William Halliwell	'The Crusaders' (Keighley)
1933	1. Brighouse and Rastrick 2. Baxendale's Works 3. Amington	William Halliwell	'Princess Nada' (Denis Wright)
1934	1. Brighouse and Rastrick 2. Black Dyke Mills 3. Wingates Temperance	William Halliwell	'Pageantry' (Herbert Howells)
1935	1. Black Dyke Mills 2. Wingates Temperance 3. Abram Colliery	William Halliwell	'A Northern Rhapsody' (Keighley)
1936	1. Brighouse and Rastrick 2. Agram Colliery 3. Luton	William Halliwell	'Robin Hood' (Geehl)
1937	1. Besses o'th'Barn 2. Slaithwaite 3. Black Dyke Mills	W. Wood	'Academic Festival Overture' (Brahms arr. Denis Wright)
1938	1. Slaithwaite 2. Black Dyke Mills 3. Luton	N. Thorpe	'Owain Glyndwr' (Maldwyn Price)
1939	1. Wingates Temperance 2. Nelson 3. Brighouse and Rastrick	W. Wood	'A Downland Suite' (Ireland)
1940	1. Bickershaw Colliery 2. Creswell Colliery 3. Brighouse and Rastrick	W. Haydock	'Clive of India' (Holbrooke)

Year	Placings	Conductor	Test Piece
1941	1. Fairey Aviation Works 2. Carlton Main Frickley Colliery 3. City of Coventry	Harry Mortimer	Choice: (a) 'Academic Festival Overture' (b) 'Robin Hood' (c) 'The Crusaders'
1942	1. Fairey Aviation Works 2. Bickershaw Colliery 3. City of Coventry	Harry Mortimer	Choice: (a) 'Lorenzo' (b) 'Pageantry'
1943	1. Bickershaw Colliery 2. Fairey Aviation 3. Creswell Colliery	W. Haydock	Themes from 'Symphony No. 5' (Beethoven arr. Denis Wright)
1944	1. Fairey Aviation 2. Creswell Colliery 3. Bickershaw Colliery	Harry Mortimer	Fantasia: 'The Tempest' (Maurice Johnson)
1945	1. Fairey Aviation 2. Grimethorpe Colliery 3. Bickershaw Colliery	Harry Mortimer	'Pride of Race' (K. A. Wright)
1946	1. Bickershaw Colliery 2. Fairey Aviation 3. Munn and Felton's	Harry Mortimer	'Salute to Freedom' (Eric Ball)
1947	1. Fairey Aviation 2. Wingates Temperance 3. Creswell Colliery	Harry Mortimer	Tone Poem: 'Henry V' (Maldwyn Price)
1948	1. CWS Manchester 2. Fairey Aviation 3. Carlton Main Frickley Colliery	Eric Ball	'Music for Brass' (Denis Wright)
1949	1. Fairey Aviation 2. Ransome and Marle's 3. Munn and Felton's	Harry Mortimer	'Rhapsody in Brass' (Dean Goffin)
1950	1. Fairey Aviation 2. Cory Workmen's 3. Carlton Main Frickley Colliery	Harry Mortimer	'Resurgam' (Eric Ball)
1951	1. Ransome and Marle's 2. Prescot Cable Works 3. CWS Manchester	Eric Ball	'The Conquerors' (Eric Ball)
1952	1. CWS Manchester 2. Foden's Motor Works 3. Munn and Felton's	Eric Ball	'Scena Sinfonica' (Geehl)
1953	1. National Band of New Zealand 2. Fairey Aviation 3. Black Dyke Mills	K. G. L. Smith	'The Three Musketeers' (George Hespe)
1954	1. Munn and Felton's 2. Ferodo Works 3. John White Footwear	Stanley Boddington	'Tournament for Brass' (Eric Ball)
1955	1. Ferodo Works 2. John White Footwear 3. CWS Manchester	George Hespe	'Sinfonietta for Brass Band' (Eric Leidzen)
1956	1. Fairey Aviation 2. CWS Manchester 3. Carlton Main Frickley Colliery	Harry Mortimer	'Tam o'Shanter's Ride' (Denis Wright)
1957	1. Black Dyke Mills 2. Carlton Main Frickley Colliery 3. Foden's Motor Works	Major G. H. Wilcocks	'Carnival' (Helen Perkin)
1958	1. Carlton Main Frickley Colliery 2. Besses o'th'Barn 3. Black Dyke Mills	Jack Atherton	'Sunset Rhapsody' (Eric Ball)

1959	1. Besses o'th'Barn 2. Carlton Main Frickley Colliery 3. Morris Motors	W. Wood	'The Undaunted' (Eric Ball)
1960	1. CWS Manchester 2. The Fairey Band 3. Grimethorpe Colliery	Alex Mortimer	'Fantasia' (Mozart arr. Sargent)
1961	1. The Fairey Band 2. Wingates Temperance 3. Grimethorpe Colliery	Leonard Lamb	'Main Street' (Eric Ball)
1962	1. The Fairey Band 2. Ransome and Marle's 3. Yorkshire Imperial Metals	Leonard Lamb	'Island Heritage' (Helen Perkin)
1963	1. The Fairey Band 2. Grimethorpe Colliery 3. Black Dyke Mills	Leonard Lamb	'Life Divine' (Cyril Jenkins)
1964	1. Foden's Motor Works 2. Lindley Band 3. BMC (Morris Motors)	Rex Mortimer	'Lorenzo' (Keighley)
1965	1. The Fairey Band 2. Brighouse and Rastrick 3. BMC (Morris Motors)	Leonard Lamb	'Saga of the North' (Cyril Jenkins)
1966	1. CWS Manchester 2. Yorkshire Imperial Metals 3. BMC (Morris Motors)	Alex Mortimer	'A Downland Suite' (John Ireland)
1967	1. Grimethorpe Colliery 2. The Fairey Band 3. Wingates Temperance	George Thompson	'A Comedy Overture' (John Ireland)
1968	1. Black Dyke Mills 2. Wingates Temperance 3. Grimethorpe Colliery	Geoffrey Brand	'John O'Gaunt' (Gilbert Vinter)
1969	1. Grimethorpe Colliery 2. Carlton Main Frickley Colliery 3. The Fairey Band	George Thompson	'Spectrum' (Gilbert Vinter)
1970	1. Yorkshire Imperial Metals 2. CWS Manchester 3. Foden's Motor Works	Trevor Walmsley	'Pageantry' (Herbert Howells)
1971	1. Yorkshire Imperial Metals 2. Black Dyke Mills 3. Grimethorpe Colliery	Trevor Walmsley	'Festival Music' (Eric Ball)
1972	1. Black Dyke Mills 2. Carlton Main Frickley Colliery 3. The Cory Band	Geoffrey Brand	'Sovereign Heritage' (Jack Beever)
1973	1. Black Dyke Mills 2. Grimethorpe Colliery 3. Brighouse and Rastrick	Roy Newsome	'The Accursed Huntsman' (César Franck)
1974	1. Black Dyke Mills 2. Stanshawe (Bristol) 3. GUS (Footwear)	Roy Newsome	'James Cook – Circumnavigator' (Gilbert Vinter)
1975	1. Wingates Temperance 2. The Fairey Band 3. Yorkshire Imperial Metals	Richard Evans	'Fireworks' (Elgar Howarth)
1976	1. Black Dyke Mills 2. Stanshawe (Bristol) 3. Brighouse and Rastrick	Major Peter Parkes	'An Epic Symphony' (Percy Fletcher)

1977	1. Black Dyke Mills	Major Peter Parkes	'Diadem of Gold' (G. Bailey arr.
	2. Brighouse and Rastrick		Frank Wright)
	3. Fairey Engineering Works		
1978	1. Brighouse and Rastrick	Geoffrey Brand	Benvenuto Cellini (Berlioz
	2. Black Dyke Mills		arr. Frank Wright)
	3. Ransome Hoffman Pollard		

National Championship Results

Year	Placings	Conductor	Test Piece
1900	1. Denton Original 2. Black Dyke 3. Wingates Temperance	Alex Owen	'Gems from Sullivan's Operas No.1' arr. J. Ord Hume
1901	1. Lee Mount 2. Irwell Springs 3. Denton Original	W. Swingler	'Gems from Sullivan's Operas, No.3' arr. J. Ord Hume
1902	1. Black Dyke Mills 2. Wyke 3. Luton	John Gladney	'Hiawatha' (Coleridge-Taylor) arr. Lt. Chas. Godfrey
1903	1. Besses o' th' Barn 2. Rushden Temperance 3. Black Dyke Mills	Alex Owen	'Die Meistersinger' (Wagner)
1904	1. Hebburn Colliery 2. Wingates Temperance 3. Irwell Springs	A. Holden	'Gems of Mendelssohn' arr. Lt. Chas. Godfrey
1905	1. Irwell Springs 2. Wingates Temperance 3. Lee Mount	William Rimmer	'Roland à Ronceveaux' (Auguste Mermet)
1906	1. Wingates Temperance 2. Linthwaite 3. Shaw	William Rimmer	'Gems of Chopin' arr. Wm. Short
1907	1. Wingates Temperance 2. Goodshaw 3. Kings Cross	William Rimmer	'Gems of Schumann' arr. Wm. Short
1908	1. Irwell Springs 2. Perfection Soap Works 3. Wingates Temperance	William Rimmer	'Rienzi' (Wagner) arr. Samuel Cope
1909	1. Shaw 2. Foden's Motor Works 3. Perfection Soap Works	William Rimmer	'The Flying Dutchman' (Wagner)
1910	1. Foden's Motor Works 2. Irwell Springs 3. Spencer's Steel Works	William Halliwell	'Gems of Schubert' arr. W. Rimmer
1911	1. Perfection Soap Works 2. Foden's Motor Works 3. Wingates Temperance	William Halliwell	'Les Huguenots' (Meyerbeer) arr. W. Rimmer
1912	1. St Hilda Colliery 2. Irwell Springs 3. Foden's Motor Works	William Halliwell	'William Tell' (Rossini)
1913	1. Irwell Springs 2. St Hilda Colliery 3. Black Dyke Mills	William Halliwell	'Labour and Love' (Percy Fletcher)
1914–1919	NO CONTEST		
1920	1. St Hilda Colliery 2. Lincoln Malleable Iron Works 3. Irwell Springs	William Halliwell	'Coriolanus' (Cyril Jenkins)
1921	1. St Hilda Colliery 2. Foden's Motor Works 3. Wingates Temperance	William Halliwell	'Life Divine' (Cyril Jenkins)
1922	1. Horwich RMI 2. Luton Red Cross 3. Hebden Bridge	J. A. Greenwood	'Freedom' (Hubert Bath)

1923	1. Luton Red Cross 2. Black Dyke Mills 3. Foden's Motor Works	William Halliwell	'Oliver Cromwell' (Geehl)
1924	1. St Hilda Colliery 2. Black Dyke Mills 3. Australia (Newcastle Steel Works)	William Halliwell	'On the Cornish Coast' (Geehl)
1925	1. Marsden Colliery 2. Irwell Springs 3. South Moor Colliery	J. A. Greenwood	'Joan of Arc' (Denis Wright)
1926	1. St Hilda Colliery 2. Carlisle St. Stephens 3. Wingates Temperance	J. Oliver	'An Epic Symphony' (Percy Fletcher)
1927	1. Carlisle St Stephens 2. Callender's Cable Works 3. Carlton Main Colliery	W. Lowes	'The White Rider (Denis Wright)
1928	1. Black Dyke Mills 2. Harton Colliers 3. Carlisle St Stephens	William Halliwell	'A Moorside Suite' (Holst)
1929	1. Carlisle St Stephens 2. Scottish CWS 3. Luton Red Cross	W. Lowes	'Victory' (Cyril Jenkins)
1930	1. Foden's Motor Works 2. Black Dyke Mills 3. Irwell Springs	Fred Mortimer	'Severn Suite' (Elgar)
1931	1. Wingates Temperance 2. Horden Colliery 3. Rothwell Temperance	H. Moss	'Honour and Glory' (Hubert Bath)
1932	1. Foden's Motor Works 2. Black Dyke Mills 3. Wingates Temperance	Fred Mortimer	'A Downland Suite' (Ireland)
1933	1. Foden's Motor Works 2. Scottish CWS 3. Creswell Colliery	Fred Mortimer	'Prometheus Unbound' (Granville Bantock)
1934	1. Foden's Motor Works 2. Scottish CWS 3. Harton Colliery	Fred Mortimer	'Comedy Overture' (Ireland)
1935	1. Munn and Felton's 2. Creswell Colliery 3. Black Dyke Mills	William Halliwell	'Pride of Race' (K. A. Wright)
1936	1. Foden's Motor Works 2. Black Dyke Mills 3. Friary (Guildford)	Fred Mortimer	'Kenilworth' (Arthur Bliss)
1937	1. Foden's Motor Works 2. Munn and Felton's 3. Black Dyke Mills	Fred Mortimer	'Pageantry' (Herbert Howells)
1938	1. Foden's Motor Works 2. Bickershaw Colliery 3. Black Dyke Mills	Fred Mortimer	'An Epic Symphony' (Percy Fletcher)
1939–1944	NO CONTEST		
1945	1. Fairey Aviation 2. Horden Colliery 3. Parc and Dare	Harry Mortimer	'Overture for an Epic Occasion' (Denis Wright)
1946	1. Brighouse and Rastrick 2. Fairey Aviation 3. Munn and Felton's	Eric Ball	'Oliver Cromwell' (Geehl)

1947	1. Black Dyke Mills 2. Fairey Aviation 3. Foden's Motor Works	Harry Mortimer	'Freedom' (Hubert Bath)
1948	1. Black Dyke Mills 2. Cory Workmen's 3. Brighouse and Rastrick	Harry Mortimer	'On the Cornish Coast' (Geehl)
1949	1. Black Dyke Mills 2. Foden's Motor Works 3. Munn and Felton's	Harry Mortimer	'Comedy Overture' (Ireland)
1950	1. Foden's Motor Works 2. Hanwell Silver Band 3. CWS Manchester	Harry Mortimer	'Pageantry' (Herbert Howells)
1951	1. Black Dyke Mills 2. Foden's Motor Works 3. Brighouse and Rastrick	Alex Mortimer	'An Epic Symphony' (Percy Fletcher)
1952	1. Fairey Aviation 2. Foden's Motor Works 3. Black Dyke Mills	Harry Mortimer	'Frogs of Aristophanes' (Granville Bantock arr. Frank Wright)
1953	1. Foden's Motor Works 2. CWS Manchester 3. Creswell Colliery	Harry Mortimer	'Diadem of Gold' (G Bailey arr. Frank Wright)
1954	1. Fairey Aviation 2. CWS Manchester 3. Foden's Motor Works	Harry Mortimer	'Sovereign Heritage' (J. Beaver arr. Frank Wright)
1955	1. Munn and Felton's 2. Ransome and Marle's 3. CWS Manchester	Harry Mortimer	'Blackfriars' (Edric Cundell arr. Frank Wright)
1956	1. Fairey Aviation 2. CWS Manchester 3. Munn and Felton's	Major G. H.	'Festival Music' (Eric Ball)
1957	1. Munn and Felton's 2. CWS Manchester 3. Carlton Main Frickley Colliery	Stanley Boddington	'Variations for Brass Band' (R. Vaughan Williams)
1958	1. Foden's Motor Works 2. Scottish CWS 3. CWS Manchester	Rex Mortimer	'Variations on The Shining River' (Edmund Rubbra)
1959	1. Black Dyke Mills 2. Carlton Main Frickley Colliery 3. Foden's Motor Works	Major G. H. Willcocks	'Le Roi d'Ys' (Lalo arr. Frank Wright)
1960	1. Munn and Felton's 2. Carlton Main Frickley Colliery 3. Black Dyke Mills	Stanley Boddington	'Three Figures' (Herbert Howells)
1961	1. Black Dyke Mills 2. CWS Manchester 3. Crossley's Carpet Works	Major G. H. Willcocks	'Les Francs Juges' (Berlioz arr. Frank Wright)
1962	1. CWS Manchester 2. Crossley's Carpet Works 3. Ransome and Marle's	Alex Mortimer	'The Force of Destiny' (Verdi arr. Frank Wright)
1963	1. CWS Manchester 2. Brighouse and Rastrick 3. GUS (Footwear)	Alex Mortimer	'The Belmont Variations' (Sir Arthur Bliss)
1964	1. GUS (Footwear) 2. Black Dyke Mills 3. CWS Manchester	Stanley Boddington	'Variations on a Ninth' (Gilbert Vinter)

1965	1. The Fairey Band 2. Cammell Laird's Works 3. GUS (Footwear)	Leonard Lamb	'Triumphant Rhapsody' (Gilbert Vinter)
1966	1. GUS (Footwear) 2. Black Dyke Mills 3. The Fairey Band	Stanley Boddington	'Le Carnival Romain' (Berlioz arr. Frank Wright)
1967	1. Black Dyke Mills 2. CWS Manchester 3. Brighouse and Rastrick	Geoffrey Brand	'Journey into Freedom' (Eric Ball)
1968*	1. Brighouse and Rastrick 2. Black Dyke Mills 3. GUS (Footwear)	Walter Hargreaves	Prelude from 'The Mastersingers' (Wagner arr. Frank Wright)
1969*	1. Brighouse and Rastrick 2. Black Dyke Mills 3. CWS Manchester	Walter Hargreaves	'High Peak' (Eric Ball)

1970 WORLD CHAMPIONSHIP

	1. Black Dyke Mills 2. The Fairey Band 3. GUS (Footwear)	Geoffrey Brand	'Benvenuto Cellini' (Berlioz arr. Frank Wright)

NATIONAL CHAMPIONSHIP

	1. Grimethorpe Colliery Band 2. Ransome Hoffman Pollard 3. Hanwell	George Thompson	'Pride of Youth' (Gordon Jacob)

1971 WORLD CHAMPIONSHIP

	1. GUS (Footwear) 2. The Fairey Band 3. Brighouse and Rastrick	Stanley Boddington	'Energy' (Robert Simpson)

NATIONAL CHAMPIONSHIP

	1. Wingates Temperance 2. City of Coventry 3. Cory	Dennis Smith	'Le Roi d'Ys' (Lalo arr. Frank Wright)

1972	1. Black Dyke Mills 2. GUS (Footwear) 3. Grimethorpe Colliery	Geoffrey Brand	'A Kensington Concerto' (Eric Ball)
1973	1. Brighouse and Rastrick 2. CWS Manchester 3. Black Dyke Mills	James Scott	'Freedom' (Hubert Bath)
1974	1. The Cory Band 2. Grimethorpe Colliery 3. Black Dyke Mills	Major H. A. Kenney	'Fantasy for Brass Band' (Malcolm Arnold)
1975	1. Black Dyke Mills 2. Stanshawe 3. Brighouse and Rastrick	Major Peter Parkes	'Un Vie de Matelot' (Robert Farnon)
1976	1. Black Dyke Mills 2. Yorkshire Imperial Metals 3. Wingates Temperance	Major Peter Parkes	'Sinfonietta for Brass Band—The Wayfarer' (Eric Ball)
1977	1. Black Dyke Mills 2. Grimethorpe Colliery 3. Yorkshire Imperial Metals	Major Peter Parkes	'Connotations for Brass Band' (Edward Gregson)
1978	1. Yorkshire Imperial Metals 2. Besses o' th' Barn 3. Grimethorpe Colliery	Denis Carr	'Checkmate' (Arthur Bliss arr. Eric Ball)

* denotes World and National Championship

SECOND SECTION

1945 Camborne Town	1956 Pontardulais Town	1967 Snibston Colliery
1946 Pressed Steel Works	1957 Langley Prize	1968 Haydock
1947 Hetton Silver	1958 Slaithwaite	1969 Thoresby Colliery
1948 Markham Main Colliery	1959 Kinneil Colliery	1970 Newhall
1949 Rhyl Silver	1960 Lindley	1971 Rogerstone & District
1950 Hoo Silver	1961 Cammell Laird	1972 Lockwood
1951 Lewis Merthyr Work's In.	1962 West Brom. Borough	1973 Tredegar Town
1952 Royston New Monck. Col. In.	1963 Skelmanthorpe	1974 Spillers (Gainsborough)
1953 British Legion (Oldham)	1964 Wellesley Colliery	1975 Northumbria Police
1954 Wharncliffe Silkstone Coll.	1965 Mirrlees Works	1976 Loughborough
1955 Chapel-en-le-Frith Town	1966 Cheetham Hill	1977 Clacton-on-Sea
		1978 Birmingham School of Music

THIRD SECTION

1945 Houghton Main Colliery	1956 Walkden Prize	1967 Rhymney Workmen's
1946 Mynyddygarreg Silver	1957 Ellington Colliery	1968 Pelton Fell Workmen's
1947 Rhos Silver	1958 Haigh Prize	1969 Teversal Colliery
1948 Storeys of Lancaster	1959 Steel Co. of Wales, Pt. Tal.	1970 Cargo Fleet Works
1949 British Legion (Oldham)	1960 Rawmarsh Prize	1971 Redbridge Youth
1950 Lewis Merthyr Work's In.	1961 Paulton Silver	1972 Wigan and District Brass
1951 John Dickinson (Apsley)	1962 Tadley Silver	1973 Haworth
1952 Wharncliffe Silkstone Coll.	1963 Poynton Brass	1974 Thornsett
1953 Barnet	1964 Romford Civil Defence	1975 Wakefield Youth
1954 Whitburn Miners' Welfare	1965 Sherborne Town	1976 St. Keverne Silver
1955 Pontardulais Town	1966 Corby	1977 Walsall Metropolitan
		1978 Carlton Silver

FOURTH SECTION

1947 Butterfield's Tank Works	1958 Elland Silver	1968 Workington Town
1948 Wincanton Silver	1959 Cammell Laird Works	1969 City of Coventry "B"
1949 Gomersal Mills	1960 Poynton Brass	1970 Harpenden
1950 Kibworth Silver	1961 Hetton Silver Prize	1971 Ebbw Vale Municipal
1951 95th (Crewe) Sq. A.T.C.	1962 Corby Silver	1972 Fishburn Colliery Welfare
1952 Ellington Colliery	1963 Cargo Fleet Works	1973 R.N.R. Dundee
1953 Ystalyfera Public	1964 Stanhope Silver	1974 West Wycombe Brass
1954 Woodhorn Colliery	1965 Guildford Silver	1975 North Skelton & District
1955 Brancepeth Colliery	1966 Hatfield Main	1976 Queensbury Music Centre
1956 Esh Colliery Welfare	1967 Chapeltown Silver	1977 Hammonds Sauce B.
1957 Gwaun-cae-Gurwen		1978 Ecclesfield

INDEX

(Folios in italic type indicate illustrations)

Acknowledgements

We are greatly indebted to the following for allowing us the loan of interesting material and historic photographs:

Alec Abram, Robert Alexander, Markus Bach (Switzerland), Mrs. Charles Badrock, Cyril Barnes, W.E. Bearchell, Don Blackburn, Francesca Brand (Switzerland), Brig. Henry A. Dries, Richard Brondell, Karl Busch, Arthur Butterworth, John Cannon (Australia), Mary Chalk, Robert Cowdroy (Australia), Ignatius Ford, John Gay, Peter Grant, Elgar Howarth, Ron Kershaw, Lt. Col. Theodore Kitching, Ron Massey, Thomas G. Middleton, E. Vaughan Morris, Sybil Mortimer, Eddie Noble, Rita Padden, Roger de Pauw (Belgium), James Rippin, William Robb, Arthur Rushworth, Ernest Sands, Joe Stanborough (Australia), E.W. Tadd, Murray Warrington (New Zealand), Stan Whiteman, Jim Williamson, Robert Wray, Maud Wright.